STUDIES ON ETHNIC GROUPS IN CHINA

Stevan Harrell, Editor

STUDIES ON ETHNIC GROUPS IN CHINA

Cultural Encounters on China's Ethnic Frontiers
edited by Stevan Harrell

Guest People:
Hakka Identity in China and Abroad
edited by Nicole Constable

Familiar Strangers:
A History of Muslims in Northwest China
by Jonathan N. Lipman

Lessons in Being Chinese:
Minority Education and Ethnic Identity in Southwest China
by Mette Halskov Hansen

Manchus and Han: Ethnic Relations and Political Power
in Late Qing and Early Republican China, 1861–1928
by Edward J. M. Rhoads

Ways of Being Ethnic in Southwest China
by Stevan Harrell

Governing China's Multiethnic Frontiers
edited by Morris Rossabi

On the Margins of Tibet:
Cultural Survival on the Sino-Tibetan Frontier
by Åshild Kolås and Monika P. Thowsen

The Art of Ethnography: A Chinese "Miao Album"
Translation by David M. Deal and Laura Hostetler

Doing Business in Rural China:
Liangshan's New Ethnic Entrepreneurs
by Thomas Heberer

Communist Multiculturalism:
Ethnic Revival in Southwest China
by Susan K. McCarthy

Religious Revival in the Tibetan Borderlands:
The Premi of Southwest China
by Koen Wellens

Religious Revival in the Tibetan Borderlands

THE PREMI OF SOUTHWEST CHINA

∾

KOEN WELLENS

UNIVERSITY OF WASHINGTON PRESS ∾ SEATTLE AND LONDON

Religious Revival in the Tibetan Borderlands is published with the assistance of a grant from the University of Oslo and the Norwegian Ministry of Foreign Affairs. Additional support was provided by the Donald R. Ellegood International Publications Endowment.

© 2010 by the University of Washington Press
Designed by Pamela Canell
Typeset in Minion Pro
Printed in the United States of America
16 14 12 11 10 5 4 3 2 1

All rights reserved. No part of this publication may be reproduced or transmitted in any form or by any means, electronic or mechanical, including photocopy, recording, or any information storage or retrieval system, without permission in writing from the publisher.

University of Washington Press
P.O. Box 50096, Seattle, WA 98145 U.S.A.
www.washington.edu/uwpress

All photographs are by the author.

Library of Congress Cataloging-in-Publication Data
Wellens, Koen.
Religious revival in the Tibetan borderlands :
the Premi of southwest China / Koen Wellens.
p. cm. — (Studies on ethnic groups in China)
Includes bibliographical references and index.
ISBN 978-0-295-99068-2 (hardcover : alk. paper)
ISBN 978-0-295-99069-9 (pbk. : alk. paper)
1. Pumi (Chinese people)—Religion.
2. Pumi (Chinese people)—Rites and ceremonies.
3. Pumi (Chinese people)—Social life and customs.
4. Ninglang Yizu Zizhixian (China)—Religious life and customs.
5. Ninglang Yizu Zizhixian (China)—Social life and customs.
6. Muli Zangzu Zizhixian (China)—Religious life and customs.
7. Muli Zangzu Zizhixian (China)—Social life and customs.
8. Borderlands—Tibet. 9. Borderlands—China. I. Title.
DS731.P844W45 2010   305.895'4—dc22   2010033489

The paper used in this publication is acid-free and recycled from at least 30 percent post-consumer waste. It meets the minimum requirements of American National Standard for Information Sciences—Permanence of Paper for Printed Library Materials, ANSI Z39.48–1984.

什么是迷信？

什么是宗教？

我们老百姓不清楚！

What is superstition?

What is religion?

We ordinary people are not sure!

—*Sixty-three-year-old Premi villager in Yunnan*

CONTENTS

Foreword by Stevan Harrell ix

Preface xiii

Acknowledgments xv

On Language and Orthography xix

Map of Research Area in Southwest China 2

Map of Bustling Township 65

INTRODUCTION 3

1   MULI

The Political Integration of a Lama Kingdom 24

2   BUSTLING TOWNSHIP

A Muli Township in the Post-Mao Era 63

3   THE PREMI HOUSE

Ritual and Relatedness 94

4 ∽ PREMI COSMOLOGY
Ritual and the State 132

5 ∽ MODERNITY IN YUNNAN
Religion and the Pumizu 188

CONCLUSION 209

EPILOGUE 217

Glossary 219
Notes 237
Bibliography 259
Index 273

FOREWORD

The Premi are one of China's smallest, most remote, and least-known ethnic groups. What can we learn from them? Koen Wellens's *Religious Revival in the Tibetan Borderlands: The Premi of Southwest China* provides copious information on the Premi as well as on contemporary China, ethnography, ethnicity, religion, and the state. As the twelfth volume in the Studies on Ethnic Groups in China series, his book continues a tradition of interdisciplinary scholarship that puts the specific into the context of the general and uses particular cases to illustrate general points.

Any book on contemporary ethnic groups must be grounded in ethnography. Until now, there has been precious little material on the Premi, most of it in obscure, minimally distributed, local Chinese-language journals and in some of the shorter chapters of general works on China's "nationalities." Most people who have written about the Premi (myself included) learned about them as a side-effect of research on a better-known group, such as the Nuosu or Naxi or, especially, the Premi's famous matrilineal neighbors, the Na or Mosuo. It seems that, except for the very few Premi who had become local scholars, no one had set out to study their history or society. As Wellens describes in his Introduction, a chance nighttime encounter with a Premi *hangui* priest led him to fill this gap. It wasn't easy. The places he went required days of upsy-downsy hiking, weeks of sleeping on hard board beds, months of subsistence on a limited diet. He had to learn a language for which there are no textbooks or even texts of any kind and deal with villagers rightly suspicious of any investigator (even a 190-cm European) as a possible agent of the Chinese state. But with the eventual help and cooperation of community members and scholarly collaborators of many ethnicities, Wellens gives us the first detailed ethnography of a Premi community.

Religious Revival, however, is not just ethnography for its own sake; it is ethnography that teaches us lessons about ethnicity, religion, and the state in reform-era China. The ethnic identity and ethnic relations of various Premi communities are extremely complex. This group of about sixty thousand people, living in two provinces, turns out to be distributed among two different *minzu*, or state-determined ethnopolitical groups. In Sichuan, where many of the Premi were traditionally subject to the Gelugpa king of Muli, they are Zangzu, for historical reasons lumped, along with their close linguistic relatives such as the Nameze and Duoxu, into the larger group whose name we translate as "Tibetan." In Yunnan, they are their own *minzu*, bearing the name Pumi, which is as close as Chinese characters can get to transcribing their name. We knew (we who knew anything about the Premi at all) that this division had consequences—Tibetans have long objected to the separate status of the Yunnanese Pumi—but Wellens's book adds two important things. One is a detailed historical account of how this came about, in a tangle of politics, language, and religion stretching back to the beginning of the Qing dynasty and forward to the 1950s, reminding us that ethnic identity is often determined by historical contingency as much as by stable genealogical and cultural traditions.

We also see for the first time how the different *minzu* statuses of Premi in the two provinces have led to very different configurations of religion, ethnicity, and religious and ethnic revival in the post-Maoist polity. *Religious Revival in the Tibetan Borderlands* enriches our understanding of the revival of religion in post-Maoist China by showing how historical contingency and the relationships among state, local elites, and communities can influence this process in locally specific ways. In Sichuan, where the Premi are Zangzu, or Tibetans, elites have promoted Tibetan Buddhism, while the revival of the indigenous *hangui* tradition has been a grassroots movement. But in Yunnan, local elites, eager to promote Pumi separateness, have been active in the revitalization of the *hangui*.

All this crisscrossing detail of history, ethnicity, and religion allows us to see the nation-building efforts of the PRC regime in light of a novel sort of complexity. It points out the delicate road that a no-longer revolutionary but still very authoritarian regime must tread as it draws leaders and members of local communities into its national body politic. At the same time, the Premi case demonstrates the opportunities that the construction of this body politic presents for local political and religious leaders as well as the limits to these opportunities. As so many volumes in the Studies on Ethnic Groups in China series have shown, the CCP goal of building a multiethnic or multicultural nation entails a project that is both worthwhile and tricky, both ideological and opportunistic, both inclusive and alienating of minority people. What the project is not, is predetermined. Every case and every community is different, and every study adds materially to our understanding of the places of these differences in the national fabric.

I am thus delighted to introduce and recommend Koen Wellens's *Religious Revival in the Tibetan Borderlands*. It is a fascinating report, from a faraway place, with lots to tell us about ethnicity, religion, and the Chinese nation.

STEVAN HARRELL
Seattle, July 2010

PREFACE

During the Spring Festival break of 1987, I was trekking through northwestern Yunnan with a fellow Chinese-language student. We had been staying mostly in small mountain villages situated several days' walk from anything resembling a road. As two foreigners visiting at the time of the Spring Festival, we found ourselves at the center of lively parties with traditional chain dancing and flute music, accompanied by copious meals of fatty pork meat and engaging in uncountable bottoms-ups of locally brewed spirits. To take a break from the strain of social obligations, we decided not to sleep in a village for one night and put up our tent in what we thought was a lonely place along the trail, far away from any village. But no sooner had darkness fallen than we suddenly realized that a person was quietly observing us. In the glow of our campfire, the old man was an impressive figure, dressed in colorful robes and wearing an elaborately adorned hat. In strong Yunnan Chinese dialect, which at that time was still hard for me to understand, he told us he was some sort of lama, a term that usually designates a Buddhist monk or lay priest, and that he belonged to the Pumi *minzu*. (For more on lamas, see chapters 3 and 4.) He wanted us to pack up all our things and join him as guests in his house. Too tired from the walking and socializing of the previous days, we refused politely but firmly, and he disappeared as suddenly as he had materialized.

Later, after having read all I could find published in Chinese on the Pumi *minzu*, or Premi people, as many of them call themselves, I figured out he was most likely not a Buddhist monk but a ritual expert, a *hangui*. Still later, during what had developed into my research project, I tried desperately to locate a village with such a practicing ritual expert, but it seemed that we had met one of the last living *hangui*. On a 1991 field trip to a village close to where we had put up our tent in 1987, I learned that the old man we had met had passed away only a few years after our nighttime encounter. The realization of this missed opportunity to visit and learn from a man whom I thought to be one of the last representatives of a unique ritual tradition made me even more determined to continue my study of ritual practice in Premi communities. In the mid-1990s, while doing fieldwork in a rather remote Premi village in Yunnan, I was told that people in the village, besides inviting Buddhist monks or people with a certain knowledge of Buddhism to perform all kind of rituals, also invited a so-called *anji* from neighboring Sichuan. They explained to me that *anji* was a local pronunciation of *hangui*. It took me another four years before I managed to get funding for my PhD project and obtain an official permit to conduct fieldwork in the county of Muli in Sichuan, a place, many Premi assured me, where the *hangui/anji* tradition was still very much alive.

ACKNOWLEDGMENTS

Many people deserve thanks for contributing to the completion of this book. I mention their names here solely to express my gratitude and acknowledge their part. None of the mistakes, omissions, or other shortcomings can be attributed to anybody other than myself.

My initial interest in Chinese and Tibetan religion was sparked by the inspiring teachings of Charles Willemen at Gent University in Belgium. While students of classical Chinese language usually dwell on the Confucian Classics, in Gent we learned Chinese largely by reading Buddhist sutras. While this might have chased away some of my fellow students, it had the opposite effect on me! Later, at the University of Oslo, I was able to draw on the extensive knowledge of Tibetan language and culture of Per Kværne, not only as the supervisor of my PhD research but also as an enthusiastic language teacher.

The University of Oslo—through its Faculty of Humanities—was also generous in awarding me a three-year scholarship and, later on, providing an inspiring research environment at its Norwegian Centre for Human Rights. The Norwegian Ministry of Foreign Affairs and NORAD, the Norwegian development agency, funded part of the research for this book through the China Programme and the China Autonomy Programme at the center. The ministry and the center also provided additional grants to support the publication of this book.

I would like to thank first of all, in China, Yin Haitao for spending innumerable hours teaching me the Premi language and for his willingness to share his expert knowledge on Premi culture. Some of the other Premi people that I have known over many years and whom I would like to thank for all the information and support they gave me are Hu Jingming, Waija Dordje Tsering, and "Matthew." Like Yin Haitao, they showed an enthusiastic scholarly interest in Premi culture that was an important inspiration for my project. But most inspiring, and surely the person to whom I owe the most in regard to my understanding of Premi culture, is Nima Anji (for reasons I explain later in this book, I have chosen not to use his real name). I was very fortunate to meet in him a person who combined extensive knowledge with great pedagogical skills, friendliness, and enthusiasm. Being with him made ethnographic fieldwork both an exciting and an enjoyable experience. Like Nima Anji, all the other people in Yousuo and Chicken Foot Village (both names are pseudonyms) who kindly answered my numerous questions have to remain anonymous, and I feel greatly indebted to them. I would like to express my heartfelt thanks to Luobu Heji, my sorely tried and much appreciated companion on most of my fieldwork trips. Although he once had to share a narrow wooden board that served as our bed for weeks and spent months without electricity and contact with his family, this did not deter him from accompanying me on still another field trip to Yousuo. Other people from my host organization, the Yi Research Institute in Xichang, whom I would like to mention with gratitude are Luocong and my other field trip companion Vugo (Qiu Wuge). I am also grateful for the help of Wang Yangzhong at the county government office in Muli.

The manuscript for this book started off as a PhD thesis. In the protracted rewriting process, I received invaluable help through the many comments of different experts. First of all, Signe Howell, Toni Huber, and Chas McKhann went beyond what can be expected of a PhD committee in providing very extensive and detailed comments as well as inspiring challenges to my arguments. A special thanks goes to Stevan Harrell for his long-standing support for my research endeavors and his very constructive advice on the initial manuscript. As one of the few Western anthropologists who has done research and published on Premi society, he has offered much-appreciated suggestions. Antonio Terrone did a terrific job of helping me check the quality of the Chinese translations of Tibetan originals. Other highly expert comments that greatly contributed to the quality of this book were made by the two anonymous readers for the University of Washington Press.

Throughout the years it has taken me to write this book, many people have contributed in several ways, either by commenting and discussing presentations of partial or preliminary results of my research or by contributing their knowledge and expertise when solicited. In addition to those mentioned earlier, I would like to thank the following people: Heidi Fjeld, Christoph Harbsmeier, Maria Lundberg, Zhou Yong, Rune Svarverud, Mark Teeuwen, Halvor Eifring, Samten Karmay, Yan Ruxian, Elisabeth Hsu, Caroline Weckerle, Ho Ts'ui-p'ing, Egil Lothe, Hanna Havnevik, David Gellner, Franz-Karl Ehrhard, Alexander McDonnald, Tashi Nima, and Katia Buffetrille. Laurel Mittenthal and Richard Armitage greatly improved the quality of my English.

At the University of Washington Press, Lorri Hagman and Marilyn Trueblood made the process from manuscript to book both highly effective and pleasant. I am grateful to Laura Iwasaki for the fantastic job she did as copyeditor and to Pam Canell for the great design.

Finally, I would like to thank my wife, Mette Halskov Hansen. Without her very competent and challenging criticisms combined with an unconditional support of my endeavor, this book would never have materialized. I am profoundly grateful that both she and my three daughters, Sine, Nele, and Hedda, put up with all the strains on family life that my work with this book has caused, especially the all too long and all too frequent absences during fieldwork.

ON LANGUAGE AND ORTHOGRAPHY

The Premi language today is spoken by approximately sixty thousand people more or less equally divided throughout the Chinese provinces of Yunnan and Sichuan. It is a Tibeto-Burman language and has two distinct dialects. The northern dialect is spoken in Sichuan and in the county of Ninglang in Yunnan. The southern dialect is spoken in the counties of Weixi, Lanping, and Lijiang, all in Yunnan. Because most Premi communities are made up of small, isolated clusters of villages spread over a large area and surrounded by speakers of other languages, local differences in pronunciation and vocabulary within the two main dialects are considerable. For example, in Bustling Township in Muli, the different autonyms "Ch'ruame" and "Premi" were used, both with the identical meaning "White People."

Premi has no script, and unlike several of the other minority languages in China without a traditional script, no script based on the Latin alphabet has been developed since the establishment of the People's Republic of China (PRC). Although it has been mentioned that some of the Tibetan texts used by Premi ritualists are in fact Premi texts written in the Tibetan script, the only texts I have encountered containing Premi words are genealogies.

The Premi terms as they appear in this book are rendered in the pronunciation of Bustling Township. Discrepancies in pronunciation or vocabulary between different areas of Bustling Township are mentioned in the text. The table on page xx shows only an approximate rendering of the pronunciation and is not linguistically precise. The Bustling Township pronunciation has both a rising and a falling tone, but because of uncertainty regarding the tone of some of the words and also to simplify the transliteration, tone-marks are not included. Most letters correspond to their pronunciation in English, with the specifications or exceptions listed in the Pronunciation Guide (below). The glossary contains a list of the Premi words in the text and their meaning in English.

The pronunciation of Tibetan words often seems rather remote from the direct transcription in the Latin alphabet: for example, the word for "incarnate lama" should be properly transcribed *sprul-sku*, although its pronunciation approximates *tulku*. In order to increase the readability of the text, Tibetan words are rendered as closely as possible to their pronunciation in English. The glossary provides the proper Tibetan spelling according to the system of romanization developed by Turrel Wylie (1959) for all the Tibetan words in the text.

Chinese terms are romanized in pinyin. All the Chinese terms in the text along with the Chinese characters and English translations or explanations are in the glossary.

PRONUNCIATION GUIDE FOR PREMI WORDS

n	nasalization of the preceding vowel, like ns in French *dans*
br	bilabial trill
jh	like j in French *je*
'	after a consonant, denotes a strong aspiration
h	a voiced aspirate
r	a voiced fricative retroflex
rr	like the Spanish r
hl	like ch in German *ach*, followed by an l.
hs	between English sh and s (like x in Chinese pinyin transcription)
a	like a in German *ja*
u	like English o in *who*
o	like English o in *log*
ö	like Ö in German *Öl*
è	like English e in *bed*
é	like English a in *lame*
e	like English u in *fun*
i	like English ea in *beat*
ü	like ü in German *fünf*

RELIGIOUS REVIVAL
IN THE TIBETAN BORDERLANDS

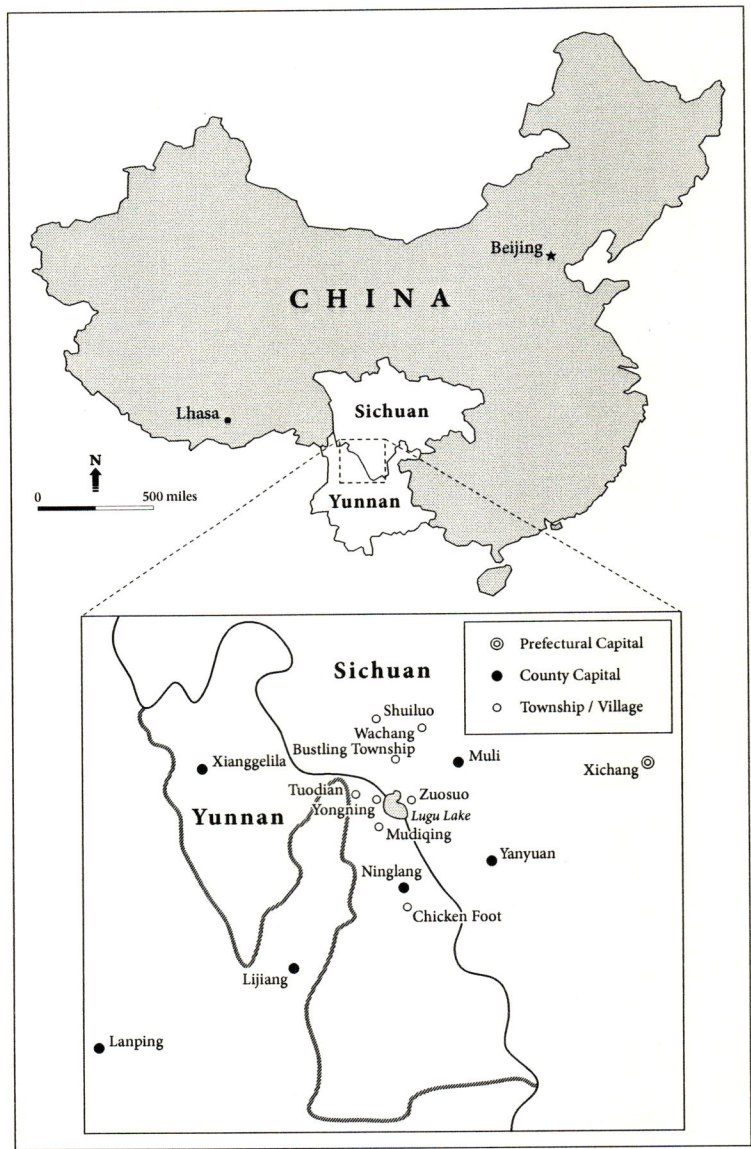

MAP 1. Research Area in Southwest China

INTRODUCTION

Only after the gradual development of the Socialist economic, cultural, scientific, and technological enterprise and of a Socialist civilization with its own material and spiritual values, will the type of society and level of awareness that gave rise to the existence of religion gradually disappear. . . . At that time, the vast majority of our citizens will be able to deal with the world and our fellow men from a conscious scientific viewpoint, and no longer have any need for recourse to an illusory world of gods to seek spiritual solace. This is precisely what Marx and Engels have predicted—that there will be an age when people will have freed themselves from all alienating forces controlling the world and will have come to the stage when they will consciously plan and control the whole of social life. This is also what Comrade Mao Zedong meant when he said that the people, relying on themselves alone, will create a new age both for themselves and for the world. Only when we enter this new age will all that shows a religious face in the present world finally disappear.

—1982 *Communist Party Document 19*

More than twenty-five years have passed since the Chinese Communist Party (CCP) expressed its confident view on the eventual disappearance of religion in China.[1] Chinese people have certainly experienced breathtaking economic growth and modernization of their society under a period of "Socialism with Chinese Characteristics." A policy shift from a planned to a market economy has had a tremendous impact on the living standard of the large majority of Chinese. Nevertheless, until now, there have been few signs that religious beliefs are declining. On the contrary, the relaxation of religious policies and the reinstatement of religious freedom in the 1982 revision of the constitution have set the stage for an explosive development of religions, whether traditional Chinese folk religion, institutionalized world religions, or new syncretic creations such as Falungong.[2] This development comes with a highly visible revival of ritual practices in Chinese cities as well as all over the vast countryside. Rather than being a waning adversary of unfolding Chinese modernity, it seems then that religion is an integral component of it. As Kenneth Dean has convincingly demonstrated in the case of Daoist ritual revival in Southeast China, "tradition" is not necessarily opposed to "modernity," but reemerging ritual practices are in a "ceaseless negotiation with the forces of modernity" (2003: 358).

The process of modernization is taking place not only in the coastal regions but all over China, although not at the same pace everywhere. While the more remote corners of the territory such as the mountains of the Southwest still lag significantly behind the rest of China, in recent years, economic development has also started to pick up momentum here. In this part of the country, where a large portion of China's ethnic minorities live, the policies of economic liberalization and ideological relaxation are having a profound effect on the lives and cultures of local communities. Interestingly, it is also possible here to observe a remarkable resurgence of religious activity.

Indeed, my initial worries about the imminent extinction of the *hangui/anji* tradition among the Premi in China's southwestern provinces of Yunnan and Sichuan have been proved wide of the mark.[3] When I visited Chicken Foot Village in Ninglang County, Yunnan, in 1998, I was told that the last *hangui* ritual specialist in the village had just passed away and none of the young people in the village seemed interested in taking over his job. On my latest visit in 2006, there was no doubt that changes had taken place in the village. Although basically still sticking to the traditional local building style, many houses now boasted windows containing real glass, and not a few were adorned with a satellite dish on top. In the enclosed courtyards, where once the family bicycles had been parked on the dirt ground, there now stood shiny motorbikes on neat concrete pavement. Other changes were less visible but no less remarkable, and some were certainly more unexpected: Chicken Foot Village now could claim seven practicing young *hangui* ritual specialists! They could be seen conducting rituals when people or animals were sick, when people had died and were cremated, when ancestral spirits had to be propitiated, or when offerings had to be made to the water deities, or *lwéjabu*, in order to bring rain for the newly planted crops. Often the *hangui* would be wearing their newly sewn, long yellow gowns, and during some rituals they would recite from photocopies of Tibetan-language scriptures. And this development was not limited to Chicken Foot: a dilapidated school building in the middle of the village had been turned into a veritable *hangui* school, training young Premi men from all over Ninglang County on becoming ritual specialists. From an almost obsolete tradition that, fifteen years ago, had been reduced to a memory in the minds of older people, the *hangui* ritual practice had turned into a vibrant cultural phenomenon spreading to all corners and layers of Premi society. Why, in a time of palpable social and economic development, were Premi villagers still not "able to deal with the world and our fellow men from a conscious scientific viewpoint," and why did they still have "need for recourse to an illusory world of gods to seek spiritual solace"?

The *hangui* tradition was not the only important religious tradition found among the Premi. As with several other ethnic minority groups in Southwest China, such as the Na, the Naxi, the Rek'ua, the Namuyi, and the Shuhi^n, non-Buddhist religious practices seem to coexist with the strong presence of Tibetan Mahayana Buddhism. These different ethnic groups live in a mountainous region situated in what today are the Chinese provinces of Sichuan and Yunnan. The area constitutes the border area of historic Tibet, and throughout their history, the people living here have been exposed in varying degrees to Tibetan culture. This is most obvious in the presence of several monasteries belonging to different schools of Tibetan Buddhism. Nevertheless, until today, many of these ethnic groups maintained their own cultural distinctiveness, apparent in the use of a number of non-Bodic (or Tibetan) Tibeto-Burman languages and the existence of ritual practices and beliefs that can be defined as non-Buddhist.

Along with Chicken Foot Village in Ninglang County, Yunnan, my main area of investigation has been the adjacent county of Muli. Even today, its high mountains and deep gorges have kept Muli relatively isolated from the outside world. Before the Chinese Communist takeover in 1950, Muli was a semi-independent monastic domain making up the southeastern border region of the Tibetan province of Kham. It was ruled by a Buddhist monk who carried the Tibetan title of "king," or *gyelpo*. Buddhism had been established in this region since at least the fifteenth century, but it was only in the seventeenth century that Muli was firmly integrated into the monastic system of the Gelugpa, a school of Tibetan Buddhism founded by Tsongkhapa (1357–1419).

The county of Muli is situated in the southwestern corner of the Chinese province of Sichuan and is designated a Tibetan autonomous county. Despite its Buddhist history, the local people belonging to different Tibeto-Burman ethnic groups participate only sporadically in monastic Buddhism. Premi and Na people from Bustling Township[4] in the south of the county visit the local Buddhist monastery once in a while during festivals, but only a few families in the township send their sons to the monastery to become monks. Nevertheless, when people in Bustling Township die or must make offerings to local deities, Buddhist lay priests or Buddhist monks living in the villages conduct rituals and recite Tibetan Buddhist scriptures. Interestingly, among the Premi within this township, such ritual occasions also involve the participation of non-Buddhist ritual experts—called *anji*—who might use the same Buddhist scriptures in their practice but are also likely to recite Bön[5] texts or orally transmitted "texts" in the local Tibeto-Burman language. *Anji* is a local pronunciation of *hangui*, the word used in Ninglang County for designating Premi religious experts.

Similar cases of religious coexistence have been reported in other peripheral areas of cultural Tibet, such as Nepal (see, e.g., Mumford 1989; Ramble 1990; Holmberg 1989; Vinding 1998). Nevertheless, it is precisely the comparison with studies on religious practice in a country such as Nepal that brings a major difference to light. In studies on the relationship between Buddhism and local cults in Nepal, the state is almost completely absent. An approach that leaves out the role of the policies, institutions, ideologies, and discourses of the state would be impossible in the case of China. In China, people's lives have been subject to one of the most widespread, radical, and comprehensive attempts at state-controlled social engineering in recent human history. Among the various aspects of social life, religious practice has been one of the selected targets of Communist attempts to change society. Even in remote Muli, in order to understand religious practice, it was necessary to take into account the area's location within the territory of the People's Republic of China. The presence of the state is therefore a connecting thread that runs through this book.

In the course of my research, it became clear that the initial questions about religious coexistence were based on debatable assumptions about religious duality and opposition between orthodoxy and heresy. They nonetheless provided an important heuristic device: by asking the "wrong" questions, I obtained invaluable knowledge and understanding and altered the direction of the research, replacing my initial exploration of religion and beliefs with a focus on the believers and their conceptions of religion. Rather than looking into the process and mechanisms of religious revival, I became concerned with Premi religion as it was practiced and how those involved understood and viewed this practice.

The monks of the major Gelugpa monastery in Muli did indeed perceive the relationship between *anji* practices and Buddhism in terms of opposition and orthodoxy. In this respect, their views were remarkably concurrent with those presented in the official Chinese state discourse on religion and ethnic identity in Muli, a discourse the local intellectual and political elites almost uncritically subscribed to and reproduced. However, once I left the monastery, the government buildings, and the state schools behind and entered the houses of Bustling Township's villages, it did not take long to discover that conceptions of what constituted religion in Muli were quite different. This was the case both with regard to cosmology and beliefs and with regard to what were correct ritual practices. Villagers and local ritualists did not view religious practices in the village as contradicting Buddhist doctrine. They were unimpressed by the fact that many village practices were condemned as heresies by the monks from the monastery, such as the worship of local so-called living deities, and the ritual killing and offering of animals.

Over the years during which I conducted fieldwork for this book, participation in monastic Buddhism was waning among the villagers of Bustling Township. The local *anji* ritualists, in contrast, had many new students, and there was increasing demand for their religious services among the villagers. It would be no exaggeration to state that at the beginning of the millennium, *anji* practice was experiencing a real revival. The resurgence of local traditional ritual practices, at the level of both the household and the village, took place at a time when villagers were experiencing increasing socioeconomic remarginalization of their community. Without wanting to overstate direct causal links between religious revival and a sense—whether justified or not—of being left out of the wonders of the booming Chinese economy, resurgence of local religious practice among the Premi of Bustling Township cannot be fully understood without taking into account the context of more general processes of modernization and economic liberalization in China.

The end of the Cultural Revolution in 1976 and the subsequent Eleventh Party Plenum of 1978 heralded the end of a period of extremist policies during which most forms of religious practice disappeared from the public sphere. Nevertheless, it was not until the new constitution of 1982 guaranteeing freedom of religion and the circulation of the above-mentioned Party Document 19 that religious practice gradually reemerged into the open. A hesitant revival developed into a veritable religious craze during the 1980s and 1990s. Some researchers—especially those studying Tibetan communities—explained this as a spontaneous resurrection of beliefs and practices that had been forbidden by the powers in charge but had continued to exist in people's minds (see, e.g., Germano 1998; Kapstein 2004). Others, focusing mainly on religion among the Han, interpreted the revival as a response to the ideological vacuum left by the debacle of the Cultural Revolution and the demise of high Maoism (see, e.g., Anagnost 1994; Feuchtwang 2000; Dorfman 1996).

Undoubtedly, all these approaches can contribute to our understanding of why and how religious practices resurfaced and quickly expanded all over China. In recent years, an increasing number of studies from different places across China's vast countryside have been more concerned with the socioeconomic context of the religious revival. They place the revival—or, in some cases, reinvention—of local practices in the context of the social insecurity that followed economic reforms and the related breakdown of the system of state-organized social security. In a new chapter on religious practice in post-Mao China, added to the most recent edition of his seminal book *The Imperial Metaphor*, Stephan Feuchtwang attributes the revival of territorial cults in the countryside to farmers who, blaming the government for mismanagement of or inaction in response to recurrent natural disasters that threaten their existence, seek relief and protection in local cults. At the same time, he points to the social dimensions of the quest for an alternative soteriology: "the resurgence of religious activity forms other communities of faith, alternative sources of moral authority and senses of security" (2001: 240). Adam Yuet Chau argues that revived popular religious activities such as temple festivals of folk religion in northern Shaanxi "encourage and facilitate a kind of sociality radically different from that of the Maoist era" and that "instead of responding to state-imposed political ideals and campaign goals, villagers today are engaged in social interactions based on kinship or community obligations and responsibilities" (2005: 237).

In studies of communities classified by the Chinese state as ethnic minorities, religious revival is viewed as having an important social aspect, in relation not only to the local community but also to the larger ethnic group. Ben Hillman makes this point in his study of a Hui community in northwestern Yunnan. Even though Islamic practice had not been in evidence in the community for many decades, villagers decided in the late 1990s to build a new mosque and revive Islam. This project was set in motion by a sense of being left behind by the county leadership's ambitious undertaking of promoting and commodifying the Tibetan character of the area. Even the name of the county has been changed from Zhongdian to Xianggelila (Shangri-la) in order to promote tourism. This Islamic revival—or, as Hillman conceives it, "invention"—becomes a socially meaningful experience for these Hui in that it produces a strong sense of community, creates economic opportunities, and enhances their sense of ethnic pride vis-à-vis the local Tibetans, Naxi, and Han (Hillman 2004).

The process of reviving local religious practice, especially traditions that were based mainly on oral transmission, is not a straightforward act of again taking up the threads that were severed in the tumultuous and traumatic years of the Mao era. The social and political context in which remembering takes place might determine much of the nature of such renewed practices. Jing Jun has compellingly laid bare the workings of social memory in a reconstruction of ritual in a village in Northwest China: "At first glance, the story of Dachuan's Confucius temple may suggest that many traditional ideas and practices prohibited under the first decades of Communist rule have been revived. But a closer look reveals a far more complicated picture. These ideas and practices are not mechanically retrieved from the past; they are blended with cultural inventions, shaped by the local experience of Maoism, and permeated with contemporary concerns" (1996: 12).

The burning of ritual texts, the destruction of sacred objects and religious buildings, the public criticism sessions of religious believers and clergy, the ridiculing of traditional practices, the humiliation of ritual specialists—all these events have left deep scars on the memories of local communities. In Bustling Township, religion and ritual were a cause of latent stress throughout the Maoist period: either because people took their chances with facing prosecution or severe criticism and continued to pray or conduct rituals in frightened secrecy or because they took chances and risked otherworldly retribution for *not* conducting rituals. The community's absorption of these traumatic experiences is an important factor in defining the shape of a revival of local religious practice. These are also recurrent conclusions from recent anthropological studies from very different parts of China. The dehumanizing consequences of Maoist collectivism are perhaps nowhere as telling and graphic as in Jing Jun's study of Dachuan (1996). The members of the Kong clan of Dachuan witnessed the literal disappearance of the physical manifestation of their existence as a community when their entire village, with its Confucian temple and ancestral graves, was submerged as a result of the construction of a hydroelectric dam in 1960. The sufferings of forced resettlement and, in addition, the political humiliation of being associated with Confucius at the wrong point in history, infused the Kongs with a strong determination to commemorate and restore through the act of remembering. It was the reconstruction of a temple and the revival of the Confucius cult that signified communal recovery for the Kongs of Dachuan.

The most elaborate narration of how ritual is intertwined with a community's suffering as a result of Maoist policies is undeniably Eric Mueggler's *The Age of Wild Ghosts* (2001). The people of a Lòlop'o[6] community in Yunnan imagine a ghostly return of an institution abolished shortly after the terrible famine of the Great Leap Forward (1958–60). This institution was a ritualized system under which local wealthy families took turns accepting responsibility for taking care of outsiders who passed through the area and carried out several of the tasks demanded by the state. In this way, the local community managed to keep some of the interference and burdens imposed by the state at bay. Several deaths during the Cultural Revolution of cadres who held posts of responsibility under the Great Leap are considered to have been caused by vengeful ghosts. These ghosts were assisted by the ancestral spirits of those who died during the famine and became wild ghosts. Mueggler's analysis demonstrates how memories of past suffering and ritual practice have been linked in many subtle ways to produce a dream of community. Moreover, one of the great contributions of *The Age of Wild Ghosts* is that it convincingly recounts how the remembering of such experiences has fundamentally altered local conceptions of the state "from personified external Other to abstract internal Other" (2001: 288). Such conceptions are furthermore connected with current concerns, such as increasingly strict birth control policies. In short, the state has lost its ideological justification of being an all-encompassing provider of feelings of community.

Shifting Chinese policies also play a central role in the revival of religious practice in Muli. From the perspective of the villagers, because the Maoist state destroyed the monastery and the sacred texts of *anji* ritualists, it appropriated the responsibility of keeping order in Premi cosmology, providing for the people's subsistence and protecting their health. This does not mean that Maoism replaced local beliefs and cosmology. For a limited but extremely confusing and disruptive period in the history of the villagers, several aspects of Maoist ideology invaded these beliefs and coexisted with them in an uneasy tension. A forty-eight-year-old villager of Downhill, in Bustling Township, asked about the consequences of not being able to hold certain rituals during the Cultural Revolution, answered in the following way: "They told us there were no evil ghosts, so performing [this ritual] was not necessary, and, anyway, we thought that if there were evil ghosts, Chairman Mao would protect us."

As elsewhere in China, the reform policies of the 1980s initially raised living standards in Bustling Township considerably. At the same time, they also moved responsibility for subsistence from the collective to the single household. Now that households again owned their animals and disposed of the production of their privately contracted land, adversities like a bad harvest or disease among livestock were not borne by the community but by the individual household. When members of a household became ill, they could no longer count on free, if basic, medical care provided by the state.

But the reforms also brought ideological relaxation. With the revision of the constitution in 1982, religious freedom became officially reinstated and policies—at least nominally—respecting and protecting ethnic minority culture replaced previous campaigns of intense ideological indoctrination. Faced with the challenges of the post-Mao period, villagers in Bustling Township felt it natural to turn to their own local traditions—or what was left of them in their memories. Gradually, the fear dissipated, and they started to openly practice rituals that had been abandoned during the Cultural Revolution. They also revamped traditional forms of social organization that had been hard to maintain during the period of collectivization, class struggle, and political campaigns. Among the Premi of Bustling Township, the shift from the collective to the household reinvigorated the traditional basic unit of social organization, the *dzè^n*, or "house." Besides constituting an economic unit, the inhabitants of a house make up a ritual community that is responsible for maintaining and mending the relationship with ancestral souls, the divine forces that control the elements of nature, and the evil spirits that bring diseases. In this task, they receive the help of local ritual specialists, the *anji*, or of Buddhist monks. But unlike the monks, the local elites, or the foreign researcher, they are not really concerned about the possible differences between these categories of ritualists or, for that matter, differences in the religions themselves. While views on religion among monks and local elites are heavily influenced by discourses of religious and political orthodoxy, such discourses have little repercussions among subsistence farmers trying to make a living in the remote periphery of the modern Chinese state.

RESEARCH

Conducting fieldwork in China, especially fieldwork based on lengthy stays in rural areas, is still a complicated matter. Since the early 1980s, the Chinese authorities have only hesitantly opened the doors to foreign fieldworkers, and there is still widespread skepticism at various levels of the government and the Party about foreign researchers staying for longer periods of time while rummaging about and asking questions.[7] Permission to stay in a village is often difficult to obtain and/or subject to several limitations. Policies, and especially their implementation, change constantly, and what is allowed one year is out of the question the next. In my case, the ideal of a stay of at least one year in one village turned out to be impossible to realize. Nevertheless, repeated medium-length stays of a few months to a few weeks in the same village, combined with similar fieldwork at other sites and interviews of Premi scholars and other important actors, can constitute an acceptable alternative to a "true" Malinowskian stay in the field of at least one or two years of uninterrupted participant observation.

Revisiting places a second, third, or even fourth time, often under changed circumstances, yielded significantly different data in more than a few cases. Between 1995 and 2007, I spent a total of around thirteen months, divided over nine stays, in Premi areas, starting with a six-month stay in 1995 in the town of Lijiang, where I worked with mainly one informant and conducted short field trips to Premi villages. In 1998, I spent two weeks conducting interviews in Premi villages in Ninglang County in Yunnan. After obtaining an official permit in 1999 to do fieldwork in Muli County in Sichuan, longer stays in villages followed: one two-month stay in 1999, one five-week stay in 2000, and two three-week stays in 2001 and 2004. Finally, in 2006 and 2007, I visited other Premi areas in Yunnan and Sichuan but did not stay in villages more than a few days.[8] During this period, I systematically collected most of the data that resulted in this book. Before that, ever since my first encounter with a Premi ritualist in 1987, I had traveled extensively throughout northwestern Yunnan, making short visits to many different Premi villages. Since Premi communities in this region were small and dispersed over a large mountainous area, this was a time-consuming activity that often involved long trekking tours but yielded rather limited and disparate ethnographic data.[9]

The basic method of gathering information in the field consisted of formal interviews, conducted in the presence of at least one assistant and recorded in notes or on tape (mainly for genealogies or ritual recitations and prayers). This resulted in 105 formal interviews. In the villages, the interviews were combined with informal conversation—during daily meals with government employees or with the host family—and observation (and, sporadically, participant observation, as during the harvest). In other places, such as the local towns of Muli in Sichuan and Ninglang and Lijiang in Yunnan, data were collected through longtime personal contacts with important Premi actors such as government cadres or scholars. Sometimes such contacts involved visiting their native villages and staying a few days with their families.

The majority of the interviews were conducted in Chinese, or in the local Yunnan or Sichuan version of it, and I asked the questions, sometimes rephrased in local dialect or Premi by assistants. Having spent half a year in the Lijiang area combining in-depth interviews with a prominent Premi scholar with the study of the Premi language in the mid-1990s, I was able to ask questions in Premi and understand some part of the answers. In a few cases, when no local assistants were present and we visited a house where only women were at home, Premi was the only possible means of communication. Complicating my task was the considerable local variation between Premi dialects, even between those spoken in villages quite close to each other. When I first arrived in Uphill and Downhill in 1999, I was disheartened to discover that I could understand only a little of the local dialect, although people could understand most of what I said. After visiting other villages and, finally, when conducting fieldwork in Walnut Grove, which is closer to Yunnan, I found out that it was easier to understand people there. This made it at least possible to get the gist of the conversation taking place around me and helped me significantly in understanding the finer intricacies of rituals and other aspects of Premi culture. Outside the villages, among cadres and intellectual Premi, my ability to engage in simple conversations created much goodwill. It also made it possible for me to challenge their views on the likeness between Tibetan and Premi languages, a frequent topic of discussion during my interviews with "urban" Premi. In the area of Walnut Grove, most people spoke three to four languages; in addition to Premi and Chinese, most also spoke Na and Naxi (Nahi^n in local pronunciation). Many of the women in Walnut Grove came from non-Premi villages but after marriage spoke only Premi at home.

Interviews with county government cadres took place either at their offices or in their homes and were often a combination of formal interview and requests for information on local conditions. The fact that the research was officially approved by the prefectural government made these cadres more inclined to hand out useful written material such as unpublished working reports and local statistics. Sometimes fortuitous circumstances made it possible to collect more in-depth information, such as the time when I traveled for two days with the cadres of the county Religious Affairs Bureau in order to visit the main monastery of Muli where we were to participate in a religious celebration. This proved to be a golden opportunity to observe how religious policy was implemented at the local level; at the same time, I would have the chance to be briefed on those aspects I wanted to learn more about or on issues I did not fully understand as they arose during the celebration.

One of the major informants for the study of Premi religion was Nima Anji, from the village of Walnut Grove. He was not only the most knowledgeable of all the *anji* in Bustling Township, with a steadily growing reputation extending well beyond the township's borders, but also a good teacher. This quality turned out to be very fortunate for me, and through numerous visits and hour-long talks, he patiently explained the intricacies of Premi cosmology, rituals, and religious practice.

Over the years, through frequent return visits, I developed closer relations with some of the Premi cadres and intellectuals, and they became important informants for my project, which I also often discussed with them. One was a retired cadre from Ninglang County in Yunnan, Waizha Dorje Tsering. He was a key figure in the establishment of a *hangui* school in his hometown, a project I followed closely and discuss in chapter 5. It is a fascinating example of how Premi identity transcends its local meaning and becomes a larger, modern form of identity shaped and reproduced on the periphery of modern Chinese society, highly affected by that society's prevalent discourses.

I carried out the main part of my fieldwork in two villages in remote Bustling Township in Muli County, Sichuan. The much more accessible village of Chicken Foot in Ninglang County, Yunnan, was a secondary field site. Except for a few occasions, I did not actually live in this village but made daily visits to conduct interviews while living in the nearby county-town of Daxingzhen. Although I did conduct more systematic household interviews here in 1998, my main method of research in Chicken Foot Village consisted of developing longtime relationships with a few people over a ten-year period in order to follow the village's development over time and, in particular, the progress of the *hangui* school established there in 2000. Fieldwork in Muli was more traditionally structured and started with a two-month stay, mainly in the twin villages of Uphill and Downhill. The government of Bustling Township was situated in Uphill, and the government-assigned assistant, or *peitong*, and I lived in the building where local government officials lived and worked.[10] When I arrived, I explained that I wanted to visit all the houses in the twin villages and register basic biographical data, family structure, and economic conditions; I said furthermore that I would like to ask people about religious practices and other customs and participate in religious ceremonies that would take place during my stay. Paying a visit to *all* families in a village in a systematic way made it possible to collect a large amount of comparable data in a survey-like way without actually carrying out a formal survey. As it turned out, insisting on talking to all the families gave me the opportunity to also talk to those families whom the local government might have preferred I not visit. Those included, for instance, polyandric families and other families typified as having "backward thinking" (*you luohou sixiang de*), or very poor families, or just families who did not particularly welcome government employees, which, maybe not surprisingly, were often families of the former categories.

In my first fieldwork period, because I lived at the government building and because, as I found out later, I was perceived as being very closely associated with the people working there and therefore with the Chinese state as a whole, I was only partly successful in establishing more informal settings in which to conduct interviews or gather information. Having experienced the hospitality of ethnic minority people in Southwest China on numerous occasions, I was surprised by how few people invited me into their homes spontaneously. In the afternoon, after I had finished writing out my notes, I usually joined some of the small groups of people sitting in the sun outside their houses or shops along the path next to the government building. After some weeks, people got used to my presence, and I became, so to speak, part of the scenery. This was the closest I got to anything resembling participant observation during my first stay in Muli.

On my next stay in 2000, I revisited Uphill and Downhill and continued fieldwork in Walnut Grove, one day's walk from Uphill and Downhill. This was also where I conducted most of my fieldwork in 2001. In Walnut Grove, my Nuosu assistant and I stayed with two different families, and in this way, we were much nearer to the life of the villagers. I developed close relations with the most knowledgeable and influential *anji* of Walnut Grove, and he became a major informant. Participation in several aspects of village life, mostly those related to agriculture (harvesting corn or threshing wheat), or larger events like the annual slaughtering of the family pig, provided excellent opportunities for talking to informants and getting a better understanding of social life.

As has been made clear, one of the major liabilities of the way my fieldwork was organized was its close association with agents of the Chinese government and the Communist Party. It should be reiterated at the outset that in China, conducting fieldwork without official permission is illegal and therefore, especially in the case of longer fieldwork in villages, practically impossible to carry out. In my case, since the county of Muli was officially closed to foreigners in 1999, I needed special permission even for a short visit. Conducting fieldwork that is officially sanctioned also entailed some consequences that I had not anticipated. Households in Communist China are very familiar with visits from official investigators, be they inspection teams for birth control or disease prevention units, registrars for the regular national population census, Communist Party propaganda teams promulgating new policies, or just members of the township government whose main function is to keep statistics on household economy or agricultural production. When a family therefore gets a visit from the local chairman of the Party accompanied by some unknown other people, this presents a familiar situation. The fact that a foreigner is part of the setup does not substantially alter the perception of the visit, namely, as an intrusion into matters that one might have good reasons for hiding from agents of the state, such as unregistered births, unlawful marriage customs, undeclared income, illegal land use, officially frowned upon practices, and so on. This realization struck me forcefully during one of my first interviews, when I tried to find out whether the family I was visiting carried out the widespread Premi custom of offering food to the ancestors before meals on a sacred stone at the fireplace. They did not understand my question, probably because I did not speak the local dialect well enough yet and because they were not prepared for such a question after having first been asked more standard questions on family composition, income, and the like. After several failed attempts at reformulation, Vugo, a Nuosu from the neighboring township and the local Party chairman, offered *his* reformulation: "You know, what he wants to find out is whether you practice all these feudal superstitious things" (*Zheixie fengjian mixin huodong*). That helped, but at the same time, it made clear to me that in a setup like this there would be severe limitations on the kind of information I would be able to obtain. Although ethnic minorities in China today are officially quite free to practice their "traditional customs" (*fengsu xiguan*), including religious practice, a certain level of official skepticism has survived the Cultural Revolution, and the belief that such customs are unscientific and hamper economic development is widespread among officials and Party bureaucrats at all levels. Somehow I had to make the best of the liability of being viewed as part of the intruding Chinese state. This was a precarious position, depressingly reminiscent of the colonial context in which late-nineteenth- and early-twentieth-century British anthropologists operated (Asad 1973).

Luckily for me, after some time, my local assistants got bored with hearing the same questions over and over again and often went out or started talking with other members of the household while I conducted my interviews. Gradually, after having learned more about local practices and sharpening my language skills and interview technique, I became satisfied with the amount of information I was able to collect. Nevertheless, it took another round of fieldwork to realize that this official arrangement limited not only the amount of information I could gather but also its reliability. In 1999, I visited the house of an old *anji* in Hill Village, which is half a day's walk from Uphill. We were accompanied by a friendly young Nuosu, the government employee responsible for running Public Security (in other words, the township's only policeman). This was my first visit to a practicing *anji*, and I was rather excited. My disappointment was therefore sizable when the old man seemed quite senile and was unable to tell me much. His son was plainly unfriendly to me and my Nuosu assistant from Xichang, so much so in fact that, at one point, the young policeman found it necessary to take him outside somewhat forcefully and keep him there. The whole visit deteriorated into a veritable anticlimax, and I would later remember it as one of the darkest moments of my research.

When I visited Uphill the following year, I decided to revisit the old *anji* in order to try to shake off the bad memories. This time I was accompanied only by a government employee who actually was from Uphill. The difference was striking, to such a degree that at first I did not recognize the hostile son of the previous year in the friendly smiling person who asked us in and prepared food for us while his father told one interesting story after the other. They explained to me that they had viewed my visit the previous year with much suspicion because I was accompanied by a government employee. Obviously, a local Premi who was also working for the township government was not viewed in the same way. He was not associated with the Chinese state, and my association with him cleared my record.

This opened my eyes to the kind of colonial-style power relations the foreign anthropologist enters into with his informants. It also alerted me to the possible means of resistance the villagers used against the unsolicited prying of all-powerful outsiders. In his "Everyday Forms of Peasant Resistance," James Scott has pointed to the "ordinary weapons of relatively powerless groups" that can be used against anthropologists: "foot dragging, dissimilation, false-compliance, pilfering, feigned ignorance, slander, arson, sabotage" (Scott 1986: 6, referred to in Metcalf 2002: 56). Among the many possible motives for such actions, most of which are definitely opportunistic, Metcalf suggests less self-interested motives, such as "trying to turn the attention of his interrogators away from practices that had caused friction with the authorities in the past. According as he understood the predilections of his hearers, he might bowdlerize traditional rituals, or suppress references to magic or shamanism—the possibilities are endless" (2002: 56).

When we started working in Walnut Grove a week later, the experience was repeated, in that there was no one from the township government with us, and we were accompanied only by the local village head on our interview rounds. As a consequence, interviews were much easier, and both quantity and quality of data greatly improved; indeed, I had to thoroughly readjust some of my previously collected data. The "official" figures I had obtained from the township government, for example, on the number of polyandric and polygynic marriages proved to be completely wrong: they were much too low compared to my empiric data. My data on school attendance also had to be revised once more. According to statistics provided to me by the head of the township school, 405 out of the 408 children between the ages of seven and eleven in the township, or more than 99 percent, were attending school. Through my participation in classes at the school and through interviews conducted earlier, I had already found strong signs that this figure might be too high, but only when township government officials were not present did people admit that they often had their children go to school for just a short time in order to have them registered as attending school and in this way avoid the fines for keeping them at home. These instances proved once more how untrustworthy official statistics in China can be, even those obtained closest to the grass roots, let alone the thoroughly edited and published versions thereof. But my experience also proves that fieldwork in itself does not necessarily provide reliable data that compensate for untrustworthy statistics. Discovering and correcting faulty data unfortunately gives one only the fleeting satisfaction of having finally gotten to the bottom of a matter, because the question remains as to which data and conclusions will withstand the next round of fieldwork.

Although the major fieldwork stays related directly to this book were allowed by the relevant Chinese authorities, I have decided to conceal the identities of most of my informants by using pseudonyms for persons and places. The majority of these people would agree that my research topic was not especially controversial. Nevertheless, Western research on religious practice and on matters relating to Tibet or Tibetans more generally have been subject to official suspicion at different levels of the administration. The March 2008 disturbances in Lhasa and other Tibetan areas, and the consequent suppression and crack-down in all places with a population officially designated as Tibetan, testify to the unpredictable development of Tibetan-Chinese relations and the shifting Chinese policies on religion and minority culture. I have therefore chosen to err on the side of caution.

Furthermore, even for an informed outsider, it is not always obvious how different people might assess one's research. I realized, to my surprise, that doing research on people officially classified as Tibetans that focuses in part on their non-Buddhist practices can be a sensitive endeavor, and not just because such research calls into question official ethnic categorizations. Even though I tried to argue that the categories of Tibetan and Premi do not have to be exclusive, I did not find much acceptance for this concept of ethnicity among members of the local elite in Muli, for example. Moreover, many intellectual Tibetans from outside Muli expressed their strong disagreement with this view, and some interpreted my studies on Premi culture as an attempt to split the Tibetan people.[11]

But I had other reasons as well for choosing to make the identification of my sources difficult. Through my fieldwork, I uncovered matters that people sometimes were not entirely comfortable with having me know, either because these matters were thought of as embarrassing or were, strictly speaking, illegal: my continuous probing into kinship relations revealed some extramarital affairs and illegitimate children and, more problematically, that the preferred form of marriage in some villages was polyandry. Many of the interviews in Uphill and Downhill were conducted with the local Public Security officer or chairman of the Communist Party present. In this way, everything my interviewees said was already "on the record." Nevertheless, even cadres at the local level might not be able to predict the impact on higher levels of authority of a systematic written presentation of data acquired under their auspices.

Naturally, hiding the identities of places and persons has some drawbacks. First of all, it reduces the verifiability of the ethnographic data. In addition, for people who have done or are planning to do research in the same region, precise geographic and biographical information could be a useful reference for their own field studies. Yet in the end, opting for full verifiability in print would force me to weigh many of my statements very carefully and leave out information in order to be sure I was not compromising any of my informants. I might also be forced to modify some of the conclusions. And even then, mistakes might be made. To keep some spirit of authenticity, I have tried to stick to Premi names for people, replacing their real names with the names of ancestors given to me in the numerous genealogies I collected. Names of local villages have been changed to the English-language translations of existing villages, but their locations do not necessarily correspond to the villages in question. Clan names and house names have been altered when they would make identification possible.

Another category of problems related to research ethics stems from the obvious differences in social background between a researcher from a rich foreign country and people who depend on subsistence farming for their livelihoods. The people of Walnut Grove and Uphill and Downhill were, by most standards, poor. Although the basic necessities of food, clothing, and housing were fulfilled, very few families managed to generate enough extra income to improve their living standards. They also did not have many resources to draw on in case of adverse events, such as bad harvests or sickness in the family or among their domestic animals. In many families, my visit was naturally perceived as a rare potential source of extra income. In view of this apparent poverty, and knowing that I benefited greatly from talking to and living among these people, I found it very difficult to find a balance in contributing financially. Practical dealings over paying for food, renting mules, lodging, and so on were the daily source of much uneasiness and minor conflicts. The matter was further complicated because my Nuosu assistants were convinced that Nuosu people, through their tradition of hospitality, would not have considered me in the same way as the villagers did (that is, according to them, mainly as a source of extra income) and would never have accepted any money from me. On the contrary, according to them, Nuosu people would have held large welcome parties in honor of my visit. On several occasions, they told me that they were embarrassed by the way the villagers behaved toward me in terms of money.

A rather striking case in point took place in a village inhabited not by Premi but by people of related ethnic origin. This village was the poorest of the villages in which I had conducted fieldwork up to that point. It was situated in a predominantly Nuosu township, and the head of the township was related to one of my research assistants. When we arrived, the village held a large party on my behalf. A goat was slaughtered and prepared, and the whole village participated in a feast, with large amounts of beer and strong spirits. In view of the extreme poverty of the village, I tried to find ways of contributing toward the expenses of the party, but the government assistant consistently tried to undermine all my attempts. Finally, he admitted that the whole thing had been organized and paid for personally by his relative, the township head. They both had wanted to keep this a secret, but my insistence on paying the villagers left them no choice. It took me the rest of the day to convince the township head to let me pay half of what he had spent, which was almost his entire monthly salary. This is but one of the more extreme examples of how my visit could disturb people's daily lives and create problems that I had few chances to anticipate and avoid.

Money would be a significant source of conflict and unease throughout my fieldwork. My assistants frequently got into agitated discussions with villagers over payments for goods and services provided to us in the village, such as board and transportation. With each revisit, these frictions seemed to increase, probably because people were now aware that my visit could mean extra income. In one of the houses where we stayed for a longer time, the daughter became ill, and I offered to pay more for our stay in order to help with her hospital costs, and this became the source of a major conflict between my assistants and our hosts.

Although I often disagreed with my assistants on the way they haggled with local people over small amounts of money, their position as intermediaries saved me from many time-consuming and embarrassing discussions. In the end, in their efforts to protect me from paying too much, my assistants took all the flak and earned a certain level of unpopularity among villagers, a fate I apparently was able to avoid. The issue of money was surrounded by a series of ongoing negotiations in which a delicate balance had to be reached between at least three interests: my interests in collecting data for my research project while also repaying the villagers somewhat for the problems my interference created and perhaps even gaining some friendship; those of my assistants, who had been given the task of helping me fulfill my goals without getting themselves or their institution into trouble but at the same time wanted to give me a positive impression of China; and, finally, those of the villagers who saw an opportunity to obtain some material advantage out of one more round of unsolicited prying into their lives.

This brings me to the final point, and that is the matter of the right of representation. Although many, mostly intellectual Premi, actively supported my project and expressed their opinions about it, I often wondered whether most people of Walnut Grove, Uphill, and Downhill would agree with my interpretations of what they said and did. I have no doubt that some of my conclusions would be contested were they able to read the final product. One reason may be that the villagers do not speak with one voice. There were families in Walnut Grove who were presumed to be possessed by evil spirits; these people were therefore excluded from common rituals in the village and were absolutely undesirable as marriage partners. They saw a religious revival of traditional practice with quite different eyes than did the *anji* whose knowledge not only was a means of making good money, by teaching *anji* rituals in Yunnan, but also constituted the grounds for his strong moral and social authority in his community and beyond. Those who criticize me for my lack of understanding of certain issues would certainly be justified in doing so in view of the relatively short time I lived in their villages. All in all, my fieldwork time was rather limited, and although it was long enough for me to get a deeper understanding of the hardships and uncertainties of life as a subsistence farmer, the realization that, at the end of the next month, I could travel back home to my secure and cozy little world was humbling.

1 ~ MULI

The Political Integration of a Lama Kingdom

The very limited number of accounts we have of Muli[1] portray the area and its inhabitants as a watered-down extension of the Tibetan cultural core. In the few instances in which Muli is mentioned in Western academic writings, it has been variously described as "a transitional zone between the Tibetan culture world to the north and the only partially sinicized tribal lands to the south" (Spengen 2002: 8–9), a "Randzone tibetischer und halbtibetischer Peripherievölker" (border area of Tibetan and half-Tibetan peripheral peoples) (Kessler 1982–: 4), and "a state on the borders of Yunnan, with an only partly Tibetanized population" (Samuel 1993: 81).

Such characterizations are undoubtedly rooted in the establishment of monastic Buddhism in the area at the end of the sixteenth century. They illustrate how a religion and its institutions—Tibetan Mahayana Buddhism—are conceived as the major ingredient in the process of acculturation or "Tibetanization." According to Samuel, such a process has been going on constantly on the margins of the Tibetan cultural region because—for the Tibetans—spreading the Buddhist dharma is a highly valued cultural goal. After adopting Buddhism, populations might gradually give up their language in favor of Tibetan dialects (1993: 147, 561).

It is true that once they had entered the region, the Tibetan Buddhist Gelugpa quickly acquired a strong and pervasive position in Muli. This was brought about by the traditionally close association of the monastic system with the political elites, whereby the support of the ruling nobility enabled Buddhism to establish itself and spread rapidly and this elite could maintain and strengthen its leading position by acquiring religious legitimation. At the same time, it is precisely this politico-religious elite that has held a near-monopoly on providing its version of Muli as a Tibetan Buddhist territory to the outside world. It was greatly helped in maintaining this control by the fact that Muli was for all intents and purposes closed off from the outside world throughout much of its recent history. The major reason for its isolation was its forbidding geography of high snowy mountains cut by steep river canyons. But other factors also complicated contact between Muli and the rest of the world: to the west of Muli are the areas of Chatring (C: Xiangcheng), Gyelthang (C: Zhongdian or Xianggelila), and Konkaling (C: Gonggaling), which had been notorious—for at least a large part of the last two centuries—for being the home of marauding Tibetan bandits; moreover, from the northeast to the southeast, Muli was partly encircled by the independent Nuosu people, who had a long-standing reputation for enslaving or killing those who ventured into their territory.

As a result, access to Muli was limited to a few easily controlled tracks in the north toward Lithang, in the south toward Yongning (T: Thar-lam), and in the southeast toward Yanyuan. Most contacts with the outside were monopolized by the Muli rulers and their immediate entourage of high-ranking monk-administrators. These were the people who concluded official agreements with their powerful neighbors, negotiated with visiting Chinese and Tibetan officials, or acted as hosts for the handful of foreign adventurers and other travelers who were lucky enough to be allowed entry. This last category of persons provides the scant sources of data that underpin the few references to Muli in Western academic publications.

One of the first Westerners to write about Muli was the Major H. R. Davies, a Briton who traveled extensively in Southwest China between 1894 and 1900, examining the possibilities of constructing a railroad link between India and the Yangzi. After spending only a few days in Muli while passing through in 1900, he classified the inhabitants as Xifan, a local Han default category meaning "Western barbarians" and designating populations that were neither Tibetan nor Nuosu. Nevertheless, the Xifan of Muli, according to Davies, "though they do not speak the same language as the Tibetans of Chung-tien, they are in other respects thoroughly Tibetan and are ruled by a lama king" (1909: 387).

The only substantial Western source on Muli consists of the writings of Joseph F. Rock (1884–1962), the Austrian American botanist and explorer who resided and traveled in Southwest China between 1922 and 1949. He had his major base in the Naxi town of Lijiang, in Yunnan, to the south of Muli. Rock visited Muli three times—in 1924, 1928, and 1929—and called himself a friend of the "Lama King," the ruler of Muli.[2] His richly illustrated articles on the "strange Lama Kingdom," published in the *National Geographic Magazine* in the 1920s and 1930s, put Muli on the West's imaginary map of highly exotic places. His presentation of the head lama, or *pönpo* (P: *boⁿ*), of Muli as a naive and self-contented local autocrat, ignorant of what was going on in the rest of the world, fits well into this colorful picture. Nevertheless, such a portrayal is belied by the fact that the head lamas were able to maintain some form of independence only by applying a highly developed sensitivity to the important political issues in China and Tibet and by carefully entertaining relationships with important actors, in the local context of the Southwest, Tibet, and the central leadership in Beijing or Nanjing.

Muli's unstrategic position as a sparsely populated and isolated monastic domain was instrumental in sparing it from becoming a battlefield where the Chinese or their Manchu overlords, the Mongols, and the Tibetans engaged in constant warfare (a fate that befell many of the other border areas of Tibet's Kham region). Muli's role in several of the wars and battles fought within the region was to provide troops to the side it felt it could least afford to refuse. The few passages referring to Muli in two Tibetan sources—the autobiography of the fifth Dalai Lama and a 1698 work by Sangye Gyatso on Tsongkhapa and the monasteries of the Gelugpa—make it clear that in the seventeenth century, Muli clearly was considered a part of the territory of the Dalai Lama: it is mentioned that the fifth Dalai Lama was able to confer the use of both land and taxes in this region (Ahmad 1970: 61). However, this did not mean that Muli was not simultaneously integrated administratively—on a nominal basis at least—into the Manchu empire, as indicated, for example, by the *Annals of Yanyuan County* (Yanyuan xian zhi) (Gu 1894) from the Qing period (1644–1911).[3]

The most extensive source for the history of Muli is *The History* [or,

The Emergence] of the Dharma in Muli (Muli chöchung). This work was compiled by an official of the Muli government, Ngawang Khenrab, in 1735 and covers the period from 1580 to 1735. It is based on several earlier writings that have been lost, such as a treatise on religion in Muli written jointly by the third *tulku*, or incarnate lama, of Muli and the fourth head lama, as well as several shorter documents written by the other head lamas during this 155-year period. The only copy of this text, a manuscript of 196 folios, was miraculously saved from a bonfire during the Cultural Revolution (1966–76). In 1992, it was published in Chengdu in a volume containing both the typeset Tibetan version and the Chinese translation (*Muli chöchung* 1993). The texts contain valuable data on the establishment and expansion of the Gelug School in Muli, on the succession of the different head lamas in the Bar clan, on the searches for the consecutive incarnations of the *tulku*, on the territorial expansion of the region, on the numerous armed conflicts in which Muli was involved, and on the relationship between the Muli head lama and the Manchu and Tibetan governments. By bestowing different official titles on the head lamas, the Qing emperor laid as much claim to Muli as did the regime of the Dalai Lamas in Lhasa.

Although the content of *History of the Dharma* greatly adds to our knowledge about Muli and its religious institutions, it was produced by the same elite that maintained its power through the association of worldly and religious power. Ironically, it was also through the introduction of Buddhism that the political elite became literate in Tibetan and thereby capable of recording its views on the history, religion, and politics of Muli. As a result of the sizable cultural differences between Tibetanized monastic elites and local village communities, the few existing sources on Muli history present a very narrow vision of Muli and its people. This is most obvious in the field of religion, in which Tibetan Buddhism occupies center stage due to its major role in the politics of the region. Although there can be no doubt that non-Buddhist ritualists in the Premi villages practiced actively throughout all of Muli's recorded history, there are no references to these practices in any of the available sources. Until the late Qing, the Premi do not exist in Muli's written history. Perhaps even more ironic, the Chinese Communists uncritically adopted the elite version of Muli's status when deciding how to integrate Muli into the People's Republic of China. The sources for this more recent chapter of Muli history are mainly oral interviews and several official publications on Muli, the most comprehensive of which is the *Annals of Muli Tibetan Autonomous County* (Muli Zangzu zizhixian zhi). One of the more interesting sections in this volume is the chapter containing detailed biographies of personages who played a relevant role in recent Muli history.

INTEGRATION INTO THE TIBETAN BUDDHIST REALM

Little is known about the religious history of Muli before 1580.[4] Beginning in the fifteenth century, several of the valleys that are now part of Muli were controlled by the Mu kings from their capital at Lijiang to the south.[5] The larger Lijiang area is inhabited mainly by the Naxi people. To the extent that Buddhism was established in the area, the prevalent form is presumed to have been that of the Karma Kagyu School, which had established several monasteries in the territory ruled by the Mu kings.[6] In addition, there was a small Sakya monastery in the north of the territory, and *History of the Dharma* mentions that a Bönpo monastery was built in the area of Liewa in the south in 1648 (*Muli chöchung* 1993: 9).[7] Most of the villages in Muli were inhabited by Tibeto-Burman–speaking people, of whom the Premi constituted the largest single group. The villages in the north of Muli were inhabited by Kham-speaking Tibetans. It is probable that village religious practice among the Tibeto-Burmans was quite similar to the practice found in many of the Premi villages today and was centered around non-Buddhist ritualists performing ceremonies related to the worship of ancestral souls and deities of nature. Although the inhabitants of Muli had no choice but to participate to a certain extent in the monasticism enforced by the Buddhist elites, it is safe to assume that local non-Buddhist practice was widespread.

Events far away from its villages were about to have profound consequences for Muli. Changes in the relationship between the Mongols and the Tibetans would reverberate all the way to Muli and have wide-ranging repercussions for politics and religion in the region. In 1578, Sonam Gyatso managed to obtain support for the Gelugpa from the Mongol khan in the politicized conflict between the different Buddhist schools in Tibet, and he acquired the title "Dalai Lama" (Ahmad 1970: 88). Sonam Gyatso was the third incarnation of the abbot of Drepung, a monastery established in Lhasa in 1416 by Tsongkhapa, the founder of the Gelug School. Since the two previous incarnations of Drepung abbots were retroactively recognized as the first and second Dalai Lamas, Sonam Gyatso became the third. The close relationship with the Mongols greatly enhanced the position of the Gelugpa and facilitated the establishment of Gelug monasteries in all areas of Tibet.

In 1580, the third Dalai Lama visited Lithang—two days' travel to the north of Muli—to preside over the celebration of the completion of the Tubchen Chamling Monastery.[8] When this news reached Muli, a small delegation composed of representatives of the local nobility went to Lithang in order to meet the third Dalai Lama and ask him to help them establish a Gelug monastery in Muli (*Muli chöchung* 1993: 2). One of the local ruling clans in Muli was attempting to gain greater independence from Lijiang, and the move to invite the Gelugpa was motivated in part by the need to find powerful allies. Sonam Gyatso was receptive to the plea of the Muli delegation and sent Sangye Gyatso to Muli. In 1584, the first Gelug monastery was built at Wa'erzhai; its full name was Lhakhangteng Ganden Dargye Ling, but it was usually called "Wachin Gompa." Sangye Gyatso became its first abbot, or *kempo*, and since he was already considered to be a *tulku*, he became the first *tulku* of Muli.

After his death in 1584, Neten Tsultrim Sangpo, a Mongolian who had accompanied Sangye Gyatso to Muli, assumed the position of *kempo* of Wachin Gompa. According to *History of the Dharma*, Neten Tsultrim Sangpo was extremely energetic in the propagation of the Gelug teaching and in establishing monasteries, even as the adherents of the Karma Kagyupa were doing their utmost to oppose the proliferation of the Gelugpa (ibid.: 3). Many smaller Gelug monasteries were built all over Muli, and in 1604, Neten Tsultrim Sangpo established the second of the three main monasteries of Muli, Debachen Sönam Dargye Ling, usually called "Kulu" (C: Kangwu; T: *khe-'ong*) Gompa. He thus became abbot at the two most important monasteries of Muli.

A few years earlier, in 1585, a boy was born into the ruling clan in the southeast of Muli. The name of this clan was Bar or Bar-sep'i, as was the name of its estate and the surrounding area;[9] Chinese sources note that they were of Premi or Xifan origin (Gu 1894: 10). The father of the boy was the bearer of the golden seal bestowed upon his ancestors by the Ming emperor.[10] This seal (*yinxin*) was the official symbol of recognition by the Chinese court as a *tusi*, a hereditary native chieftain, "a unique sub-bureaucratic institution created during the early Ming to extend nominal Chinese state control over the non-Han peoples located just beyond Beijing's administrative reach" (Herman 1997: 50). The system of native chieftains was divided into two categories: military chieftains, or *tusi*, and civilian chieftains, or *tuguan*. *Tusi* tended to be appointed in areas where the emperor's control was most tenuous. While the *tuguan* often had to accept a Chinese official at his side and meddling in his administration, the *tusi* had a considerably higher level of autonomy in the way he or she ruled the territory.[11] Especially during the Ming (1368–1644) and the early Qing, the imperial bureaucracy did not interfere with *tusi* administration and demanded only a nominal level of tribute. A more important task for the chieftain was to maintain an army that the emperor could muster for his military campaigns in the region. For the native chieftain, the title helped legitimate his position locally, since the *tusi* could ask the court for support when his position or territory was threatened, and those who trespassed against his decrees were in principle subject to imperial legal code rather than the customary law. In addition to the seal, the *tusi* was also required to have an official charter (*haozhi*) as proof of his title. Each time a *tusi* died, the heir had to be acknowledged by the imperial court as the rightful successor, and in principle the charter had to be renewed (ibid.: 15–36).

According to the animal cycle of the Tibetan calendar, the boy from the Bar clan was born under the same animal as Tsongkhapa. This and other signs convinced Neten Tsultrim Sangpo and other leading monks that the boy must be a reincarnation of Sangye Gyatso, the monk sent to Muli by the third Dalai Lama, who was the first *tulku* of Muli. That the reincarnation was "discovered" among members of the leading clan was no coincidence, according to the introductory article in the Chinese translation of *History of the Dharma*: "[They] knew that if they wanted the Gelug teaching to take root in Muli and develop they first of all had to develop and rely on the local upper strata"(*Muli chöchung* 1993: 2). The boy, who later would be given the monk name of Jamyang Sangpo, was groomed by Neten Tsultrim Sangpo to take over the leadership of the Gelug monasteries in Muli and combine this position with his inherited *tusi* position, entitling him to political rule of the area. The religious aspect of his role was not neglected, however, and at the age of twenty, Jamyang Sangpo set out on the first of three study tours to Lhasa, during which he stayed at Drepung, Sera, Ganden, and Tashilhunpo monasteries (ibid.: 5).

But once again, events in the outside world would profoundly alter the political and religious landscape of Muli for years to come. In 1604, as part of a drive to strengthen the waning powers of the Ming dynasty in the Southwest, the Wanli emperor supported the Naxi *tusi* of Lijiang, Mu Zeng (1587–1646), in sending an army up the Chongtian River to occupy the area of Muli, Daocheng ('*dab-pa*), and Lithang. He consolidated the gains of his military campaign in Muli by stationing Naxi troops and building stone watchtowers.[12] Mu Zeng, or Mu Tian Wang (Heavenly Mu King), as he also was called, was a devout Buddhist and patron of the Karma Kagyu School of Tibetan Buddhism.[13] Although his father, Mu Wang, had shown a certain respect for the Gelugpa, Mu Zeng was probably too aware of the strong connection between the Gelugpa and the powerful rulers in Lhasa not to fear their political role.[14] Whether this was his primary motivation, or whether he was spurred on only by his religious convictions, is unclear. In either case, Mu Zeng is infamous in Muli history for his relentless campaign of spreading the Karma Kagyupa while attempting to destroy the Gelugpa. This ruthless undertaking involved the burning of monasteries and the massacre of numerous monks. According to *History of the Dharma*, sending a son to a Gelug monastery to become a monk at the time of Mu Zeng was the equivalent of cutting off his head and limbs (*Muli chöchung* 1993: 4).

This state of affairs made Jamyang Sangpo reluctant to leave Lhasa and return to Muli. In the meantime, he had attained the Buddhist scholarly degree of *geshe* and was planning to spend the rest of his life in retreat somewhere in Tibet. But the fifth Dalai Lama was concerned about the threatened position of the Gelugpa in the southeastern corner of Kham, and he finally convinced Jamyang Sangpo that his task was to spread the Gelug teaching and wipe out the Karma Kagyupa in his home region. Because of the situation in Muli, it was impossible for him to return immediately though, and he had to bide his time in neighboring Yanyuan, a county and military post under direct imperial rule, which officially administered the territory of Muli. In 1640, he established a Gelug monastery in Jueluo in Yanyuan, which subsequently became a safe haven for the sixty surviving Gelugpa monks who had managed to flee Muli (*Muli chöchung* 1993: 5).

Again, events far beyond its borders were about to have important consequences for Muli, especially in relation to religion. In 1642, Gushri Khan of the Koshot Mongols took the title King of Tibet but installed the fifth Dalai Lama as the worldly ruler of Tibet. In this way, Tibet became unified, and the Gelugpa's position was greatly strengthened (Smith 1996: 107). At the same time, important events were taking place in China as well: in 1644, the Manchus established the Qing dynasty, and three years later an army loyal to the Qing captured Lijiang and weakened the position of the Mu clan once and for all. Jamyang Sangpo had been waiting for precisely this kind of opportunity, and in 1648, he left Yanyuan and returned to Muli with an army and defeated the remnants of the troops of Mu Zeng (*Muli chöchung* 1993: 7).

Soon after his return, Jamyang Sangpo convened a large meeting at Wachin Gompa, where he was able to muster broad support for his position as both religious and political leader of Muli. Moreover, he managed to find acceptance for the rule that from then on, the position of head lama would be heritable only by members of the Bar clan. The position of head lama would go to the oldest brother; the youngest brother would become the lord of Bar, the manager of the manorial estate of the Bar clan, and—since the head lama was not allowed to marry—the provider of an heir to the head lama. If the lord of Bar had no offspring, his own position and that of the head lama could be inherited by the sons of his sister. The year 1648 then became the first year of the unbroken line of nineteen head lamas belonging to the Bar clan, which lasted until 1950. Besides holding the post of head lama, Jamyang Sangpo had also been recognized as the second *tulku* of Muli. Such concurrent holding of positions was not the rule in Muli, however, and subsequent *tulku* were recognized in different families, several of them poor farming or herding families. *Tulku* enjoyed enormous prestige throughout Muli's pre-Communist history, but they generally refrained from directly interfering in politics, although their advice was sought in all major decisions made by the head lamas.

Also in 1648, Muli received a visit from two officials dispatched by the Dalai Lama. They were traveling through eastern Kham to conduct a population census and collect taxes, which indicates that Muli was considered an integral part of the Tibetan regime in Lhasa. Muli is mentioned as one of the places visited by officials in the autobiography of the fifth Dalai Lama, but there is no direct reference to the visit in *History of the Dharma*,[15] which mentions that a small Tibetan force assisted Jamyang

Sangpo in suppressing the remaining resistance in Liewa, in the southwest of Muli, in that same year (*Muli chöchung* 1993: 8). It is possible that these soldiers were accompanying the two officials from Lhasa.

Jamyang Sangpo firmly established the Gelug School in Muli, largely to the detriment of the Karma Kagyupa. *History of the Dharma* contains little reference to direct religious suppression, but, when mentioned, opposition to the rule of Jamyang Sangpo is often framed as opposition to the true teachings of the Buddha and to the beneficial rule of the (Gelugpa) monasteries. The leader of the Liewa resistance, for example, happened to be an adherent of Bön. His crimes included the killing of several Gelugpa monks, and, the record states, when he was finally captured, "as a punishment for opposing the Gelug, he is executed by ripping his heart out from the back-side" (*Muli chöchung* 1993: 9). In 1656, Jamyang Sangpo died after being poisoned by one of his close followers who tried to usurp the leadership of Muli. The attempt failed when the Bar clan managed to summon the support of the fifth Dalai Lama. He sent an envoy to Muli to ensure that Samten Sangpo of the Bar clan was officially installed both as the next head lama and as the person to be recognized by the Manchu emperor as the rightful *tusi* (ibid.: 3). One of the first important feats of the new head lama was the establishment of the large monastery of Ganden Shedrub Namgyel Ling—namely, Muli Gompa—near the present-day town of Wachang in the center of Muli.

For the next three hundred years, the system of government in Muli would remain largely unchanged. As in many other monastic domains of the Gelugpa, worldly and religious authority went hand in hand. The triumvirate of the head lama, the *tulku*, and the lord of Bar (the clan that provided the head lamas) held all power in Muli. Major decisions regarding Muli had to be agreed upon by these three people (*Muli Zangzu zizhixian zhi* 1995: 544). There were several levels of administration.[16] The highest level was part of the rotating staff of the head lama and the *tulku*. All posts at this level, except for the Chinese-language secretary (C: *shiye*) and the hereditary position of *bazong* (T: *barzung rabyampa*), had to be filled by monks. The Chinese-language secretary was involved in handling relations with the Chinese—official and nonofficial—and was responsible for translating and drafting documents in Chinese. There was also a Tibetan-language secretary, the *trungyi* (C: [*da*]*zhongyi*). In addition to drafting official letters in Tibetan, one of his most important tasks was to issue, renew, and file land deeds within the territory of Muli. The different *bazong* were stationed in border areas of the territory. They were responsible for monitoring and reporting the situation at and beyond Muli's border and for engaging in and maintaining relations with the outside world, including neighboring *tusi*, the Nuosu headmen, and Chinese officials. The *bazong* would also assume responsibility for outside visitors and therefore were expected to master different languages, including Chinese and the languages of the Naxi and Nuosu. There were four major *bazong* and two minor *bazong*, each ruling an estate at the borders of Muli containing from ten to more than two hundred tenant families.[17]

The highest formal position under the head lama was that of gatekeeper (C: *mengong*; T: *dzasa*). The person who held this three-year position was responsible for carrying out the head lama's orders and handling relations with local headmen and the outside world. The gatekeeper was also responsible for overall military affairs. Other officials at this central level were an individual responsible for finances, a head clerk, and the leader of the head lama's personal bodyguard. Below this level, each of the three monasteries had its own administration, which largely followed the general Gelug monastic system. Managing the religious affairs of the main monasteries and their subordinate monasteries was the office of the *umdze* (lit., "master of rituals") under the leadership of a *kempo*. Another office, the *labrang*, administered all other affairs within its territory under the leadership of an attendant, or *kuchar*, and a manager, or *chantsö*, who took care of the economic aspects. The last level of administration was based in the villages and included an administrator sent by the monastery, the *rongpo rabjampa*, or *rongban* for short. The *rongban* was a monk, and his term of office was three years. He worked with two local administrators, a hereditary village chief and a *baise*. The *baise* was responsible for collecting taxes, organizing corvée labor, and collecting rent from tenants. The *baise*'s period of office was not fixed and depended on whether the office of the head lama was satisfied with the way the tasks were performed.[18]

This administrative system resembled that of other semiautonomous monastic domains under the control of the Lhasa government, yet in Muli it had a few peculiarities, reflecting some of the local conditions. For example, the territory was not ruled from a fixed monastery; rather, the seat of the head lama and his administration rotated each year between one of the three main monasteries of Muli, Wachin, and Kulu. Muli furthermore had its own local system for accommodating cultural differences among some of the ethnic groups: the Naxi living in Eya, a strategic border area in the southwestern corner of the territory, were granted a high degree of autonomy and were ruled by their own hereditary native chiefs, the *muguan*. A *muguan* had his own administration, but his staff had to be approved by the monastic bureaucracy (Guo 1986: 6). In the few Miao villages of Muli—established by refugees who had escaped the suppression of the Miao Rebellion of 1855–72 in Yunnan and Guizhou—the *baise*'s powers were limited in comparison to those of *baise* in other villages.

The Dalai Lama's Tibetan government recognized the authority of the head lama as that of a *gyelpo*, or local king, under the rule of Lhasa. At the same time, the head lamas were recognized by the Qing administration as *tusi*, a hereditary native chieftain. Both titles implied a substantial level of independence. As a remote border area, Muli enjoyed greater actual autonomy from Lhasa than did other monastic domains such as Chamdo. The relationship between the head lamas and the Manchu empire was also very loose, especially in the early period of the Qing. In the seventeenth century, the emperors were too busy consolidating their regime to pay attention to the Southwest. Furthermore, the Qing accepted Gushri Khan's administrative power over Tibet and were weary of upsetting the balance of power with the Mongols (Y. Dai 1996: 79). But even a nominal inclusion into these two larger polities was not entirely without consequences: Muli was regularly forced to provide soldiers to assist either the Qing or the Tibetans and their Mongol allies in fighting battles in the region.

When Wu Sangui (1612–1678) rebelled against the Qing in 1673, Muli was indirectly drawn into a major conflict.[19] The Kangxi emperor requested assistance in suppressing the revolt, but the fifth Dalai Lama was reluctant to become involved, according to documents on the correspondence between Lhasa and Beijing.[20] In 1674, in a very limited response to the Qing request, he sent a Tibetan-Mongol expeditionary force to attack some of Wu's troops who had penetrated Gyelthang, to the southwest of Muli. The Dalai Lama ordered the second head lama of Muli, Samten Sangpo, to aid this force in the attack. An army of monks and laypeople was hastily assembled and subsequently invaded Gyelthang from the northeast. According to *History of the Dharma*, the Muli troops performed very well, compared to their Tibetan and Mongol allies, because they were familiar with the terrain. A year later, the Dalai Lama rewarded Samten Sangpo with five villages in the Naxi-inhabited territory of Eya to the southwest of Muli. The retaking of Gyelthang was the only real action the Tibetans undertook in response to the requests of the Kangxi emperor.

According to the autobiography of the fifth Dalai Lama, Wu Sangui also tried hard to win the support of the Tibetans, sending several delegations to Lhasa, some of them laden with gold and other treasures. The rebels even renounced their claims to the territory of Gyelthang and the whole of Lijiang Prefecture (Lijiang Fu) in the hope of forging an alliance with the Tibetans (Ahmad 1970: 216–17). This presumably contributed to the Dalai Lama's willingness to try to convince the Kangxi emperor to enter into a truce with Wu Sangui (Y. Dai 1996: 105). But the attempt failed and greatly displeased the emperor. Suspicious of the Dalai Lama's motives, he ordered all correspondence between the rebels and the Tibetans to be collected and studied. In order not to upset the Qing even more, during the final phase of the rebellion, the Dalai Lama issued a directive to all local rulers dependent on Lhasa to block any attempt by the remnants of the rebel armies to escape toward Kham. When a thousand rebel troops entered Muli in 1680, the head lama hastily sent troops to block the invading rebels; ill prepared, Muli troops were initially defeated. After regrouping and waiting until the rebel army was concentrated at the Yu River crossing, Muli troops launched a surprise attack and annihilated the rebels. Those captured alive were handed over to the Qing in Chengdu (*Muli chöchung* 1993: 32).

The Wu Sangui Rebellion and its suppression marked the start of a new phase in the history of the Southwest. One of the most important lessons for the Qing was that it had to become more directly involved in the administration of this region. The *tusi* system was closely scrutinized, and many native chieftains were replaced by Qing administrators (the so-called *gaitu guiliu* system). The Qing emperor drew another lesson from the rebellion, namely, that it was necessary to keep a much closer watch on the regime of the Dalai Lama and become more involved in monitoring and controlling the border regions of Kham.[21] This policy only intensified in the following decades, when the Kangxi emperor and the Tibetans were unable to agree on a common policy for handling a major conflict between the Oirat, or Dzungars, and the Khalka Mongols, which spilled across the northern frontier of the Qing (Ahmad 1970: 254–85). The fact that the death of the fifth Dalai Lama in 1682 was kept secret from the Kangxi emperor for fifteen years by the regent, or *desi*, of Tibet did nothing to improve the relationship between the Manchus and the Tibetans.

MAINTAINING AUTONOMY IN A CONTESTED AND CONFLICT-RIDDEN BORDER REGION

In 1720, Qing forces occupied Lhasa to chase out the Dzungars. They stationed troops there, and installed a local government under the nominal control of a Qing representative, the *amban*. Kham was detached from Lhasa's jurisdiction and placed under the control of the Manchu emperor through the *tusi* system (Smith 1996: 127–35). Qing control over Tibet reached its zenith in 1792, when the powers of the *amban* were considerably extended, and from that time onward, the Qing emperors had the final say in recognizing new incarnations through the system of the golden urn.

The broader sociopolitical changes of the eighteenth century did not leave Muli unscathed. The Gelug monastic system dominated by the Dalai Lama remained firmly in place and was even strengthened through the active patronage of the Manchu emperors, but the political dimension of the system was reduced to a locally significant legitimation of worldly authority. The larger political picture for Muli was now dominated by the close presence of the Qing, through its active administration of Kham and Yunnan and its control over central Tibetan politics. In order to maintain a high degree of independence, the subsequent head lamas of Muli were forced to skillfully cultivate their relationships with the Qing court. At this, they were rather successful, and in 1729, the Yongzheng emperor rewarded Lobsang Thutob, the sixth head lama, for his assistance in the Qing campaigns against the Nuosu of Liangshan with the official title of "pacification commissioner" (*anfushi*), and he was given the official seal in the following year (Gu 1894: 12).[22]

Starting in 1781, during the term of office of the ninth head lama, the Bar were awarded the Chinese family name Xiang by the emperor.[23] The ninth head lama, Xiang Niancha, was the first ruler of Muli to be mentioned in the official *Annals of Yanyuan County*. This Qing record also clearly states the rules of succession, namely, that the position of pacification commissioner would be inherited by the younger brother of the officeholder or, if there were no younger brother, by the son of a brother (Gu 1894: 12). Xiang Niancha left no opportunity unexplored in his attempts to bolster his relationship with the Qing court, and in 1787, he undertook the long journey to Beijing accompanied by a large mission from Muli.[24] They carried numerous precious gifts with them and were rewarded for their efforts with an audience with the Qianlong emperor at which Xiang Niancha received several honorary titles.

It would be wrong to conclude, however, that the closer relationship with the Qing meant that Tibetan influence had vanished from Muli. The Gelug monastic system brought with it a strong link to the main Gelug monasteries in central Tibet. Monks from Muli regularly participated in ceremonies in other Gelug monasteries, and at any given time a number of monks from Muli were studying in Lhasa. Since head lamas were also monks, they were required to follow certain religious regulations; as the head lama was the highest religious authority, succession to this position had to be recognized by religious leaders in Tibet. Each time a new head lama ascended to the throne in Muli, delegations would be sent bearing gifts to the Dalai and Panchen Lamas, in order to obtain approval and blessings from the new head lama. When seen in the light of the head lama's worldly powers, this meant that Lhasa continued to play a political role in Muli, even during periods when the Manchu empire exercised stronger control in the region. This was important: although succession to the position of head lama remained the exclusive monopoly of the members of the Bar clan, their leadership did not always go unchallenged. Muli's history is full of internal fights initiated by high-ranking monks and other local power holders who were attempting to usurp the throne in Muli. Such contenders often allied themselves with the forces of neighboring local rulers, several of whom were in almost constant conflict with Muli—and with one another—because of territorial disputes. The times when the succession passed from one head lama to the next therefore constituted vulnerable periods for Muli and its continued existence as a semi-independent political entity.

One major incident occurred in 1867, when a conflict between one of the higher-ranking monks and the twelfth head lama, Xiang Zhashi,[25] escalated after the monk managed to get help from a Han opium dealer and his well-armed troops. The result was disastrous for Muli. Several hundred Muli soldiers were slaughtered, Wachin Gompa was destroyed by fire, and Xiang Zhashi was strangled and the official seal of the pacification office was lost (*Muli Zangzu zizhixian zhu* 1995: 706; Gu 1894: 13). In spite of these adversities, the Bar clan managed to cling to power, and in 1868, Xiang Zhashi's younger brother Xiang Songlang Zhashen was installed as the next head lama. In the same year, because of his achievements during a Qing campaign in Yunnan, the Tongzhi emperor awarded Xiang Songlang Zhashen with the title of "control commissioner" (*xuanweishi*), which Hucker defines as "one of the most prestigious titles granted aboriginal tribes in south-western China and their natural, mostly hereditary chiefs" (1985: 251).[26] The appointment expressed the Qing's appreciation of the head lamas' valuable contributions and would prove an important asset in the final years of the dynasty.

Over the course of the nineteenth century, Qing influence in central Tibet and Kham gradually waned. The emperors were fully occupied with major conflicts threatening the survival of the dynasty, such as the Opium Wars and the Taiping Rebellion. Qing interest in Tibet was dramatically aroused again in 1904 by the British military expedition into Tibet led by Francis Younghusband. The Guangxu emperor realized how exposed Tibet was to foreign intervention and decided that more troops had to be stationed in Tibet and that Kham had to be brought under direct imperial rule. More effective control of the major towns in Kham would safeguard the route to Lhasa, protect the Qing's income from taxes on the lucrative trade in tea and salt, and open up the region for economic development (Coleman 2002: 37).

In Bathang, Sichuan authorities had planned a small-scale project under which Chinese farmers were to constitute the vanguard of a process of economic development in Kham. When a Qing official passed though Bathang on his way to Chamdo in 1904, he decided that the time was ripe for implementing the project (Sperling 1976: 12–13). With great zeal, he imported Han farmers, enlisted local Tibetans in his army, allowed French missionaries to set up a mission station, and punished bandits, all without consulting the local rulers. Not surprisingly, these actions provoked an uprising, and the Qing official was killed by a monk-led mob. The reaction of the Sichuan government was as heavy-handed as could be expected: the local rulers and all the principal monks were killed. Zhao Erfeng was one of the Qing magistrates who led the punitive action. In hindsight, it is clear that this was just the occasion Zhao had been waiting for in that it provided the opportunity to implement a series of radical changes in Kham and establish firm control in the whole area. Over the next few years, he abolished the *tusi* system in the whole of Kham and replaced these native rulers with Qing officials, forcefully curtailed the power of the monasteries, initiated the establishment of Chinese schools to "civilize the natives," and promoted permanent Han migration to the region (ibid.: 19–21). All opposition was brutally suppressed: large numbers of Tibetans, whether local rulers, monks, or ordinary villagers, were killed, and not a few monasteries were burned to the ground.[27]

The fall of the Qing in 1911 effectively undid many of Zhao's reforms (he was murdered in the same year), but the ensuing chaos was not necessarily an improvement for the people of Kham. The Qing administration installed by Zhao crumbled, but the traditional Tibetan system of indirect rule by local hereditary rulers (*depa* or *gyelpo*)[28] or monasteries had been thoroughly dismantled and could not easily be resurrected to provide alternative power structures that would provide some stability for local populations. After the death of Yuan Shikai in 1916, Yunnan and Sichuan declared their independence and then went to war against each other. Eastern Kham became part of the battlefield. In 1917, after the debacle of the Simla Conference, conflict between Tibetan and Chinese troops erupted in Chamdo and escalated into a full-blown war over territorial authority in central Tibet and Kham. This time, the main battlefield was western Kham. The de facto border between the Tibetan regime in Lhasa and the Chinese Republic stabilized after a truce in 1918, although neither side accepted the status quo as a definitive solution to Tibet's status in relation to China (Teichman 1922: 58). Armed conflict between the two sides broke out intermittently—as in 1931—but otherwise this state of affairs lasted until the Communist takeover in 1949.

However, the absence of major wars did not mean that the region became peaceful: banditry and minor local conflicts were rife. The areas immediately to the west of Muli, Chatring and Kongkaling, were especially affected.[29] This development, too, could be attributed largely to Zhao Erfeng. His removal of the *depa* of Lithang and destruction of the monasteries in the region effectively eliminated functional authority, and agriculture almost came to a standstill since nobody protected the harvests. This left villagers with only two alternatives: to leave the region or to join the numerous bands of armed bandits and live off the booty they obtained through attacking caravans passing through the region or raiding some of the richer areas surrounding Chatring, Kongkaling, and Gyelthang. In addition to banditry, the whole Southwest region was a theater for petty conflicts between local warlords: eastern Kham was for several decades ruled by the warlord of western Sichuan, Liu Wenhui, who regularly engaged in conflicts with other warlords vying for control of Sichuan and the Southwest (Peng 2002: 62). In 1939, Kham was officially designated the Chinese province of Xikang.

Events in this macro-level context of political upheavals, forced reforms, uprisings, and border wars did not leave Muli unaffected, although it managed to retain its autonomy and members of the Bar clan remained the undisputed autocrats of their kingdom. There are very few references to Muli in the available literature, and consequently one can only speculate as to why Muli escaped from direct political or military interventions such as those conducted by Zhao Erfeng and his officials.[30] Most likely, several factors were responsible: First of all, Muli was not situated on major trade routes and was a small area with a small population. Second, the position of control commissioner held by the head lama conferred a certain prestige and a well-developed network that included ties with elites in the Southwest and Nanjing. Third, Muli might have been overlooked because of its administrative status: although Muli was part of Kham from a Tibetan point of view,[31] the Chinese officially classified it as part of Yanyuan County, which was one of the counties of Ningyuan Prefecture (corresponding more or less to present-day Liangshan Prefecture). A final reason was surely the astute diplomatic skills of the head lamas, who avoided confrontations they could not win and constantly built alliances with the strongest parties. Although Muli avoided many of the major upheavals of this violent half century, it could not escape the occasional disturbance. The turbulent career of the sixteenth head lama, Xiang Cicheng Zhaba (1877–1934), presents a telling illustration, not only of how developments in the larger region affected Muli, but also of the need to carefully balance relationships with important regional players and that the inevitable occasional miscalculation could have fatal consequences. Xiang Cicheng Zhaba was the head lama visited by Joseph Rock and mentioned in several of his writings (see, e.g., 1925). Originally, Xiang Cicheng Zhaba's older brother was in line to take up the position of head lama. Moreover, at a very young age, Xiang Cicheng Zhaba had been recognized as the reincarnation of the Miji Tulku of Molashog Gompa just north of Muli, halfway to Lithang. After receiving a thorough education in Buddhism and visiting Tibet on several pilgrimages, he began traveling around Kham to expound Buddhist teaching. But when fate struck, he was pulled back to Muli. As his biography in the *Annals of Muli Tibetan Autonomous County* tells us:

> His reputation steadily increased, and he developed a large network within Kham. When the fifteenth head lama [his brother] died in 1924, Xiang Zhaba Songdian [his nephew, the next in line] was too young to take over, so Xiang Cicheng Zhaba returned to Muli and convinced local religious leaders that he should become the acting sixteenth head lama of the Muli Pacification Commission. As was customary, this succession had to be recognized by the Dalai and Panchen Lamas. At that time, the eighth Panchen Lama happened to be in Inner Mongolia, and people from Muli had to travel the whole way through Yunnan, Vietnam, and Nanjing to reach him and present gifts. . . . At the same time, people were sent to the Yi areas to purchase good horses to send them as gifts to the thirteenth Dalai Lama.
>
> After Xiang had usurped the post . . . he expanded the military. As to relations with the outside, he enlarged ties with army and government officials and important social figures in Xikang, Tibet, and Yunnan. He became a celebrated personality, with the power of a *tusi* of the nine *suo* [military commanderies] of Yanyuan. After some time, Xiang received the order from the Sichuan frontier commissioner Chen Xialing[32] to come and assist him in suppressing a rebellion in Lihuo. They were victorious. The Xiang army captured a small cannon and 250 rifles. Xiang escorted them personally to Chen in Kangding [Dartsendo] and received his praise.
>
> During his time in office, Xiang did not submit to the jurisdiction of Yanyuan at all; he did not obey orders and acted like a king. He even went so far as to threaten to break away from Yanyuan in Sichuan and become part of Yunnan Province. In 1928, the Preparatory Committee for the Establishment of Xikang Province listed Xiang's nine major crimes in its "Survey of Muli *tusi*." At the same time, it announced that troops would be sent to abolish the *tusi* system in Muli. . . .

In 1930, the Yunnan army was engaged in fierce battle.[33] The Thirty-ninth Infantry Army of the Nationalist Party stationed in Yunnan was defeated by the army of [warlord] Long Yun, and the survivors—led by commander Hu Ruoyu and vice-commander Meng Kun—fled to Muli. Xiang received orders from Long Yun to send troops to make surprise attacks at strategic passes and exterminate soldiers who fell behind. They captured more than one hundred guns. The soldiers led by Hu suffered tremendous losses while under way, and when they crossed the Yarlong Zangbo River in their retreat to Jiulong, they were blocked by the Long and Xiang armies and then almost completely annihilated. Only four hundred of the men originally led by Hu found refuge with Liu Wenhui. As a result, Xiang's relationship with the Sichuan and Xikang militarists worsened further.

In March 1931, Xiang Cicheng Zhaba sent [two high-placed officials from Muli] to Jiang Jieshi [Chiang Kai-shek] in Nanjing carrying many gifts. Although they did not obtain the audience with the president they had hoped for, Jiang granted the official title "Nomihan"[34] for Xiang. [After a subsequent delegation visited Nanjing], Jiang Jieshi gave one hundred rifles and ten thousand bullets to the Muli *tusi*.

In 1933, [a] Nationalist army [under the command of Liu Wenhui] dispatched troops to Muli to begin mining gold in order to pay the soldiers. Xiang was not pleased and did his best behind the scenes to stop the project. He petitioned the Republican government to stop the mining and promised to pay compensation. At the same time, he gave support to [local bandits] to harass the miners and the accompanying soldiers. They wiped out these troops, forcing the mining to stop. Xiang never paid any compensation.

In Republican times, bandits constantly attacked the [eastern part of Muli]. In 1933, Xiang organized a standing army of one hundred well-equipped soldiers and transferred twenty contingents of regular soldiers to this region, each contingent being made up of twenty-five people. They were placed to guard strategic spots....

In 1934, Xiang, through Long Yun's recommendation, received the title "Lieutenant General of the Ground Forces" from the central Nationalist government.... In November of the same year, the army commander Liu Wenhui retaliated against Xiang for Xiang's rapprochement with Yunnan and for the mining incident. He dispatched [an army commander] with a company of soldiers to Muli under the pretense of carrying a letter stating that Xiang had been appointed control commissioner together with the appropriate official seal. When Xiang Cicheng Zhaba came out to meet the commander near Kulu Gompa, he was shot dead by Liu's soldiers. He was fifty-seven. (*Muli Zangzu zizhixian zhi* 1995: 937–39)

Clearly the good relationship Xiang Cicheng Zhaba had cultivated with Chiang Kai-shek could not save him from his local warlord enemies.[35] Liu's troops moreover seized the Muli *tulku* and Xiang Zhaba Songdian, Xiang Cicheng Zhaba's nephew and successor, and transported them to Xichang. According to its official gazetteer, Muli was also forced to pay Liu between four hundred thousand and six hundred thousand silver dollars as well as large quantities of precious medicinal herbs as ransom (*Muli Zangzu zizhixian zhi* 1995: 708, 949), to which the villagers of Muli had to contribute. After his release in 1935, Xiang Zhaba Songdian was instated as the seventeenth head lama. Xiang continued the difficult task of building alliances to maintain Muli's independence. Nevertheless, he had learned from the tragic death of his uncle and his own abduction to Xichang. Soon after taking up his post, he contacted Liu Wenhui and managed to mend fences. At the same time, he sent a delegation to Kunming to strengthen his alliance with Long Yun, the Yunnan warlord. In 1936, Long Yun provided Xiang with modern military equipment and recommended to the government in Nanjing that he receive a high military post. One of his tasks would be to block the Red Army in its advance in the Southwest. This responsibility involved the maintenance and training of a large army. According to a Chinese visitor to Muli in the late 1930s, one young man in each family in Muli was forced to participate in a one-month training session each year, and if there were no men in the family, a woman had to work for the army by taking care of provisions (Liu 1939: 66).

In the years just before the Communist takeover, Xiang was embroiled in a prolonged armed conflict with the *tusi* of Zuosuo, also one of the nine chieftains classified within the territory of Yanyuan County. This conflict erupted when the Zuosuo *tusi* interfered in a local succession feud in Qiansuo—a third chieftaincy under Yanyuan—and in this way provoked the Muli *tusi*, who claimed a legitimate interest in the conflict due to his close religious ties with a Gelug temple in Qiansuo. Over the next two years, the standing armies and conscripts of the chieftaincies fought several battles, which resulted in many casualties (*Muli Zangzu zizhixian zhi* 1995: 80–82). The conflict is worth mentioning because the older people in Bustling Township still had vivid memories of the fighting. An eighty-year-old man from the village of Ten Houses recalled:

> There once was a big fight between Muli and the Zuosuo *tusi*. I was twenty to twenty-five then. There was no way to escape; every family had to send one soldier to fight Zuosuo. Even the Han had to participate. Nobody from here died though. The idea was to muster as many people from Muli as possible to demonstrate to Zuosuo how strong we were. We, the common people, only had single-shot rifles that had to be filled with powder up front and fired by a piece of burning wood. This [participation in military actions] we had to do several times in that period.

Reading about the lives and exploits of the head lamas of Muli is like reading about the lives of celebrated generals or warlords in the Chinese historiographical tradition. Of course, to a large extent this impression may be attributed to the form of historiography available, in which wars and related events are considered to be the information most worthy of being recorded. Nonetheless, in between listings of weapon purchases, records of battlefield merits, or the reception of military titles, there are references suggesting that the head lamas and their entourages were also preoccupied with activities more aligned with their role as Buddhist monks. For example, the *Annals of Muli Tibetan Autonomous County* mentions that in 1940, Xiang Zhaba Songdian went on a pilgrimage to Lhasa during which he visited all of the major monasteries and paid his respects to the fourteenth Dalai Lama (*Muli Zangzu zizhixian zhi* 1995: 950). In fact, Xiang stayed in Lhasa for fifteen months to pursue religious studies and build close contacts with the religious elite. But no details were written down about his stay. In 1944, Xiang Zhaba Songdian resigned, and his nephew Xiang Songdian Chunpin became the eighteenth head lama.

While the few sources on Muli history give us at least a limited insight into some aspects of the lives of the pre-Communist elites, there is very little to be found about village life during this period. There are few traces suggesting the existence of separate local cultures within villages inhabited by Premi, Na, Shuhi^n, or other ethnic groups. In contrast to many other ethnic minority areas of China, Muli was the subject of only a few sporadic research projects in the early PRC period that might have documented social organization before the Communists arrived. Some patchy data on village life can be found in the Muli gazetteer, but as could be expected, most of the data included appear to have been selected in order to expose the hardship borne by ordinary villagers under an oppressive regime that combined religion and politics and consequently to legitimate the toppling of the head lamas' regime. That does not belie the fact that life probably was quite difficult for the majority of the inhabitants of Muli. One of the very few surviving eyewitness accounts about life in Muli before 1949 is the short article by Liu Lirong, who stayed there for a month in 1938. Liu does not paint a rosy picture of village life under the head lama and his administration. There were 3,700 commoner households, including the Xifan (Premi), the Gami (Kham Tibetans), and the Moxie (Naxi, Na, Rek'ua).[36] The commoners (*baixing*) had to pay taxes and perform corvée duties, called *ulag*.[37] The approximately 3,000 other families living in Muli in 1938 were almost all tenant farmers who were migrants or descendants of recent migrants. About one-third were Han, and the remainder mainly Lolo (Nuosu) and Miao. Tenant farmers were free of corvée duties but had to pay around 40 percent of their harvest as rent for their land as well as taxes to the head lama (Liu 1939: 67–68). Some of the old people in Bustling Township still remembered trying to hide some of their goods when the taxman came on his yearly visit after the Premi New Year period. In each house, he would make an inventory of the family's possessions and calculate the taxes due, and the villagers then had to deliver the taxes to the monastery.

In addition to taxes and corvée duties, commoners also had to send their sons to the monastery or to fight in the countless conflicts in which the head lamas were involved. In special circumstances, tenant farmers could also be called to arms, as described by the Ten Houses villager who took part in the war between Muli and Zuosuo. An effective system of public security ensured draconian enforcement of these duties and the regulations of the local penal code. Consequently, according to Liu, there was little crime, at least until the arrival of several hundred migrants in the early years of the Republic (1939: 68). Those who broke the laws met with cruel punishment, such as being skinned alive, as the Muli gazetteer is careful to mention (*Muli Zangzu zizhixian zhi* 1995: 672). Nevertheless, bandits from neighboring territories regularly raided people living in the border regions of Muli. In the west, these bandits were Tibetans from Chatring and Kongkaling. In the east and south, villagers were attacked by Nuosu people plundering and capturing slaves. But not all Nuosu bandits came from outside Muli, and sometimes they even had accomplices among the non-Nuosu population. People did not wait for the monastery's judicial system to settle the case, as my eighty-year-old Rek'ua informant from Ten Houses revealed:

> [In the 1940s] I was wounded by the Ga^{n}yè [Nuosu]. A bullet went right through my lower arm. One other person was wounded and two died; one of them was my relative. This happened when about twenty Ga^{n}yè came from [the neighboring township, also in Muli]. They had been called in by two Premi from [Flowery Valley, in Bustling Township]. These two Premi knew the region well, so they could inform the Ga^{n}yè precisely where they could steal what. These Ga^{n}yè stole everything, that is, including all domestic animals in [Walnut Grove] and [Ten Houses]. They gave part of the booty to the two Premi from [Flowery Valley]. The Ga^{n}yè also kidnapped two children to make them into slaves. Afterward, the people from [Ten Houses], [Walnut Grove], and [Uphill and Downhill] went to [Flowery Valley] and killed the two Premi.

In the final decades of the Republic, the relative stability of Muli attracted refugees from the more volatile regions around its perimeter, doubling its population, according to Liu (1939: 68). Many newcomers were Han and Nuosu people. The Nuosu from the Liangshan area were pressed ever closer to Muli in their search for more arable land, and in 1940, the head lama granted a Black Nuosu[38] leader from Guabie in Yanyuan a "red permit" (*hongzhao*), allowing him to open up land in Muli and move in Nuosu tenant farmers in exchange for a considerable amount of money. Relations between the Nuosu and their neighbors were not very cordial, though, and in 1950, a disagreement between the Nuosu clan leader and the Muli administrators about payment of land taxes led to a major armed conflict. For several months, both sides conducted raids and counter-raids into each other's territory, resulting in scores of casualties. According to the villager from Ten Houses, some of these raids extended as far into Muli territory as Bustling Township: "Another time when the Ga^{n}yè attacked, the Muli army was in [Gaku]. I ran as fast as I could to

[Gaku] to call for help. The Muli army came immediately and killed one Black Ga^{n}nyè, but two from the army were wounded, one of them got a bullet through his mouth which went out through his neck. The others ran off." Only under strong pressure from the new Communist regime was the conflict resolved, in June 1951, more than a year after the "liberation" of Yanyuan and Muli (*Muli Zangzu zizhixian zhi* 1995: 82–84).

INTEGRATION INTO THE PEOPLE'S REPUBLIC OF CHINA

At the beginning of 1950, the cornered Nationalists in the Southwest sent a delegation to Muli to convince the retired head lama Xiang Zhaba Songdian to organize a military blockade against the advancing People's Liberation Army (PLA) and prepare for resistance in case the Communists took over.[39] Xiang Zhaba Songdian had abdicated in 1944 in favor of his nephew, Xiang Songdian Chunpin, the eighteenth head lama, who in turn abdicated on 1 January 1950, leaving the Muli throne to his own nephew Xiang Peichu Zhaba—also known as Pencozaba—the nineteenth and last head lama. Xiang Zhaba Songdian nevertheless still played an important role behind the scenes, and he had excellent connections with the Nationalists. The Muli leadership was initially favorably inclined toward the request, but opinions diverged after Xichang fell to the PLA at the beginning of March 1950. While one faction of the elite advocated a plan to mobilize a force of three thousand men at arms to block the PLA from entering Muli from the southeast, another faction under the leadership of Gatekeeper Wang Peichu Qudian strongly opposed such an action, believing that it would be utterly futile. According to the *Annals of Muli Tibetan Autonomous County*, Wang argued that "fighting the PLA with lama soldiers was like smashing rocks with eggs" (*Muli Zangzu zizhixian zhi* 1995: 84). The thirty-eight-year-old Wang enjoyed a high level of prestige in Muli and the trust of the nineteenth head lama, Xiang Peichu Zhaba. Wang had been sent to a monastery at the age of seven and made a brilliant career in the monk-bureaucracy of Muli, becoming gatekeeper in 1947. During a longer stay in Kangding (Dartsendo) in 1949, on official business, he came to understand that the days of the Nationalists were numbered. Nevertheless, he was unable to convince either the other faction or the two Xiangs. In this stalemate, the two factions agreed to request that the ninth *tulku* of Muli, Jiayang Zhigu, perform a divination, and the result would prove auspicious for Muli's elite: "do not dispatch troops!" (ibid.: 84). While the *Annals* gives the impression that the outcome of the *tulku*'s divination tipped the balance, it is hard to believe that a result supporting the momentous decision to militarily oppose the PLA would have been accepted. In view of the long-standing tradition of pragmatism and realpolitik the head lamas followed when faced with unwinnable military challenges, compliance and submission were the sole logical reactions.[40]

After taking Yanyuan at the end of March 1950, the PLA was keen to avoid having remnants of routed Nationalist forces escape through Muli. Mu Wenfu, a local Tibetan accompanying the PLA, sent a letter to Wang Peichu Qudian.[41] Extolling the wonders of the Communists' ethnic minority policy, he asked Wang to assist the PLA in blocking the Nationalists and to prepare for the PLA's entry into Muli. Finally, in its pursuit of the fleeing Nationalists, the PLA marched unopposed into Muli on April 25. Wang managed to convince those members of the elite who had fled into the mountains to return and meet the PLA officers. Both he and the head lama Xiang Peichu Zhaba received letters of recognition for their contribution to the "liberation" of Muli (*Muli Zangzu zizhixian zhi* 1995: 939).

The smoothness of the Communist takeover in Muli was not without significance for the manner in which the area would be further integrated into the new People's Republic of China. It was especially important in determining the role the former elite would be allowed to play in rebuilding Muli within the narrow frame of a Chinese Communist state. Under the United Front policy of the early years, the Chinese Communist Party (CCP) committed significant resources to the effort of winning over so-called progressive former elites in ethnic minority areas. Melvyn Goldstein argues that this was one of the principal policies shaping the Sino-Tibetan relationship between 1951 and the Tibetan uprising in 1959. He underscores this by referring to instructions the Party's Central Committee sent to the Chinese leaders in Lhasa in mid-1952 regarding the three monastic seats of Drepung, Sera, and Ganden:

> The united front work of the three main monasteries is like other united front work in Tibet. The emphasis should be on the upper hierarchy. We

should try to win any of those close to the top of the hierarchy, provided that they are not stubborn running dogs of imperialists, or even bigger bandits and spies. Therefore, you should try patiently to win support among those upper level lamas whom you referred to as those full of hatred to the Hans and to our government. *Our present policy is not to organize people at the bottom level to isolate those at the top.* We should try to work on the top, get their support, and achieve the purpose of building harmony between the masses and us. (Telegram from the Central Committee of the Chinese Communist Party, 19 May 1952, cited in Goldstein 1998: 23, Goldstein's emphasis)

The Communists did not consider Muli to be part of Tibet and were therefore technically not required to use these indirect methods of imposing their regime. Nevertheless, the establishment of Muli Tibetan Autonomous County unfolded in such a way to make it clear that the Communists rigorously followed a policy of co-opting the local elites. In view of the strong link between religious and worldly rule, this policy would have important consequences for how religion would be defined in Muli under the new Communist regime.

In January 1951, the military control commission in Xichang sent two high-ranking cadres to Muli—one of them the Tibetan Mu Wenfu—to convince Xiang Peichu Zhaba and Wang Peichu Qudian to send students to the Xichang Nationality Cadre School (Xichang Minzu Ganbu Xuexiao) and to send a delegation to the second Conference of Representatives of People of all Ethnic and Other Groups (CRPEOG) (Ge Zu Ge Jie Renmin Daibiao Huiyi) in Yanyuan. They were successful, and at the beginning of April, Wang led a delegation of forty representatives from the three main monasteries of Muli to Yanyuan to participate in the conference. There, Xiang Peichu Zhaba was elected the vice chairman of Yanyuan County, of which Muli was still officially a part, and Wang was elected a permanent member of the conference. A week later, Wang participated in a Yanyuan delegation of minority *minzu* to Xichang, where he was received by high-ranking CCP cadres.

A month later, on 20 May 1951, the Xiangs and the other elites must have realized that a radical new era had begun when a twenty-member delegation arrived and initiated a comprehensive reform agenda that would keep them in Muli for almost two months. The delegates organized mass meetings during which the propagation of CCP policies was accompanied by gifts of tea, salt, and cigarettes. They set up several committees for different purposes such as organizing education, recruiting students for cadre schools, mopping up remnants of the Nationalist armies, preparing to abolish the corvée system, and resolving the dispute over land taxes between Muli and the Black Nuosu headman from Guabie, which had resulted in armed conflict the year before. The delegates were careful to involve the head lama and other members of the elite, such as Wang and Lin Jiayong, the lord of Bar, in most of this work and, in particular, in the creation of a preparatory committee for the establishment of a Muli Tibetan Autonomous Region at the county level. Xiang Peichu Zhaba became its head, and Wang Peichu Qudian, Mu Wenfu, and a Yanyuan CCP vice chairman were made its vice-leaders.

After the departure of the delegation, Wang worked to involve the lower echelons of the old Muli administration—such as the abbots of the smaller monasteries and the local headmen—in the reforms of the PRC regime. But his revolutionary zeal was not shared by everyone in Muli, and on 27 August 1951, he was shot and killed on his way to work at the preparatory committee. As the *Annals of Muli Tibetan Autonomous County* reports: "The progressive activities of Wang Peichu Qudian were looked upon with hatred by a small number of reactionary upper-strata" (*Muli Zangzu zizhixian zhi* 1995: 940). Through the organization of large-scale ceremonies in Muli, Yanyuan, and Xichang, the new regime took great care to display its appreciation for a member of the former elite who had made the ultimate sacrifice for the "New China."[42]

The preparatory commission continued its work without Wang. According to Hu Jingming, now a retired Premi cadre from Yunnan, who participated in one of the meetings of the commission, Xiang Peichu Zhaba wanted to establish the Tibetan Autonomous Region at the county level, since this would make Muli independent of Yanyuan County (Hu Jingming, pers. comm., 18 May 2004). He found support for his wishes when he visited Party leaders in Beijing in 1951 (Harrell 2001: 210). Opinions were divided, though, and there were several conflicts within the group; one of them—between Lin Jiayong, the lord of Bar, and two of the former head lamas—had to be settled with a visit from a special working group from Xichang. Finally, at a large meeting at Muli Gompa on 19 February 1953, the Xikang provincial government officially declared the establishment of Muli Tibetan Autonomous County. The new county was divided into three "districts" (*qu*) according to the domains of the three monasteries: first district, Muli; second district, Kulu (Kangwu); and third district, Wachin (Wa'erzhai). Below the district level, nineteen townships were established. Xiang Peichu Zhaba, the nineteenth and last head lama, became the county head, and both Xiang Songdian Chunpin, his predecessor who ruled Muli from 1944 to 1949, and Tulku Jiayang Zhigu, were each given one of the four vice-leader posts. Han Jiayang, the former gatekeeper for the seventeenth and eighteenth head lamas, became vice-head of the Chinese People's Political Consultative Conference (CPPCC); Shu Yuanyuan, the former Naxi *bazong* of Baiwu and attendant for the head lama, was made vice-head of the civil administration of the autonomous county. In all, nine members of the former high-level elite were given leading posts in the new administration, almost thirty of those categorized as medium-level leaders were given positions, and more than one hundred headmen and local administrators of the old regime were given positions such as heads and vice-heads of townships (*Muli Zangzu zizhixian zhi* 1995: 87–88). As elsewhere in China, members of the former elite were also given posts in the CPPCC; although this organ has limited direct political power, membership carries a certain prestige and provides access to important personal networks. Besides co-opting the Muli elites by drawing them into the new political system, these appointments served another purpose: in order to obtain their support in carrying out more radical reforms such as the abolishment of the corvée and tax systems (also called the "thirty-three burdens" [*sanshisan zhong fudan*]), it was necessary to provide the former leaders and administrators with a regular income in place of their traditional source of income. The 1,100-strong monk population living in the monasteries needed a source of income now that the Muli villagers were no longer forced to provide for their livelihoods; therefore, each monk was allotted a fixed amount of 25 *jin* of grain per year.[43]

The integration of Muli into China followed a model the Communists had used in other areas inhabited by majority non-Han populations who had enjoyed a high degree of de facto independence and would therefore be more difficult to integrate, for example, the Shan/Tai kingdom of Sipsong Panna (Xishuangbanna), on the Burma border, and the famed independent Lolo (Nuosu/Yi) of Liangshan. The approach was different with many other ethnic minority areas in the Southwest, where local autonomy vis-à-vis the Chinese state had long since withered because of such factors as large-scale Han in-migration or the Qing's *gaitu guiliu* policy of replacing native rulers with its own administrators. Rather than risking a bloody takeover that might generate resistance in other ethnic minority areas and jeopardize the Party's ethnic minority policy throughout the sensitive border regions, the Communists chose not to carry out radical reforms in the initial phase of their regime and instead worked to co-opt the local elites.

One of the results was that these elites were able to exercise considerable influence on the process of integration. Normally, the establishment of so-called autonomous areas for ethnic minorities—one of the cornerstones of the ethnic minority policy—was based on thorough ethnographic research and consultation with many different representatives of the population concerned, potentially giving rise to the official classification of a "minority *minzu*" (*shaoshu minzu*).[44] Since most of this research was published in the 1980s and articles based on fieldwork in Muli are almost totally absent from these publications, it is reasonable to conclude that no such ethnographic research was carried out.[45]

A census conducted in 1952 divided the population of Muli as follows: the Zangzu (Tibetan *minzu*), 18,057, or 33.26 percent of the population; the Hanzu (Han *minzu*), 13,265, or 24.45 percent of the population; the Yizu (Yi *minzu*), an umbrella label designating several linguistically related groups, one of which is the Nuosu of Muli, 12,450, or 23.14 percent of the population; and the remaining 20 percent consisting mainly of the Mengguzu (Menggu *minzu*) (meaning Mongol, the *minzu* label given in Muli to the people known as Mosuo by the Chinese and who call themselves Na and Rek'ua), the Miaozu (Miao *minzu*), and the Naxizu (Naxi *minzu*). Based on these statistics, it must have seemed logical to establish a so-called Tibetan *minzu* autonomous county (*Zangzu zizhixian*) in the area, since the people labeled as Tibetans were the largest ethnic group. Nevertheless, there could have been good reasons to reach a different conclusion concerning the ethnic makeup of Muli. The Qing gazetteer from Yanyuan differentiated between five kinds of "barbarians" (*yiren*) living within the territory of Muli (among the people counted as commoners), and excluding, for example, the Nuosu/Yi): the Gami, the Yuegu, the Xumi, the Moxie, and the Xifan (Gu 1894: 13). The 1987 fieldwork of

Long Xijiang would also confirm that the 1952 classification perhaps did not follow the more rigorous principles applied in other parts of China inhabited by ethnic minorities. According to Long, the people whom the local Chinese called "Xifan" and who ended up being officially classified as Tibetans consisted of several groups with not only distinct, mutually unintelligible, languages but also other distinguishable cultural attributes such as religious practices. Extrapolating from his data and those in a few mainly linguistic studies[46] and combining this information with the township population figures and other data in the *Annals of Muli Tibetan Autonomous County*[47] yields the following breakdown of the 35,000 people classified as Tibetans in the year 1990: roughly 22,000 Premi speakers living in central and southern Muli; about 10,000 speakers of Kham or eastern Tibetan dialect who call themselves Pöpa (as Tibetans in other regions of Tibet call themselves) or Ba (Harrell 2001: 212), called "Gami" by other Muli inhabitants, and who live mainly in the north of the county; about 2,500 Shuhi^n (also Xumi, Shumu) people, all living in the western township of Shuiluo (T: Sulu); approximately 2,000 Liru and Lamuzi (also Namuyi) in the eastern township of Luobo.[48] All these people were called "Xifan" by the Han before the ethnic classification project of the 1950s and 1960s. In Yunnan, the Xifan, who almost all spoke Premi, were classified as a separate minority *minzu*, the Pumizu.

It is possible that one important argument for not recognizing the Premi as a separate minority *minzu* was that doing so would make the number of Tibetans in Muli too low to establish a Tibetan autonomous county. But it is likely that other factors played a role in determining the official classification of the Premi in Muli as Tibetans. The whole process of setting up an autonomous county was to a large extent left in the hands of the former elites, namely the former head lamas and their top administrators, such as Wang Peichu Qudian. They were the leading members of the committee charged with preparing the establishment of a Muli autonomous county, and in view of the United Front policy, it is reasonable to believe that their opinions carried great weight. Although most of them were of Premi origin, they had a vested interest in identifying Muli as a Tibetan area because this "naturalized" the Gelug monastic tradition as an integral part of Muli culture and, by implication, legitimated their leadership positions. Moreover, the elites would be inclined to identify themselves as Tibetans, since their long-standing participation in monasticism and Buddhist studies implied familiarity with the Tibetan language and entailed frequent, long stays in central Tibet. In this way, they were also instrumental in defining the major religion of Muli as Buddhism.

When Long Xijiang, one of China's experts on Tibeto-Burman cultures in Sichuan and one of the few anthropologists who has conducted fieldwork in Muli, addresses the intriguing incongruity of the Premi-speaking Tibetans of Muli, he is not in doubt about the role the pre-Liberation elites played in the ethnic classification process. In a Web publication (which perhaps did not fulfill all the criteria of political correctness that would be required in another form of publication),[49] he writes:

> According to our fieldwork, the upper strata [*shangceng*] of the Pumi of Muli (meaning mainly the cadres [*ganbu*]) all held the opinion that they were Tibetans [Zangzu], but the broad masses of the lower strata [*xiaceng*] all held the opinion that the Pumi were one separate nationality and that they were not Tibetans. The Pumi from Muli County and the Pumi from Ninglang County in Yunnan were the same nationality, but in the ethnic classification [*minzu shibie zhong*], the Pumi from Ninglang County in Yunnan were classified as a separate nationality and as one of the fifty-six nationalities of our country. But the Pumi in Muli were classified as Tibetans. Muli Gompa, the large Gelugpa monastery in Muli, was the largest monastery within the county, it was where a disciple of Tsongkhapa expounded the teachings to the Pumi of Muli, and it was constructed by the Pumi people. The Ba'er clan to which the Muli *tusi* belonged were Pumi people; in Tibet he was called "Muli Jiabo," meaning "King of Muli." The Pumi are the oldest inhabitants of the area of Muli. Muli Gompa and the Ba'er clan of the Muli *tusi* had a high position and reputation among the upper strata in Tibet and within the three large monasteries. (1997)

Indeed, it would be no exaggeration to claim that the pre-Liberation elite also became the elite in Muli after the establishment of Muli Tibetan Autonomous County.[50] Besides holding top government posts and leading positions within the CPPCC in Muli, some elites even obtained positions beyond Muli.[51] It is not surprising then, that their version of Muli as a Tibetan territory also becomes the politically correct PRC version of Muli's ethnic and, by deduction, religious makeup. The *Survey of Muli Tibetan Autonomous County*, published in 1985, states that 29.9 percent of Muli's population are Tibetans and that the majority of them speak the Kham Tibetan dialect (*Muli Zangzu zizhixian gaikuang* 1985: 2, 18). Nothing in this 165-page-long description of Muli, which addresses its history and the cultures and societies of its different minorities, points to the existence of the Premi.

The year 1956 heralded a dramatic new phase in Muli history and a new test for its old ruling class. In February of that year, on the basis of instructions from Beijing, the Democratic Reforms (Minzhu Gaige) campaign was launched. Its purpose was to push ahead with Communist reforms, especially in the area of land and property redistribution and the abolishment of what were dubbed "leftovers of feudalism." The attribution of class labels to the entire population was not without importance in light of later developments in revolutionary China. In Muli, the campaign was to be carried out "through the method of peaceful consultation and in a mild way" (*Muli Zangzu zizhixian zhi* 1995: 88). Nobody would be struggled against, participation would be voluntary, and some form of compensation would be paid; the positive assessment of the Muli elite as progressive was certainly a factor in this decision. And, at least according to the narrative of the *Annals of Muli Tibetan Autonomous County*, once again the elite did not disappoint and took the initiative in carrying out the campaign. Although the Communists had expressed their intention to slowly dismantle the corvée, land tenure, and slave-holding systems, figures from the campaign reveal that in 1956 not much progress had been made. At one of the first meetings of the campaign, Xiang Zhaba Songdian, Lin Jiayong, Shu Yuanyuan (the former Naxi *bazong*), and forty-five others freed 534 slaves. By 1959, when the reforms ended, 3,682 slaves had been set free and almost 50,000 *mu*,[52] or 3,335 hectares, of land had been confiscated (ibid.: 89). The annals also mention that members of the former *minzu* and religious upper strata who showed a patriotic attitude after education and reformation were rewarded with positions within the administration.

The *Annals of Muli Tibetan Autonomous County* clearly aims to give the impression that members of the Bar clan, such as the Xiangs and Lin Jiayong, as well as many other members of the elite, such as Shu Yuanyuan, were actively engaged in the Democratic Reforms campaign and did their best to push ahead faster than was expected. From a more cynical perspective, it could be argued that they had no choice and were forced to demonstrate revolutionary zeal in order to keep their positions of influence. Nevertheless, a large part of the religious and political elite, as well as many people further down the hierarchy, did make radically different choices. Indeed, in view of how these people fared—many were killed—and with the wisdom of historical hindsight, it must be said that the former head lamas and other members of the Bar clan once again made a pragmatic and wise decision to support the Democratic Reforms campaign.

In March 1956, when the campaign was being implemented, a triumvirate consisting of a Gami landlord from Donglang, in the north of Muli (at that time the vice-leader of the Third District), the *kuchar* of Wachin Gompa (at that time the district leader of the Third District), and a high monk from Kulu Gompa banded together with several Black Nuosu leaders from the southeast of Muli and rose in rebellion. They obtained arms and quickly assembled a force of three thousand men. Initially, they attacked government buildings in the northern Gami region of Muli, but the rebellion soon spread to other areas, and by the middle of April, there was fighting in fourteen of the nineteen townships of Muli, although the south and southwest of Muli, inhabited mainly by Naxi and Premi, and the majority of the monks of Muli Gompa were not involved.

This uprising was not an isolated event but part of a pattern of revolt among Tibetans all over Kham and among the Nuosu of Liangshan, to a large extent provoked by the enforcement of the Democratic Reforms campaign.[53] While the Communists had initially proceeded very slowly with initiating reforms in ethnic minority areas, including the Tibetan areas outside central Tibet, they believed their rule was now sufficiently established to start the process of radical social change and did not foresee the extent of the opposition this would provoke. The attempt to divide the clergy and the elite from the "lower strata" through class struggle in many cases had the opposite effect and united the Tibetans in armed struggle. The move to force the Khampas to hand in their guns did nothing to defuse the explosive situation in the area. Since both the Tibetans in the rest of Kham and the Nuosu in the areas surrounding Muli had revolted, it is likely that the conflict spilled over into Muli to some extent. It took three and a half years to completely suppress the rebellion in Muli.⁵⁴ According to the minute statistics of the *Annals of Muli Tibetan Autonomous County*, 661 battles were fought, 432 rebels were killed, the PLA lost 8 officers and 55 soldiers, and 49 local militia lost their lives (*Muli Zangzu zizhixian zhi* 1995: 94). Although no specific data are given about ethnic affiliation of the rebels beyond the recognized minority *minzu*, such as the Tibetan and the Yi people, it seems the uprising was most pronounced among the Gami and the Black Nuosu. One of its main leaders was a Gami from northern Muli, Jiayang Chunpin. A monk at Wachin Gompa who held the high position of *umdze*, he had been co-opted by the new regime and given the position of head of the Third District. The uprising began in the Third District, which is adjacent to Lithang, where, in the spring of 1956, the PLA committed one of its worst atrocities, killing hundreds of Tibetans, laypersons, and monks by bombing Lithang Gompa from the air (Smith 1996: 409–11). Several survivors fled to the safety of the mountains south of Lithang; some came to Muli, where they found support among the local Khampa, the Gami.

It is noteworthy that the areas in Muli with the densest Premi, Naxi, Na, and Miao populations were the ones that did not experience any fighting (including Bustling Township, as was confirmed by my interviews). While there are strong indications that ethnicity might have played a role in drawing the battle lines in Muli—placing the Gami and the Nuosu on the rebel side—there is not enough data to fully substantiate this claim. The *Annals of Muli Tibetan Autonomous County* does mention that the rebels did not succeed in attracting the *tulku* Jiayang Zhigu, the Xiangs, or Lin Jiayong to their cause. On the contrary, the authors claim that Lin Jiayong, Xiang Zhaba Songdian, and Xiang Peichu Zhaba (all from the Premi Bar clan) were actively engaged first in trying to convince rebels to switch sides and later in providing arms to suppress the rebellion. Shu Yuanyuan, whose former position as *bazong* had involved military training by the Nationalists, became actively engaged in suppressing the rebellion, for which he was officially commended. As a result of their active collaboration with the Communists,⁵⁵ these members of the former elite kept their positions throughout the Democratic Reforms period and also managed to emerge relatively unscathed from subsequent campaigns such as the Four Antis (Si Fan) movement of 1959. Except for Xiang Peichu Zhaba, who was still alive in 2004, almost all the pre-Liberation leading elite died of natural causes in the early 1960s and did not have to experience the Cultural Revolution nor witness sad events like the destruction of Muli's monasteries.[56] The local leader of the revolt, Jiayang Chunpin, was captured by forces including Shu Yuanyuan in the summer of 1958 and executed in public in Wa'erzhai in March 1959. A similar fate befell eight other captured rebels in the following two months. In September of the same year, the last twenty rebels were shot dead in a concerted military action, effectively ending the rebellion in Muli.

Muli's remoteness did not protect it from the different political campaigns that took place all over China at the end of the 1950s and the beginning of the 1960s. Some were only mildly implemented in Muli, such as the Rectification and Elimination of Counterrevolutionaries campaigns of 1958, in which only nineteen people were labeled "rightists." Others hit especially hard, such as the Four Antis movement launched in March 1959 by the Muli Party Committee. The Four Antis movement—anti-uprising, anti-lawbreaking, anti-privileges, and anti-oppression—was directed specifically against religion and focused on controlling and curtailing the influence of the monasteries; the title of a Party document issued on April 18, "Resolution on Launching the 'Four Antis' Movement among the Lama Community in Muli County," leaves no doubt about the campaign's target (*Muli Zangzu zizhixian zhi* 1995: 891). One major outcome was the virtual destruction of organized religion in Muli: the monks were forced to leave their monasteries, and soon afterward, many of the territory's religious buildings were destroyed or fell into disrepair.

Profound changes were also taking place in the villages. In 1957, the first People's Commune was established and collectivization reached its zenith during the Great Leap Forward (1958–60), when domestic animals became the property of the commune, common kitchens were established all over Muli, and small steel factories sprang up everywhere. The older people in Bustling Township still had vivid memories of this period, especially the consequent famine of 1960 and 1961. It was a terrible time when many people became ill and there were more deaths than usual. Large-scale slaughter of livestock to supply the common kitchens with meat at the start of the Great Leap inevitably led to disaster. When the common kitchens were finally abandoned in Muli in August 1960, food shortages were rampant, especially in the towns. In spite of the obvious disastrous effects of the radical new policies, those clear-sighted cadres and others who bravely opposed the Great Leap were viciously attacked in the Anti-

Right Deviation campaign, which began in November 1959. According to the *Annals of Muli Tibetan Autonomous County*, 375 cadres from all levels of government and the Party in Muli were "wrongly" labeled as "right deviationists and opportunists" (*Muli Zangzu zizhixian zhi* 1995: 102). Many were "progressive" members of pre-Liberation elites who had been given government positions to reward them for collaborating in the transition from the old monastic structures of government to the new Communist administration. But worse was still to come…

After a few years of more relaxed policies in the first half of the 1960s, such as allowing households to keep a limited number of domestic animals, in 1966, the Cultural Revolution once more turned people's lives profoundly upside down. Students at two middle schools in the district-town of Wachang, near Muli Gompa, initiated the movement, and it soon spread to every corner of Muli. In the autumn of 1967, guided by the slogan "Smash the Four Olds!"[57] the remnants of Muli Gompa, including bronze Buddha statues and most of the scriptures, fell prey to the local Red Guards. The former elites were paraded at gunpoint through the streets, publicly criticized and beaten up, and had their property confiscated. Most were sent to the countryside to the so-called May 7 Cadre Schools, where they were forced to do hard manual labor while living under very basic conditions; occasionally they were rolled out and subjected to verbal and physical abuse. In 1970, many were able to return home and not a few of the former government and party cadres were reinstated in their former positions. One of them was Da^{n}qu Ya^{n}p'i from Bustling Township. He was a monk and former manager, or *chantsö*, of Muli Gompa and had been given a high position in the new administration of Muli. In 1967, he was labeled a "feudal leading monk" (*fengjian da lama*) and sent from the county-town to the countryside to work the land. He was fortunate to survive his ordeal, and his family in Bustling Township was only mildly criticized. After the Cultural Revolution, he was rehabilitated. Many other members of the former elite were not that lucky. The *Annals of Muli Tibetan Autonomous County* gives the official figure of ninety-eight people killed by the Red Guards (*Muli Zangzu zizhixian zhi* 1995: 107). This number does not include the many casualties sustained during the heavy fighting that took place in 1968 and 1969 between different factions, including well-armed Red Guards who had raided the local army weapons depots.

While the campaign was less violent in the villages, few households were left untouched. Red Guards from the county- and district-towns also found their way to remote Bustling Township and mobilized local youth in starting "revolutionary activities" such as organizing study groups and criticism sessions for people from "bad classes." The families who bore the brunt were the few that had been classified as "rich peasants" (*funong*) and the one "landlord" (*dizhu*) family. Villagers in the township insisted that none of those criticized—or sometimes even beaten—were significantly richer than the others. The so-called landlord family had simply saved a bit more silver than its neighbors, "all through hard work and certainly not by stealing or exploiting anybody," as other families in the village insisted. These "revolutionary activities" were usually carried out by youths from the neighboring villages. People mostly did not dare to attack their fellow villagers, many of whom were also close relatives or fellow clan members. In smashing the Four Olds, the Red Guards directed their revolutionary zeal toward destroying the few visible signs of religious practice in Bustling Township, such as the *mani* (piles of stones erected on ritually important places), the *zaⁿbala* (Tibetan Buddhist picture or relief found in all houses in Bustling Township), and the ritual paraphernalia of the local *anji*, such as scriptures and effigies of deities. In order to avoid criticism, many *anji* took the initiative or participated actively in the destruction. The collectivization of livestock also precluded the ritual sacrifice of animals. Religious activities disappeared from the public sphere. At the height of the Cultural Revolution, afraid of exhibiting any trait that could be viewed as belonging to the "old feudal society," the women in the township stopped wearing their traditional plaited skirts, and both men and women modeled their haircuts on those of the Han.

In late October 1976, when news of the arrest of the Gang of Four—the leadership group held responsible for the Cultural Revolution—reached Muli, a big spontaneous celebration took place in the county-town (*Muli Zangzu zizhixian zhi* 1995: 109). Not long after, the Chinese Party-state under the leadership of Deng Xiaoping embarked on a radically different course, heralding once again a new period in the history of Muli. From being all-encompassing and meddling in the minutest details of people's lives, the state permitted economic liberalization and ideological relaxation. Villagers in Muli were free to decide what to grow in their fields or even to leave and try their luck in one of China's booming cities. The women could again wear plaited skirts and adorn their hair in the local traditional fashion. But when somebody got sick, there was no barefoot village doctor providing free medical care. And when the new seedlings were threatened by heavy spring rains, the people of Muli could rely only on the benevolence of the water deities.

2 ⌘ BUSTLING TOWNSHIP

A Muli Township in the Post-Mao Era

Although the pace of economic growth has been markedly slower in China's western regions, in recent years, the forces of the globalized economy have also reached the smaller cities and county-towns, even in the more remote mountainous areas of the Southwest. This development has been facilitated by the many infrastructure projects resulting from the central government's Opening Up the Western Regions (Xibu Da Kaifa) policy, initiated by Jiang Zemin in 1999, such as building roads to all corners of this part of China, constructing airports in smaller cities or in the many popular but often hard-to-reach tourist destinations, and upgrading and expanding railroad links. Nevertheless, change is slow to come in many villages that are farther away from towns and cities. These are often villages inhabited by ethnic minorities, many still living a precarious existence as subsistence farmers. They can observe the marked success enjoyed by local and in-migrating Han who are able to grasp the opportunities created by the new capitalist economy. At the same time, they can no longer count on the social security system and other principles of solidarity of the socialist state to help them when they are threatened by misfortunes such as bad harvests, floods, landslides, or illness. And to add insult to injury, while it is retreating in several areas vital for people's livelihoods, this same state is increasingly interfering in areas in which people used to have more freedom, such as family planning, state education, and land management. Under these conditions, communities such as those in Bustling Township turn their gaze inward and rediscover the values of their own cultural traditions. Ritual practices related to traditional cosmology and religious beliefs are reclaiming some of the terrain that was lost in Premi society during the previous decades.

ECOLOGY AND SUBSISTENCE

Bustling Township has a rugged, mountainous landscape with high peaks, deep-cut river gorges, and very little level land. The difference between the lowest and highest points is almost 3,000 meters, from a little more than 1,500 meters to a mountaintop at 4,500 meters. Roughly a third of the township is covered with forests, while the higher areas, or about 10 percent of Bustling Township's surface, are grasslands. Agriculture is possible only on those mountain slopes that are not too steep and were not covered by forests in 1998, when a general ban on logging was introduced. This amounts to less than 1 percent of the total surface of the township. The main crops are maize, wheat, and potatoes; other important crops are barley, highland barley, buckwheat, and beans. In and immediately around the villages, people tend pear, apple, walnut, and other trees. On the lower-lying slopes, there are some rice paddies (occupying less than 5 percent of the total arable land) and mandarin trees. The few cash crops are chili pepper (*haijiao*) and hemp. The average annual temperature of 15°C makes it possible for large parts of the township to have two annual harvests: maize, harvested at the end of October, and wheat, harvested in April or May. On sheltered south-facing slopes, wheat and maize can be grown at altitudes as high as 3,000 meters. In spite of moderate average temperatures and sufficient seasonal precipitation, the average yield of wheat in the whole township is still significantly below the national average.[1]

The forest areas provide the approximately three thousand inhabitants of Bustling Township with much-needed fuel for cooking and heating as well as materials for house construction. Forests also yield some medicinal plants and mushrooms as well as small game such as wild fowl. Extensive overhunting in the past as well as more recent, tighter controls on the possession of firearms and the enforcement of strict nature-protection

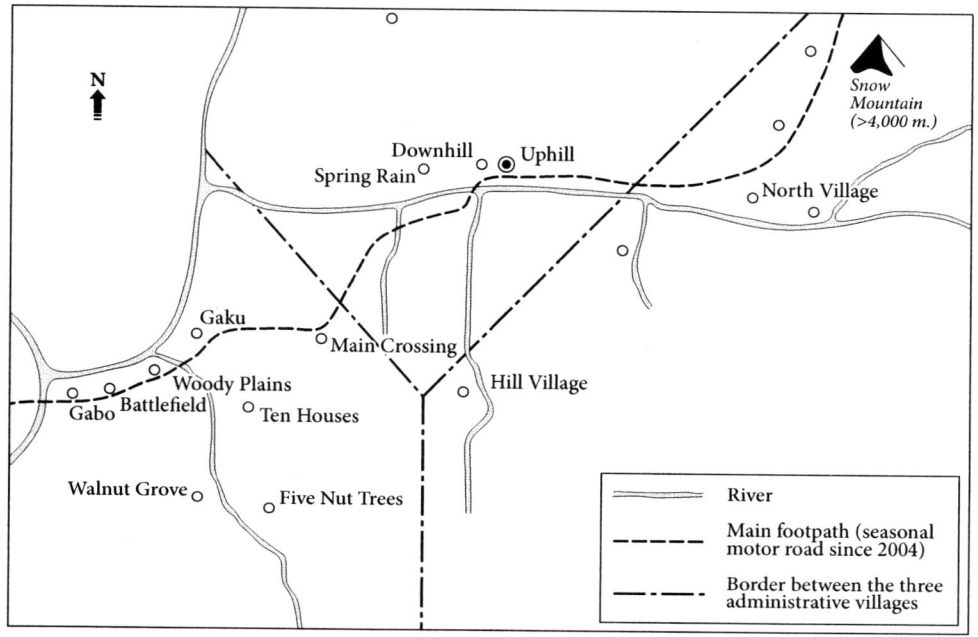

MAP 2. Bustling Township

regulations have combined to reduce the importance of wild game as a source of animal protein.

In addition to agriculture, people depend on animal husbandry for their livelihoods. Almost all households keep one or two oxen for plowing and threshing as well as pigs, goats, and chickens. Many households also keep a few mules or horses for transportation of goods and people. Variations in the number of animals depend mostly on the number of people in the household. A state-run yak breeding station (*guoying muchang*) employs some of the local people and provides families with daily necessities such as the yak butter they use in large amounts for making butter tea (P: *modyè*).

After de-collectivization in 1982, individual households received the rights to use collectively owned land. Under the "household responsibility system" (*jiating lianchan chengbao zerenzhi*), land in Bustling Township was allocated according to a ratio of 1.1–1.3 square *mu* per person in a household, with the quality of land and the micro-climatic conditions determining the difference. In higher areas, people needed more farmland because of harsher climatic conditions, while in some of the lower valleys, including in Uphill and Downhill, yields per *mu* were higher, and households in these areas did not need as much land.² As elsewhere in China, the rural collectives (mostly the villages) remained the nominal owners of the land, and land could therefore be neither sold nor bought. Households were given only the right to use it and initially had no formal contracts substantiating their rights. The local government or Party could readjust the size of household lands when people died or when households increased in size. Since the enactment of the Land Management Law of 1986 (subsequently revised several times), households have been able to sign formal contracts with the rural collectives, allowing them to lease the land for thirty years and creating a more stable situation for households that depended mainly on agriculture.

Under normal climatic conditions, people in Bustling Township manage to produce enough food for subsistence, and 1998 was the last year the township received special funds for the "alleviation of poverty" (*fupin*).³ Nevertheless, there is little left over for selling or bartering. Moreover, of this surplus, only a few products can be transported conveniently on people's backs or on mules to the nearest market town, at least two days' journey away. Depending on the number of family members of working age, a household in Bustling Township typically generates between ¥2,000 to ¥5,000 a year, mainly by selling chili peppers at the market and also occasionally selling a mule or a horse. Another possible source of income is the collection and sale of Chinese medicinal plants. In 2003, one kilo of *songrong*—a pine mushroom used in Chinese medicine and known in the West under its Japanese name, matsutake—could be sold for ¥200 at the market in Yongning (P: Lingwu). The well-known Tibetan medicinal plant *yartsa gunbu*, or caterpillar fungus, is known locally as *nadzawèⁿwu* and is used in Bustling Township as a general-purpose medicine and tonic.⁴ One small fungus of about five centimeters can bring in ¥10 at this same market.⁵ Since *nadzawèⁿwu* is found higher up in the mountains, collection is a time-consuming job, and although the possibility of a lucky find keeps people looking for the fungi, sales do not generate substantial income for the township. Fungus harvesters usually spend part of the extra income on rice, yak butter, clothes, and a few other necessities and save the rest in case they have to pay for medicine, visit the hospital, or suffer bad harvests.

Although some rural areas in the richer coastal provinces began experimenting with limited medical insurance schemes in 2004, no such programs were available in Bustling Township. The impoverished township government also had no funds to set aside for welfare assistance. As a consequence, serious illness or chronic disease could quickly ruin a household and put a strain on families related to the household. My host family in Walnut Grove had to pay a hospital bill of ¥5,000 when their daughter had an operation for kidney stones. This not only drained their savings but also tapped the savings of many closely related kin. One family in Walnut Grove, whose head of household had a chronic disease, spent between ¥200 and ¥300 on medicine each year. This family was already one of the poorest in the village because one of the household's main wage earners could not work at full capacity. Their yearly income from selling products at the market did not exceed ¥800. When the margins for subsistence are that narrow, a little adversity can push many families into dire straits for a long time. The weather may wreak havoc, as when a landslide in 1998 washed away more than fifteen *mu* of good agricultural land and several families lost their major source of subsistence. Many of the ritual practices of the Premi in Bustling Township are directly related to controlling those forces deemed responsible for disease and the weather.

There is a limited local economy in which people sell or barter some of the surplus of home production, such as *arje*, locally distilled spirits. In general there is very little artisanal specialization, except for wood carving, some aspects of house building, and smithery. In Walnut Grove, there were four men who had special skills in woodworking and four in smithery, but they were first and foremost farmers and did not make a living from their crafts. The women in each family weave the traditional cloth that is still used in men's and women's clothing on the house-loom, which is found in every household. They make smaller items such as belts on a small foot-driven loom. A few people turn their craft into a business, albeit on a very modest scale. One of them, Adzarra, the "village head" (*cunzhang*) of Walnut Grove, made Tibetan-style knives using deer bone and yak horn. He made an average of ¥600 a year selling them to the local villagers, but even after adding his yearly wages of ¥150 as village head, his family still depended primarily on the products of their fields and animals for survival. The story of how he learned his craft does not indicate a tradition of inherited trades and crafts, as in villages in nearby Tibetan areas:

FIG. 2.1. Brewing *arje*, the local spirits.

When I was young, my father came home one day from Shuiluo [an area in the east of Muli with several villagers inhabited by Gami, or Kham Tibetans] with a Tibetan knife. He was very happy with his knife, and tragedy struck the family the day his knife broke. My brothers and I tried to repair the knife, and finally we developed a technique and were able to make other knives as well. Now I sell some knives to people on demand. The small ones cost ¥30, the large ones ¥100. I can make around ¥600 a year. Actually, I have now taught the trade to somebody else in the village as well.

A friendly and self-effacing middle-aged man, Adzarra just laughed at my suggestion that he could try to start selling his knives at the nearby market town: "No, no, I am too old for that!"

The township included a number of younger people who had spent some years in other places such as the district- or county-town. Some were former students who had not passed the examination for higher secondary education. Others had worked in the logging industry or had jobs indirectly related to logging, for example, in transportation or road construction. All told, more then one hundred people from the township had worked outside Bustling Township in logging-related jobs, generating a yearly total income of ¥400,000. After the general ban on logging enacted by the Natural Forest Protection Program (Tianranlin Baohu Gongcheng), or Tianbao, in 1998, only a few of those people managed to find new jobs, mostly in reforestation projects funded by the county.[6] The township government initiated a few projects for returnees, such as collecting and selling forest products and making small agricultural tools. For many people, the Tianbao policy not only had a devastating effect on their economic situation but also severely limited their prospects for establishing a life outside of agriculture. One of the returnees was a young man who lived in the house next to our government building in Uphill. He regularly came over to talk to me and my assistant, and we discussed issues relating to international politics or social issues in China and abroad. He had been working at a "state-run logging company" (*guoying linchang*) for several years and had finally saved enough money to buy his own truck. The end of logging made his prospects as a truck driver rather bleak, so he had abandoned the project and returned to Uphill, resigning himself to life as a farmer. He did not conceal from us his unhappiness with his lack of choices.

It is among people who have some outside experience and hope to make a living by doing something other than farming that the new entrepreneurs are to be found. There are perhaps not more than a few dozen such people in the township, and many of them live near the township government buildings. At the beginning of the new millennium, in Uphill, Downhill, and Walnut Grove, six families had obtained videocassette recorders (VCRs) that they operated with generators or very small water-driven power stations that produced just enough electricity to power the machines. For one or two *mao*, all members of one family could come and watch prerecorded TV programs or movies. This was clearly the highest price people were willing to pay, and the owners of the VCRs admitted that it would take a long time to earn back their investments. The smallest power station alone cost ¥3,000, and the generator-operated VCRs required expensive gasoline that had to be carried in by mule. Resigned to the tough laws of the marketplace, these enterprising families continued to run their business, viewing it as a service to the community rather than focusing on profit. One VCR owner explained to me that he liked having many people in his home. In villages without general access to electricity, books, or newspapers, and with few occasions to socialize beyond the family network, these video gatherings were especially valued by the younger people. After weeks without television, restaurants, telephone communications, or new things to read, my assistants and I easily empathized with young government cadres or returnees from the district- or county-town who would gather regularly to watch videos, drink beer, play cards, and complain that there was nothing else to do in Bustling Township.

The presence of the township government and the boarding school at Downhill and Uphill also created prospects for generating small amounts of additional income by meeting the needs of government employees, schoolchildren, and teachers. People came to take care of errands at the township government building, such as paying taxes, participating in official meetings, or obtaining official documents or certificates, and circulating officials from the district or county governments also visited. There were no fewer than seven "small shops" (*xiaomaibu*) next to one another in front of the government building. Several had been made by simply cutting a hole in the wall of a house along the path between the village and the government building and putting up a rack with two or three shelves behind it. The seller would sit inside, and buyers did not enter the house but made their purchases through the hole. All the shops offered approximately the same limited assortment of items: two kinds of cigarettes, one kind of beer, one kind of fizzy drink, candles, batteries, candy, and soap. But with supplies being brought in by mule from the market town on an irregular basis, more often than not many items within this limited assortment were sold out. In Uphill, where only a few families had electricity, it had once been impossible to buy candles for several weeks. None of those shops could support a family in the long run and are considered a source of extra income for a family, typically bringing in between ¥1000 and ¥1500 annually. Three of the shops are operated by old men who are unable to work in the field; the other four are run by young people. Two of those four had invested the money they had earned by working outside Bustling Township to buy their first stock, hoping they would sell enough to stay in business. The other two are young, unmarried women who work in the shops owned by their families. Both women had studied at the junior middle school in the district-town and had convinced their

2 ⁘ Bustling Township

families to invest in a shop so that they could make enough money to avoid the fate of becoming a farmer.

Another brick building stands next to the government building, both in a similar state of disrepair. This used to be the state-run shop, and it houses several rooms that surround a courtyard. After the state shop closed sometime in the early 1990s, a farmer in Uphill leased the building from the government, intending to rent out rooms to temporary residents or the occasional traveler. During my stay in Uphill in 1999, his only customers were a teacher employed at the boarding school and a young woman who ran a little private health service. A young returnee also used a room for showing video films. All the other rooms were empty, and the whole place was in a terribly run-down state, with countless holes in the roof and a courtyard full of litter and empty beer bottles. The building stood as the sad embodiment of one more failed attempt at setting up a nonagricultural business in the township.

According to statistics compiled by the township government, 1,700 people in the township work in agriculture, but only 71 are employed in other sectors. These are mostly people working in the administra-

FIG. 2.2. There is little mechanization of agriculture in Bustling Township: threshing is done mostly by animal and human power.

tion, the schools, and in the small shops. More than half of them live in Uphill.

In 2001, the government built a motor road connecting Bustling Township to the district-town of Wachang and to Yongning in Yunnan. The road is unpaved and impossible to drive on when it rains. The cost of ¥26 per meter was financed with funds given to the county as part of the Opening Up the Western Regions policy. Although the main construction team consisted of Han from outside, two hundred local people were employed on temporary contracts, so-called *mingong*, and as such the construction of the road provided a temporary source of income for people from Bustling Township. The road passes through the township and village of Uphill, but many of the villages higher up in the mountains are still a long walk away from the road; it takes one and a half hours to reach it from Walnut Grove. Three years later, in 2004, only a handful of people had acquired motorcycles, and only one family in the whole township had scraped together ¥10,000 to buy a well-used Beijing Jeep. Because of the rough terrain, the unpaved road, and the large detour it makes, it takes a whole day to reach Yongning and a very long day to reach Wachang. This is only slightly faster than the traditional horse and mule transport, which remains the major form of transportation. Since people are not willing to pay enough for renting his car, the owner of the Beijing Jeep does most of his driving in and around the district-town of Wachang and only occasionally takes the long road to Bustling Township. As with many of the projects financed by the central government, the local government must pay for maintenance and incessant repairs to the road. In view of the generally bad condition of roads in Muli, Bustling Township is not a high priority, and local volunteers often make repairs to the final stretch of road to Bustling Township.

By 2004, it was not clear whether the road had brought benefits to Bustling Township, although it nevertheless represents the means for developing contacts with the outside. One of the more unexpected results was an influx of several hundred poor migrant workers from Guangxi who had come to tap the pine trees for resin.[7] The workers live in temporary encampments in the woods—sometimes with their families—and buy a portion of their food and other supplies from the local population in Bustling Township. The company that collects the resin does not hire local workers, but these purchases provide families close to the encampments

2 ◦ Bustling Township

a welcome opportunity to sell some of their surplus, and in this way, the new road has brought some economic benefits.

POPULATION AND ETHNIC RELATIONS

The twenty-odd "natural villages" (*zirancun*) are organized into a number of "village groups" (*cunminzu*) and are then further grouped into three "administrative villages" (*xingzhengcun* or *cunweihui*). Following the official PRC categorization of *minzu*,[8] 60 percent of the approximately three thousand inhabitants of Bustling Township are classified as Zangzu, or Tibetan *minzu*; the second-largest group is the Mengguzu, or Mongol *minzu*;[9] the third-largest is the Naxizu; and the Hanzu, or Han, is the smallest. In terms of local categories, using local ethnonyms in the language of the ethnic group, these official labels are unproblematic in the case of the Han and the Zangzu. The Han are called "Hsyè" by the Premi. The Zangzu correspond to "Premi" or "Ch'ruame" ("Ch'ruame" is the term used in Uphill and Downhill, but people there and in the rest of the township agree that it is just a dialectal pronunciation of "Premi"). The official *minzu* label of "Naxizu" corresponds to the people who call themselves "Nahin" in Bustling Township, and they are culturally closely related to the Naxi of Yunnan. The label of "Mengguzu" is a bit more problematic. Many of those classified as Mengguzu in Sichuan are people who call themselves "Na" or "Naze." In Yunnan, where most of the Na live in the area of Yongning, they have been lumped together with the Naxizu.[10] A small group of about fifteen families in Bustling Township are Na people who migrated from Yongning to the area in the neighborhood of Walnut Grove eleven generations ago. The other Mengguzu are more closely related to the Naxi and call themselves "Rek'ua."[11] The close connection with the Naxi is clear in their language and religious practice. The Rek'ua in Bustling Township also have *dtô-mbà* religious specialists who use pictographic texts in their rituals.[12] Most Na in Bustling Township have either integrated their religious practice with the Rek'ua or use *anji* ritual specialists from the village of Walnut Grove.

The most general term used by the Premi in many areas to designate Na, Naxi, and Rek'ua is "Nyè-me" (Black People), which is in contrast to the autonym "Pre-mi" (White People). Such is the case in the northern villages, where people do not differentiate between—or are not even aware of—different subcategories of Nyè-me. In Walnut Grove, in contrast, distinctions are made. Here, the term "Nyè-me" is reserved for the Rek'ua; these people are also sometimes designated by their own ethnonym "Rek'ua," while the Na from Yongning are called "Lihè^n." The Naxi of Bustling Township call the Na "K'uma." Na, Rek'ua, and Naxi use the word "Be" or "Bo" for the Premi.

The township can be roughly divided into three regions (see map 2). The northern villages, situated in the highest region, are inhabited entirely by Premi. The villages in the central region are also mainly Premi villages (some of the in-married women are Na or Rek'ua). This is also where the twin villages of Uphill and Downhill, and the seat of the township government, are situated. The southern villages are ethnically much more complex and comprise Rek'ua, Naxi, Han, and Premi villages, all in relative proximity to one another. One village, Ten Houses, is ethnically mixed and inhabited by Premi, Na, and four Han families. Two of the Han families are there because Han were sent to the village as cadres and teachers during the Democratic Reforms period of the 1950s. Walnut Grove is also one of the southern villages. These three regions are separated from one another by geographical obstacles, be they distance, steep mountains, or deep river gorges. The divisions correspond to the three administrative villages and are also reflected in patterns of social interaction such as marriages. None of the wives in Walnut Grove, for example, came from Uphill or Downhill. The Premi of the central and northern villages, who call themselves "Ch'ruame," speak a dialect that is quite distinct from the ones spoken by those living in the southern villages. They held that their pronunciation, which is more nasalized and has a significant number of Tibetan loanwords, is more "pure" and not as influenced by the languages of other ethnic groups as compared to the pronunciation of the Premi from the southern villages. These differences do not create problems of mutual understanding within the township but testify to the relative isolation of the two microregions and to a different history of settlement.

While historical notions of migration and village establishment are rather vague in Uphill and Downhill, the Premi of the southern village of Walnut Grove know the history of their village. According to Mesé Galo^n, the Party secretary of Ten Houses, to which Walnut Grove belongs:

Walnut Grove was established only six generations ago when Ya^{n}dra^n Yishi, an *anji* from the Mesé clan, arrived with his wife and son from Yunnan at this sloping mountainside above the Naxi village of Battleground. The original inhabitants [of what would become Walnut Grove] had been wiped out by disease, and since more or less level land was scarce, it was a good place to build a house. The son married two wives: a Naxi woman from Battleground and a Premi woman from Ten Villages [also within close walking distance]. One of his daughters married a Naxi from Battleground who moved to Walnut Grove and built the first house of the Ak'ua clan. In the next generation, another Naxi man started neolocal residence in the village, marrying a Mesé girl, and this became the third of the three clans of Walnut Grove, the Bot'a clan.

Ethnic identity is largely defined and upheld through residence in separate villages and through notions of common patrilineal descent. In Bustling Township, there is extensive intermarriage between Na, Rek'ua, Naxi, and Premi. Ethnic categories are not of much consequence in daily life, and cultural differences are limited largely to language and ritual practice. People consistently downplayed cultural differences among these four categories, and although three of the four groups speak their own language, people also usually speak the language of the other groups. When Na or Rek'ua women marry into a Premi household, they start speaking Premi and vice versa. In view of the large number of such mixed marriages, the assertion that the Premi language spoken in the southern villages is less pure than that spoken in the northern villages may have some truth to it. During the fieldwork for this project, we often heard it said that there are some differences in the style of the women's traditional clothing or hairdo, and that the Na women usually wear larger earrings. Nevertheless, several times, people made mistakes when guessing whether an approaching woman was Na, Rek'ua, Premi, or Naxi. Linguistic differences are only the most obvious sign that three of these four groups were culturally more differentiated in the past. It seems that Premi are longtime inhabitants of the central and northern regions, but in the southern region, not only Premi but also Na and Naxi have histories of relatively recent migration. Although the ritual practice has some remarkable similarities, there are also obvious differences, the most prominent being the active *dtô-mbà* religious specialists of the Naxi and the use of pictographic texts by the Rek'ua. The Na invite both *dtômbà* and *anji* ritualists.

The village of Woody Plains is also situated in the southern region. It is inhabited by twenty-five Han families. Woody Plains was founded five generations ago by Han migrating from Yunnan, and today it counts five different family names. At first glance, the village does not look much different from other neighboring villages. A slightly closer look suggests that this may be a wealthier place. People are dressed a little bit better, children seem healthier, many houses have glass windows and concrete floors, and some families share a small power station that provides enough energy to power a few lightbulbs and a television set with satellite dish. The village boasts a couple of mechanized plows and a mechanized threshing machine. An even closer look reveals a markedly higher rate of school attendance and a higher level of education. But why would a village of Han farmers be wealthier than its close non-Han neighbors? The Han were not given more land in 1981, and before that, they had been as poor as any of the other villagers. The answer to this question can be found by mapping out some of the family networks in Woody Plains.

Zhang Wenming was nearing his thirties in 1999. Both his parents were from Woody Plains, but his family had migrated from a small village in Yunnan four generations ago. They still had relatives in Yunnan and kept in contact. He was the only one of the four children who had stayed at home, and he was gradually taking over all farming activities from his father. Both his parents spent most of their time in Uphill, where the family owned a shop. Besides running the shop with the help of their younger, unmarried daughter, they also provided banking services in Uphill. Zhang Wenming's older sister was married and lived in a neighboring township, and his older brother had settled down in the market town of Yongning where he was making a living by trading. Zhang Wenming's wife came from a village in Yunnan, which was close enough that they were able to maintain regular contact. They had a small boy of five months and a girl of six who stayed with her grandparents in Uphill in order to attend the township school. Although there was a school in the neighboring village that provided classes up through the second grade, the township school was thought to provide better education.

This family is no exception in Woody Plains. Many more households have family members working outside, most of them in market towns or administrative centers. Several other families have marriage relations with Han families far beyond the borders of the township. Such networks were established by maintaining family ties with the place where these families had migrated from and through further expansion of these links. Networks are instrumental in finding jobs outside the township, but language skills and a certain educational level are even more useful. Being Han and speaking Chinese are significant assets, even in areas with a majority non-Han population. In the small district-towns and market towns in multiethnic areas, Chinese serves as a lingua franca, especially when none of the many linguistic groups dominates either socially or numerically.[13] Han children do not start school with the handicap of not knowing the language of education, and their rate of participation in secondary education is considerably higher. Outside income has created possibilities for investment in better agricultural production methods. Wide networks also provide better access to goods, and it was no coincidence that the shop with the most extensive assortment of products, lowest prices, and most consistent availability of goods in Uphill is run by Han, the Zhang grandparents. Zhang Wenming's brother who was working in the market town provided steady access to better and cheaper products. The Zhangs' shop is the only one in Uphill not run by local Premi, and a certain anti-Han sentiment among their potential customers is probably the sole reason that it does not completely overshadow the other shops.

There is a clear ethnic divide between the Na, Rek'ua, Naxi, and Premi on the one side and the Han on the other. Although the Han have been living in Bustling Township for at least five generations, there is not one mixed marriage between Han from Woody Plains and non-Han. Nevertheless, people in Bustling Township insist that relations between Han and non-Han are cordial and that there are many cases of friendship between the two "groups." Local Han are also fluent in at least one of the other local languages. Zhang Wenming stated that people from the neighboring Rek'ua village often came to watch TV in his specially built TV room. The one night I stayed at his place and watched TV, however, all of the twenty or so visitors were Han from Woody Plains. But there are more serious signs that relations between Woody Plains and the surrounding villages are not as smooth as people described. On a visit to the village in the company of the local police officer, Zhang told us that people from the neighboring Rek'ua village had been throwing stones at his house that afternoon. This appears to be only one small incident in a long line of conflicts between people in Woody Plains and those in the neighboring Rek'ua and Premi villages. Some of these conflicts involved real mob violence. On several occasions, there had been raids by large crowds, sometimes more than a hundred people from the neighboring villages. During such raids, people went from house to house and took whatever they could carry, including clothes and animals. On other occasions, groups of Premi and Rek'ua had surrounded several houses, one of which was Zhang's, and thrown stones until they were given some money.

Although nobody had ever been seriously hurt in such incidents, the Han villagers complained that they did not dare to travel alone anymore through the neighboring villages. Other Woody Plains villagers agreed with Zhang's assessment that all of this had started around the late 1980s and was caused by the ever widening economic gap between the Han village and its neighbors; before the privatization of agricultural production, everybody had been equally poor. Through their networks and by being part of the dominant culture in China, Han villagers are clearly in a better position to profit from economic liberalization. The other ethnic groups are left with many fewer opportunities to compensate for the loss of jobs directly or indirectly related to the timber business.[14] At the same time, they see a steadily deteriorating level of state support, epitomized by the disappearance of free health care. Furthermore, the persistence of endogamy among the Han and non-Han communities in Bustling Township provides fertile ground for establishing a clear ethnic divide. That exogamy can cement peaceful relationships between different communities is a point made by Tylor more than hundred years ago (cited in Holy 1996: 124).

BUSTLING TOWNSHIP AND THE CHINESE POLITY

There can be no doubt that Bustling Township has been firmly integrated into the Chinese Communist state. In the village of Uphill, several brick buildings with white plastered walls stand out from the traditional log houses characteristic of this part of Southwest China. These buildings house the institutions the Chinese state has brought to one of its more marginal corners: the township government building, the state shop, the medical dispensary, and the township's full primary school. The buildings themselves could be viewed as highly visual symbols of Bustling Township's relationship to the Chinese state. They constitute a dominating presence in the landscape of Uphill, as a result of their rather disproportionate scale and the alien character of their architecture. At the same time, one is struck by their dilapidated state: only a few window panes have glass in them, the roofs are marred by missing or broken tiles, and the courtyards of several buildings are littered with broken beer bottles and other garbage. One might be tempted to extend the use of visual symbolism and see the sad condition of the buildings as a telltale sign of the retraction and consequent diminished prestige of the Party and the state in post-Mao China.

A "township" (*xiang*) is the lowest administrative level in China at which a complete set of government and Party functions is normally present. It is also the point of contact between the top-down system of administration of the Chinese state and the grass roots. It is through the cadres of the township government, the township Party leaders, and the township schoolteachers that the villagers are confronted with a personification of the Chinese state, which they refer to simply as *guojia* (country, nation, state). In Bustling Township, the local government and Party administration consists of fourteen people. As in other townships in China, at the top of the hierarchy stand a Party secretary and a vice-secretary, a township leader and a vice-leader. The township government counts an additional fifteen administrative posts at the central level, but this quota of "authorized personnel" (*bianzhi*)[15] was never filled in the period 1999–2004. In 1999, only ten of the fifteen posts were filled, and in 2004, this number had fallen to six. All these cadres lived and worked at the township government building, a two-story structure with single rooms facing a courtyard. During the day, these rooms served as offices, and at night they were the sleeping quarters of the government employees. Cooking and eating took place in a separate building consisting of a row of tiny kitchens, each with its own fireplace. Three to four people shared a kitchen. Such a kitchen group also shared the tasks of buying rice, cutting firewood, and providing vegetables from the common plot of land belonging to the township administration. Overall, the people working at the government building were surprisingly isolated from the people in the village. Most interactions related to the work of administration, and there was little socializing between the two groups.

Some years ago, a small power station had provided electricity for the government building and the other state-owned buildings. Electricity was but a faint memory after the power station broke down and the county government did not have it repaired. The same sad story applied to the telephone connection: until several years ago, it was possible to make phone calls from the government building to the outside world. But when the telephone line—which stretched over tens of kilometers of formidable terrain, crossing deep gorges and steep mountains—was cut a few years ago, no money was available to make the necessary repairs, and the line continued to deteriorate. During my stay at the township government building, a radio powered by a small generator enabled communication with the outside world. Every morning at nine o'clock, a short report was broadcast to the district-town and information or instructions were received. Bad connections and recurring defects with the radio or generator made this an unreliable means of communication, but in addition to facilitating official business, it gave the people of the township a way of exchanging important information with relatives in the district-town, such as when someone in the family had become seriously ill or died.

The employees working and living in the government building came from all over Muli County, but mostly from within the district in which Bustling Township was situated. These cadres rotated between different administrative positions within Muli County and usually did not stay longer than the minimum three-year term. Except for the one employee who was responsible for providing practical assistance to the local administration, such as arranging for transport, none of these cadres was from Bustling Township. The policy of filling positions in local governments with people from outside the administered area and rotating them after the standard three-year term, or *lunhuan*, is the default over most areas in China. Several recent studies have pointed out that the job-rotation system, far from being on the decline, has been strengthened in recent years, enabling the center to maintain control over the lower levels of government and Party (Edin 2003; Pieke 2004). Holders of a "top position" (*lingdao ganbu*) at one level of the government or Party often hold another position at a higher level. In combination with the rotation policy, this means that, for example, a township cadre will be more loyal to the district or county than to the township (Edin 2003: 42, 47). While this policy may at first have been upheld in recent years as a means of countering corruption, it has also functioned as a very effective way to avoid empowering local communities. It is not entirely clear whether this is a conscious policy in Muli. In his study of the Lianmu Menggu in Shuiluo Township, also in Muli, Roland Naef wrote that seven of the local men worked as "Kader der chinesischen Partei" (cadres belonging to the CCP) and get regular wages from the state, which could indicate that they work for the local township government or the Party (1998: 88), although Naef does not specify further. It is also possible that things have changed since he collected his data in 1996 and that the situation in Bustling Township was more in line with official policy in the late 1990s compared to the situation in Shuiluo as described by Naef.

When government employees at the prefectural level were asked specifically about the policy of job rotation and filling township-level positions with people from outside the township, they replied that only the positions of Party chairman, township leader, and head of police had to be filled by people from outside the township.

In any case, the fact that most cadres in Bustling Township came from outside the township and only stayed there a short time has had serious drawbacks for the local people. People from outside Bustling Township often have a very limited understanding of local conditions and cultural practices. In 1999, only two of the fourteen cadres were Premi and two were Na, but none were from the township. The "township head" (*xiangzhang*) was a Premi from the neighboring township, and the vice-head was a Na.[16] The rest of the cadres did not speak any of the local languages and most of them were not really interested in understanding local customs such as marriage patterns, clan relations, or religious beliefs. Some of the things the villagers told me were unknown to the township government workers who accompanied me on my interviews.

Moreover, the uncomfortable working and living conditions for government employees, even in the context of an already poor and underdeveloped county such as Muli, make Bustling Township a hardship post, and consequently, young men make up the majority of workers assigned to this township. Although it is possible to prolong one's assignment beyond the three-year minimum term, most seek a transfer as soon as their terms are up. Most cadres know at the start of their stay in Bustling Township that they intend to seek a job at a higher level of the administration that will involve transfer to the district- or county-town or to a township closer to their hometowns. Consequently, they usually are not interested in obtaining a deeper understanding of the place or learning any of the local languages. This cultural divide only strengthens local perceptions of the Chinese state and its representatives as agents of outside interference and control.

At first sight, it is not immediately obvious how the local government exercises its political power. One of its major tasks seems to be to fill a symbolic role similar to the buildings in which it is housed: in other words, to constitute a visual sign that Bustling Township is part of the Chinese state. Most of the routine activities are related to registering and monitoring all kinds of data: detailed figures of agricultural production and land use, number of births, income generated outside agriculture, and the like. During my stay in Bustling Township in 2000, all government employees were busy organizing and carrying out China's fifth population census. Another major occupation consisted of calling meetings in the villages once in a while in order to stress the importance of fire prevention, forest protection, birth control, hygiene, and children's school attendance. I participated in several such meetings, and in view of their ritualistic and uninspired nature, it is hard to see any but a symbolic reason for the meetings, to remind the local villagers that they are part of the People's Republic of China.

But several other modes of governance are clearly more than symbolic. The direct power of the administration becomes more apparent in its authority to issue permits and licenses, such as marriage certificates or permits to cut down trees or build or repair houses, which interferes with the villagers' social life and livelihoods in very concrete ways. Furthermore, the township government issues fines in cases of, for example, breaching the quota of three children per couple or illegally felling trees.

At the time of my visit, the most powerful person in Bustling Township was Secretary Vugo. He was a Nuosu in his late thirties and originally from the neighboring township, where a considerable part of the population was Nuosu and where his family was living. Besides being the township Party secretary, Secretary Vugo was concurrently filling the post of "chairman of the township National People's Congress (Renmin Dabiao Dahui)" (Ren Da zhuxi). As Party leader, he decided at any time what was the correct policy; consequently, no major decision concerning the township was made without his consent. Secretary Vugo mediated and propagated new policies and regulations from the higher Party and government levels to the people in the administration, the school, and the village. At several long meetings with villagers, government employees, or teachers at the township school, the Party secretary read aloud documents containing new policies formulated at the county level. At the same time, as chairman of the local National People's Congress, Secretary Vugo had a final say in local legislation, that is, the rules set by the villagers for local issues, in controlling the working of the government and approving candidates for the positions of, among other things, township head. Government employees solicited his opinion on all major issues, and he mediated conflicts between villagers or between villagers and the government.

In general, throughout my stays, which totaled almost half a year, I witnessed relatively little direct intervention by government bureaucrats in Uphill in the lives of the people of the township and even less in communities farther away from Uphill, such as Walnut Grove. Although people's lives were clearly affected by the policies of the Chinese Communist state, the lowest levels of its representatives meddled surprisingly little in village affairs. Many concrete issues were decided at the village level, either by the village head or at ad hoc meetings of village elders. Most conflicts were also solved at this level. Only very few conflicts or criminal acts had to be brought to higher levels. There was very little crime in Bustling Township, and most were minor cases of fighting related to alcohol abuse. One of the very few serious cases involved a native of Walnut Grove who had a career as a thief outside the township and was imprisoned in Xichang, the prefectural capital.

Once every month, a traveling district judge and his assistant arrived in Uphill. They toured continuously between the outlying townships of the district, on horseback and visibly armed. They stayed one or two days in the government building in order to settle unresolved conflicts and decide whether criminal cases needed to be taken to court. But such cases were rare, and during the three visits I observed, the judge had to settle only one conflict, which had started when two young men from a village close to Uphill got into a brawl after drinking heavily. Although heavy drinking among young men and the occasional fistfight were recurring problems in the township, they seldom escalated. But in this case, the parties involved had simply refused to budge, and in the end, the traveling judge had to broker a settlement.

The villagers most directly encounter state-imposed restraints in areas related to land use. They are not permitted to log additional forest areas, and people have been compelled to reforest some of the fields on the steeper slopes in order to counter erosion, reducing the amount of arable land. While geographical conditions already excluded most of the surface of Bustling Township from cultivation, the rigorous implementation of land use regulation in relation to marginal lands and forests provides a latent source of friction between the villagers and the township cadres. I learned that one small stretch of steep land at the edge of Downhill had been at the center of many heated debates between the cadres and the villagers, and that it had taken several meetings before the villagers agreed not to cultivate maize there but to plant fruit trees instead. Several times when I passed by the orchard with one of the local cadres, they pointed out the place as one of their more important achievements in educating the villagers in scientific land use.

In 2003, the Tuigeng Huanlin (Return Farmland to Forest) campaign reached Bustling Township, and the county government offered incentives for planting chestnut trees, peach trees, or Sichuan pepper. This campaign started in 1999 across Southwest China, and, like the Tianbao campaign, which banned logging, was a result of the 1998 flooding of the Yangzi. It targeted the mountainous areas of the upper Yangzi and Yellow Rivers, specifically, cultivated land on slopes of twenty-five degrees or more.[17] In Bustling Township, the government was to provide the trees and compensation for loss of income for a period of five to eight years, depending on the kind of tree planted. Because large tracts of denuded but uncultivated land were available on the mountain slopes, the rationale behind this policy was poorly understood by the villagers, and people were worried about whether compensation would be paid in full and what would happen after five or eight years.[18]

At the same time, the strictly enforced rules on tree felling have created a veritable bottleneck for families who want to split their households and build new houses or expand their old ones. Yearly quotas for the number of trees to be felled are distributed from the county level down to the township and village levels. If a village has filled its yearly quota, it must wait until the following year to build. This is one of the main sources of tension between villagers and the Chinese state, especially because a real building boom has been taking place since the late 1990s (created partly by the need to make room for laid-off forestry workers and their families). For several years, township authorities tried to compensate for local conditions by taking a less restrictive attitude toward the felling of trees for house construction and repair. But in 2003, inspection teams from the provincial forestry department began to show up unexpectedly and fined people for chopping down trees without proper authorization. One family in North Village was fined ¥1,000 for felling a couple of trees to add a room to their house. Such bypassing of local authorities—and especially the size of the fines—caused consternation among the villagers and was a major topic of discussion during my visit in 2004.

Limited possibilities for expanding arable land can put a severe strain on growing families, especially when a son moves out of the parental home and needs a piece of land on which to support his own family. One traditional solution to such problems is the practice of adelphic polyandry (see also chapter 3). When two or more brothers marry one wife, and as such establish only one family, the land does not have to be divided. Polygamy, be it polyandry or polygyny, is officially forbidden in China, but in those ethnic minority areas where it has been widespread, the local authorities tolerate it to some degree and hope that intense propagation of marriage laws will gradually eliminate the practice.[19]

On the one hand, the practice of polyandry, and, to a lesser extent, polygyny, is clearly an issue with which the township government prefers not to interfere too much. On the other hand, local government officials are aware that it is forbidden and therefore downplayed its prevalence in the township when discussing these issues with me. The numbers of such marriages do not figure in official township statistics, and the few cases of polyandry in Uphill and Downhill were presented as holdovers from the old days. Nevertheless, at the level of the administrative village, the picture looks quite different. In the administrative village in which Walnut Grove is situated, the local Party secretary told me that of the 191 non-Han families in this area, 51 (or 26.7 percent) were polyandrous families: such marriages were very common and even a highly preferred form of marriage. In this case, the township government mediates between state policies and local customs. On the one hand, the government acts out its part in proclaiming marriage laws to the villagers, while, on the other hand, officials do not interfere with local practices and such marriages are generally registered by declaring only one of the brothers as the legal husband.

The same pragmatic attitude has prevailed in the case of birth control. Ethnic minorities are allowed three children, while the Han in the township are permitted only two. The government cadre responsible for birth control travels constantly to the villages to try to convince people to follow these quotas. He is also responsible for explaining and propagating birth control methods, a daunting task for a young, single man, but has not been particularly successful, and besides monitoring a birth rate that far exceeds the official limit, he also enforces the fines levied on above-quota births. Patrilineal inheritance means that it is still highly desirable for a family to have at least one boy, and therefore people kept trying to have a male heir even if the house is filled with girls. Of the forty-four families in Walnut Grove, there were eleven with at least four children; of those, four had four girls. Until 2003, the fine of ¥1,000 was considered stiff but obviously was not insurmountable, as testified by the unrestrained attempts to have boys.

However, starting in 2003, directives from the provincial authorities began to be strictly enforced, incorporating fines of at least ¥14,000. Villagers agreed that this would have the desired effect, because nobody in the township could ever afford such an amount. Township cadres vehemently denied that women were offered inducements to be sterilized. Although I did not pursue the matter through specific questioning, I came across no data that contradicted their claim. Sterilization campaigns have been conducted in many poor ethnic minority areas in Southwest China, and it is often one of the issues that create friction between the local community and the Chinese state. In Mueggler's study of an impoverished Lòlop'ò community in Yunnan, his account of the painful relationship between the local community and the intruding Chinese state begins with a description of a merciless campaign of forced sterilization of women under the age of forty (2001: 24).

Below the level of the township government and Party cadres, as elsewhere in China, there is the level of the "villagers' committees" (*cunmin weiyuanhui*), also called "administrative villages." This level includes a Party secretary, a vice-secretary, a village head, a vice-head, a militia leader, the chairperson of China's Women's Association, and a few minor officials, all appointed by the township government.[20] Top posts at this level provide a monthly salary of ¥30. Below this level is the level of the "villagers' small groups" (*cunmin xiaozu*). In Bustling Township, this level corresponds to the level of the natural village, except for two of these small groups, one that consists of two separate villages (the twin villages of Uphill and Downhill, fifteen minutes' walking distance from each other) and one that comprises three. These are collective units, meaning that the villagers choose the "group leaders" (*zuzhang*), who receive a mere ¥150 a year. Both these levels are staffed with local people and act mainly as facilitators between the township government and the villagers.[21] They perform tasks of registration related to income, agricultural production, and population; call meetings of villagers when requested by the township cadres; and explain some of the government's policies to the villagers, mainly in the areas of land use and agricultural practice. But these officials also wield more substantial power through their role in advising the township government on land use issues, as when a family has no heir and the land must be redistributed. Unlike many other areas of China, in Bustling Township, there were no regular rounds of general land redistribution.

BECOMING SOCIALIZED AS CITIZENS OF THE PEOPLE'S REPUBLIC

Many of the inhabitants of Bustling Township first encounter an embodiment of the Chinese state in the official state school, either in the form of one of the twelve "local village schools" (*jiaoxue dian* or *cunxiao*) or the "full primary school" (*zhongxin wanquan xiaoxue*) in Uphill. The village schools offer only the first two grades. Teachers at these village schools were almost all locals, and most taught in one of the local languages. After these two grades, the children could continue their education up to the sixth grade at the full primary school in Uphill, which was a boarding school. The school had eighteen teachers and more than 120 registered students. Here most teaching was done in Chinese, but teachers often would use Premi for explanations, especially in the lower grades. From the third grade onward, all children were taught Tibetan as well.

According to the school head, 99 percent of all children in the township between the ages of seven and eleven attend school as they are supposed to, in accordance with county and prefectural regulations that aim to implement six years of compulsory primary school. This is well below the national target of nine years stipulated in China's 1986 law on compulsory education.[22] The children attend either the village school or the township boarding school.

Systematic household interviews in Uphill, Downhill, and Walnut Grove revealed that the 99 percent figure did not say much about actual participation in education. Most parents registered their children at school to avoid being fined, but many children did not attend school regularly. During my visits, at the school serving the village of Walnut Grove and a neighboring village, there were usually not more than twenty children present, five of them girls. At the same time, the village of Walnut Grove alone counted almost twenty girls between seven and eleven who should have been at school according to the county regulations. The situation was even worse in the higher grades: during my stay in Walnut Grove in 2000, none of the girls in the village was attending classes at the boarding school in Uphill. Reasons given for not sending girls to school were that they were needed to help care for the younger children or to take the family's domestic animals to pasture. If girls participated in education, they usually attended only the local village school, and this on a highly irregular basis. This pattern resulted in a marked age difference among the girls at the Walnut Grove village school, who were between nine and twelve years old in the second grade. Most of the boys in the village were also not attending school on a regular basis. In periods when all hands were needed at home or in the fields, classes were almost empty. This was typically during harvests or just after the autumn harvest when all families slaughter pigs in preparation for the Premi New Year.

The reason most villagers gave for not sending children to school was the financial burden involved. Although there is no tuition fee, there are administrative fees, including the cost of schoolbooks, of ¥150 a year. Fees are reduced for very poor families, but they still have to pay for schoolbooks. For the first five grades, books cost ¥24 per year, and the cost in the sixth grade is ¥32.5. There are also extra costs related to having children at boarding school. Here it seems that girls risk drawing the shortest straw: among the families I spoke with, when it was deemed too expensive to let all school-age children go to school, girls are the ones who usually stayed home.

While there is a significantly higher rate of participation in education for boys, the numbers for both girls and boys drop drastically from the third grade onward. This is especially true for children not living in

Uphill and Downhill. It is a tough affair for a ten-year-old to make the half- or full-day walk twice every week to the boarding school, carrying all their food for the week, and then, moreover, to cook it themselves. Sometimes families solved this by waiting until children were a bit older before sending them to school. Two of the third-grade boys from Walnut Grove were thirteen, while pupils would normally be nine or ten years old. It is not surprising then, that the rate of participation in the higher grades of primary school and, consequently, in secondary education was markedly higher for Uphill and Downhill than for places like Walnut Grove. While the two areas have approximately the same population (a bit more than forty families each), more than twice as many people in Uphill and Downhill had finished "technical secondary school" (*zhongzhuan*) or "junior middle school" (*chuzhong*) or were in the process of completing such an education than was the case in Walnut Grove (twenty-two in Uphill and Downhill combined, and nine in Walnut Grove).

Poverty, traditional practices related to gender roles, and logistical impediments such as distance to the township school explain to a large extent the low level of participation in official state education. Asking people why they had dropped out of school also revealed other problems with the Chinese educational system in ethnic minority areas. Even though several teachers spontaneously used local languages in teaching at the village level, they were neither trained in nor had adequate schoolbooks for providing a truly bilingual education in which children are gradually introduced to Chinese through the use of their mother tongue. Since Premi and Na were not recognized languages in Muli, no such materials existed. Most education was centered on learning Chinese using normal Chinese-language schoolbooks. None of the children in the township, except for those in the Han village, knew any Chinese before entering the village school. The limited level of proficiency they attained during the first two grades did not prepare them for their continued education at the complete primary school in Uphill. Here much of the teaching was done in Chinese, since three of the teachers were Han and one was Nuosu; none could speak Premi or Na. But Chinese was not the only challenge: in many areas of Muli, children also had to learn Tibetan at school.

One of the few areas in which the Chinese system of autonomy for recognized ethnic minorities functions is in organizing courses in languages other than Chinese. In 1992, the county government began to implement a regulation adopted by the National People's Congress on teaching spoken and written Tibetan at various levels of the educational system.[23] Since Premi were classified as Tibetans and constituted an absolute majority in Bustling Township, the township's full primary school introduced Tibetan courses in 1992. In the third and fourth grades, students have only one hour of Tibetan a week, but in the fifth and sixth grades, instruction in Tibetan increases to two hours a week. During these four years, the pupils work through two Tibetan schoolbooks, part of the national curriculum for teaching Tibetan in areas outside the Tibetan Autonomous Region. Unfortunately, for the Premi in Muli, Tibetan is basically another language rather than a related dialect. Because of the limited scope of teaching and the traditional teaching methods used, results were not really impressive.[24] I observed one hour of Tibetan-language teaching at the sixth-grade level (the term had started two months before I arrived) and recorded the following field notes. The class consisted of ten Premi and one Han, all boys.

> The students stand up when the teacher comes in and greet him in Tibetan. The teacher then starts writing a poem on the blackboard in Tibetan. He reads the poem word by word, first in the Tibetan way of spelling by which each letter is pronounced by its name, then by reading the whole word. The students repeat after him. When they have to read together aloud without him doing it first, it does not go very well. Then he explains the meaning of some words using Premi. The next fifteen minutes the students have to work by themselves, copying the poem on a sheet of paper first and then translating it into Chinese with the help of their textbook. They have clearly obtained a certain proficiency in writing Tibetan letters, but seem to struggle with the translation. One by one they go to the teacher's desk and present him with their translation. Then the class ends with the students standing up and greeting the teacher.

Because of the double language handicap, it is not surprising that very few students in Bustling Township pass the examination for entering junior middle school. In 1998, eight students passed the examination and went on to the "district junior middle school" (*qu chuzhong*) in Wachang. Almost two-thirds of the students in this school are official Tibetans—in this case, mostly Premi—and the rest are mainly Han. Tibetan is also taught two hours a week, and Han children are included in these lessons.

But at this stage, another new language is introduced: English. As would be expected, very few Premi students manage to pass the final exam at the end of junior middle school. In 1998, none of the forty-seven students passed the examination for senior middle school; twenty-six had enough points to continue with a teacher training school, or "normal school" (*shifan xuexiao*), or a technical secondary school. In the latter category, the most frequently attended schools are the Muli Tibetan Autonomous County School of Hygiene (Muli Zangzu Zizhixian Weisheng Xuexiao) and the Muli Tibetan Autonomous County Agricultural School (Muli Zangzu Zizhixian Nongye Xuexiao), both in the county capital. Of these forty-seven students, nine were from Bustling Township, but only two were able to continue. The Premi and other Zangzu students who do not score high enough on general topics like Chinese language or mathematics to enter a teacher training school have another option if their Tibetan-language scores are reasonable: they can enter the Tibetan Language Section of the Kangding Normal School (Kangding Shifan Xuexiao)[25] and become Tibetan-language teachers, usually in the full primary school in their home townships. This was the case with the two Tibetan-language teachers at the Bustling Township full primary school. But most students in Bustling Township do not obtain results good enough to be able to continue studying. As they are fifteen or sixteen years old when they finish junior middle school, they would have few other options than to return to Bustling Township. Before 1999, some of these people were able to find jobs as local village teachers, the so-called *minban* teachers. In 1999, this system was abolished, and all *minban* teachers had to pass a test to become regular teachers, a promotion that greatly improved their income. Since no new positions were filled during my visits to the school in the following two years, it was unclear whether people with junior middle school degrees were capable of passing this test immediately and taking up a teaching position.

As a result, there is limited participation in education in the township. Many children who attend school do not continue past the second grade offered at the village schools. The little that has been learned of, for example, Chinese language is never made operational and is quickly forgotten. Those who make it through their entire primary education obtain some workable skills in Chinese. In conversations with sixth graders, I could make myself understood in Chinese, but they had great difficulty in speaking it themselves. Probably more important than language skill is the basic knowledge they obtain, through the Chinese language, about the country and world they live in, albeit the officially sanctioned version propagated in national curriculum schoolbooks, explained by teachers imbued with this same version. I have not specifically studied how this education affected the views and understanding of children who drop out of the school system after the sixth grade, as the majority of Bustling Township children do. Interviews with people from Bustling Township who had different levels of education beyond primary school revealed a correlation between the number of years of education and the extent of internalization of official Chinese discourses on ethnicity, social evolution, politics, and so forth. People with only junior middle school degrees presented very diverse opinions on whether they were official Tibetans or Premi, or both, and showed very little consistency in their views of the difference between Buddhism as it was taught at the monastery and their local ritual practice. In contrast, Tibetan-language teachers at the township school in Bustling Township had thoroughly accepted official stances on religion, ethnic categorization, and social and cultural development. According to those views, there was no doubt that the Premi were Tibetans and therefore Buddhists. In their opinion, it was consequently also only natural that Tibetan is taught at school, and in this way, they were instrumental in perpetuating one of the more exotic results of the Chinese ethnic classification project.

The school system is the arena in which the state in principle has the greatest potential for making its presence felt in Bustling Township. Nevertheless, both as a project of mass emancipation and enlightenment and as a means of propagating the Chinese nation-state project, the impact of Chinese education is minimal in Bustling Township. At the same time, villagers experience a state that is retracting from several areas crucial for their livelihoods, including a partial breakdown of the social security system, the disappearance of job opportunities in the state logging company, and the removal of price guarantees for some agricultural products. Although local farmers in many areas of China view migration to find work in urban areas as a way out of their predicament, Bustling Township farmers lack education and language skills and know they cannot compete with the countless Han farmers flooding the towns and cities of the Southwest and beyond. Living standards have increased since de-collectivization, and this improvement has made it possible for people to become aware of an increasing gap between Bustling Township and "the rest of China," thereby quickly eroding their initial satisfaction with the policy changes.

While the state is retreating from some domains of social and economic life and its ideological impact is waning, its interference in several other domains is mounting. In their article "Taxation without Representation in Contemporary Rural China," Thomas Bernstein and Lü Xiaobo write about a "deconcentration of the state" in China, describing a shift in state power during the Reform Period by which the state's presence does not evaporate but instead vertical decentralization goes hand in hand with horizontal expansion (2003). In Bustling Township, new, stringently enforced birth control policies as well as increasingly stricter regulations on land use and tree cutting are causing growing resentment. All these issues are national priorities in China, and therefore the local administration is under strong pressure to implement the dictates coming from the center. In other matters that—although clearly illegal—are concerns of a more local nature, such as the persistent custom of polyandry, regional representatives of the Chinese state show much greater tolerance.

In short, the role of the Party-state in guaranteeing people's livelihoods is quickly fading. At the same time, it is incapable of enforcing its version of cosmological truth through the school system. In a context of feeling marginalized and left behind, the subsistence farmers of Bustling Township turn increasingly to their remembered traditional cosmology, values, beliefs, and ways of organizing their social life. The relatively more relaxed official policies on the practice of religion and on ethnic minority culture during the Reform Period provide a political climate that enables a veritable revival and revitalization of local traditions. This is what the next chapters will address.

3 ∞ THE PREMI HOUSE

Ritual and Relatedness

Understanding religious practice in Bustling Township is impossible without examining the ways people conceive of social relationships. Ancestor cults are inextricably intertwined with notions of kinship or "relatedness"—to use a recently introduced alternative term.¹ Care and respect for lineage members continue after their deaths, while the souls of the deceased continue to interfere with the lives of their surviving descendants. In order to understand religious practice and cosmological beliefs in Bustling Township, it is therefore necessary to understand how relatedness is socially constructed.

There are two clearly prominent principles of social organization in Bustling Township. The first is the exogamous unit created through patrilineal descent, called *jhü*, probably best rendered as "clan." The second principle, which is particularly central in the structuring of daily life, is a residential unit called *dzè^n*, or "house."² Traditional anthropological concepts like those of "kinship" and "household" are not very helpful in explaining these empirically encountered forms of social organization. To a certain extent, the *dzè^n* are coterminous with the anthropological concept of households. They constitute domestic groups that share tasks of production and consumption, and they are tied together by descent and alliance (Carter 1984; Netting, Wilk, and Arnould 1984). But as several anthropologists have noticed, household members are not necessarily co-residents (Harrell 1997);[3] moreover, one house may contain several households. The Premi in Bustling Township also have a word for the domestic group, the "single, bounded, multi-activity group" found in the villages (ibid.: 50): *k'a* (in Walnut Grove) or *ga* (in North Village). But while *dzè^n* clearly refers to the built structure, the term is fully interchangeable with *k'a* when it comes to designating the inhabitants of a house. Keeping to the indigenous concept of *dzè^n* in this analysis of Bustling Township society avoids the chicken-or-egg controversy of whether residence is a generative factor for the creation of the domestic group or co-residence is the result when such a unit exists (Levine 1988: 128; Carter 1984: 77).[4] But Premi *dzè^n* not only constitute a local category for the "conceptualization and practice of social relations"; they also make up the primary centers of *ritual* practice and symbolic meanings (Thomas 1996: 281). Having names and being ascribed with the magical power to provide its inhabitants with prosperous lives, the Premi *dzè^n* furthermore possess animistic qualities.

FIG. 3.1. Cluster of houses in Bustling Township. The roofs are made of planks kept in place with stones. While these houses are made partially of stone, in many areas of Bustling Township, houses are made entirely of logs.

Houses conceived as basic units ordering social life are not unique to Bustling Township Premi. Ethnographic data on communities within the larger region of the Himalayas and their foothills actually confirm that patrilineality as a structuring principle often is combined with residentially based principles of social organization, or houses. The Kachin word *htinggaw* literally means "people under one roof" (Leach 1970). It can refer to one household and, interestingly, also to several households belonging to the same patrilineage. According to Barbara Aziz, in conceptualizing social relations in Tibetan D'ing-ri, the idea of residence is more important than that of descent (1978: 117–24). Elisabeth Hsu finds in the concept of "the house" an alternative framework for understanding kinship among the Naxi and the Na, both close neighbors of the Premi. These two ethnic groups are closely related culturally, and their kinship systems have been described as patrilineal for the Naxi and matrilineal for the Na.[5] While the Naxi are virilocal or neolocal, the Na are traditionally duolocal or natolocal. Comparing the ethnographic studies of McKhann (1992) on the Naxi and Shih (1993) on the Na, Hsu discerns two coexisting local ideologies: a hearth-oriented ideology and an alliance-oriented ideology. The hearth-oriented ideology is concerned with harmony and consequently stresses the prominence of the house as the basic unit for all kinds of social relations (Shih 1993: 135). Alliance-oriented ideology is concerned with honor, rank, and hierarchy and is expressed in the distinction between *raka* (bone), which stands for the exogamous patrilineage, and *na* or *she* (flesh), which stands for the lineages of the affines. Making a clear distinction between ideologies and practices, Hsu sees the interplay between these two *ideologies* as creating the conditions for the flexible implementation of kinship *practices* (1998: 90).

In the anthropological literature in many other areas of the world, however, "houses" also turn up as central concepts in the study of social organization. Claude Lévi-Strauss was the first to put forward "the house" as a specific form of social organization.[6] He proposed the theoretical concept of "house-based societies," which several writers subsequently elaborated on and criticized.[7] Relatedness is not necessarily the sole result of fixed descent rules; it is continuously "under construction" through shared participation in everyday activities by, for example, the inhabitants of a common residence (Carsten 2000: 18). Everyday activities in a

Premi house involve ritual offerings of food to the ancestors, thereby constructing and strengthening ties between the co-residents.

MARRIAGE AND RELATEDNESS IN BUSTLING TOWNSHIP

The traditional age for marriage in Bustling Township, as in many other Premi areas, is thirteen. At that age, children also enter into the world of adults. In Bustling Township, boys and girls go through a ceremony called "wearing trousers" and "wearing skirts," respectively. When Premi girls become thirteen, they start wearing the traditional pleated skirts as well as braiding their hair and interweaving it with black thread in the typical and recognizable style of Bustling Township. The current age for marrying is now slightly higher, around seventeen on average. I registered marriage ages between fifteen and twenty-one. Although the official age of marriage is eighteen for women and twenty for men, people get around the limits by waiting to register their marriages or by not registering them at all. In cases of brothers or sisters marrying one spouse, they would register only the oldest sibling. Often, when I asked about how partners were chosen, people gave the standard answer that marriages were based on free choice. In Walnut Grove, where I got to know people well enough to make such political correctness unnecessary, several people told me that parents were in charge of choosing marriage partners for their children. They usually made these arrangements at the ceremony held when the children turned thirteen. There were only three well-known cases of couples in Walnut Grove who had married after choosing each other. Although I did not specifically pursue the matter, premarital and extramarital sexual relations do also occur, as testified by a few unmarried mothers and persons with uncertain clan identity.

There is no word in Premi for "marriage." This does not mean that there is no concept of a legitimated sexual union in Premi society. When expressing the fact that one is married, Premi people say, "A pri getyè^{n}sa^n," which literally means "I have drunk *pri*" (*pri* or *tri* is a locally brewed beer). When saying, for example, that one got married at the age of eighteen, one would say, "A ga-hsüè-go k'o-nyè pri getyè^{n}sa^n," which means "In the year that I turned eighteen, I drank *pri*." The explanation for this way of describing a formal union between two or more partners is that *pri* was consumed only rarely in the old days, and the drinking of *pri* was a major part of the marriage ceremony, which celebrated not only the relationship between the partners but also the establishment or strengthening of relationships between two families and two *jhü*, or exogamous clans. Asked to describe how they were planning to marry off the last of their four daughters in the coming spring, the parents in my host family explained that they would invite an *anji* to preside over the ceremony and perform several rituals to bless the union. The whole celebration would last six days: three days at their house and three days at the groom's house. On her journey to the house of her future husband, their daughter would be escorted by her brother and ceremoniously handed over to her new house and new clan. They would not have to pay any real dowry, but their daughter would not be entitled to any share of the land. The families would exchange only a few symbolic gifts: *arje*, or homemade distilled spirits, dried pork meat, and homespun hemp cloth. If they managed to save some money in the coming months, they might give her a bit as a dowry, but they would never pay more than ¥100, since this was not the custom in the village. After marriage, their daughter would move in with her new husband, either in his parental home or in a new house when they found some land to build on. In Lévi-Strauss's scheme of elementary structures of marriage, Premi marriages are definitely of the symmetric exchange type in which clans exchange women but no material goods. The major advantage of establishing affinal ties is that it facilitates future exchanges of women. Once families in two neighboring villages— whether they are Premi, Na, Naxi, or Rek'ua—have established their first marriage relationship, they will try to continue the exchange of women, and cousin marriages constitute the most obvious opportunities for such exchanges.

There is at least an ideological preference for cross-cousin marriages, which is also reflected in kinship terminology that makes the distinction between parallel and cross cousins. On the male side, the term apo^n is used for father, father's brother, father's sister's husband, and mother's sister's husband and also designates the father of one's wife, but one's mother's brother is called *agu*. On the female side, the women in one's mother's generation are all called *ama*—or *ma* for one's mother—except for one's father's sister, who is called *ane*.[8] Such distinctions do not exist in one's own generation, in which there is no distinction between cousins and siblings: *pep'ei* is used for one's older brother, older sister, and older male and female cousin, while *gwè^{n}gwè^n* is used for the cousins and siblings younger than oneself, also without regard to sex (see fig. 3.2). In practice, cross-cousin marriages are not all that frequent. Among forty-six marriages in Walnut Grove, I registered only five such marriages. With only two registered cases, there were even fewer marriages between parallel cousins.[9]

Polygamous marriages were frequent in Bustling Township. These were mainly instances of fraternal or adelphic polyandry, in which two or more brothers take one wife, with a few cases of sororal polygyny, in which sisters marry one husband. A prevalence of more than one-fourth of all marriages in the southern villages—one of which is Walnut Grove—suggests that fraternal polyandry is a preferred form of marriage in this part of the township. This is also the most ethnically diverse part of the township, and polygamy was as prevalent in Na, Rek'ua, and Naxi villages as in Premi villages (see table 3.1). All four instances of sororal polygyny I recorded were from the northern villages, two of them in one family from Hill Village: one of the two *anji* in the village had two mothers who were sisters and was married to two sisters himself.

While I have no data substantiating that this form of marriage has been practiced among the Premi in the neighboring province of Yunnan, Muli and the adjacent Litang (Lithang) area have long been known for the practice of polyandry. According to a survey by Wu Wen in 1956, the prevalence of brothers or sisters marrying a single spouse was more than 20–30 percent in Muli,[10] where the practice is prevalent among Premi,

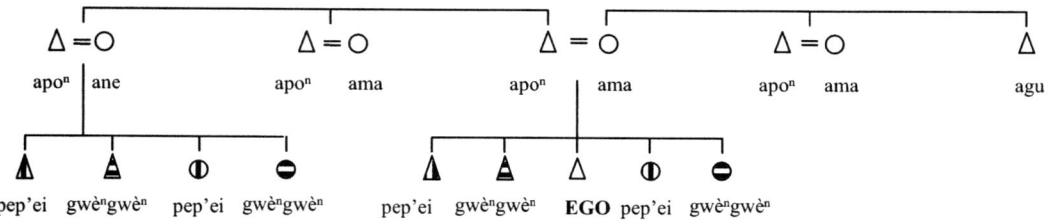

FIG. 3.2. Kinship chart showing Premi terms of relatedness.

TABLE 3.1 Number of Polyandrous Marriages in Southern Villages in 1998

Southern villages*	Ethnic group(s)	Polyandrous marriages	Households/ houses
Walnut Grove	Premi	3	43
Five Nut Trees	Premi	5	14
Ten Houses	Premi/Na/Rek'ua	10	32
Main Crossing	Premi	5	20
Battleground	Naxi	17	44
Gaku	Rek'ua	8	43
Gabo[n]	Rek'ua	9	30
TOTAL		52	191

*The Han village of Woody Plains and the four Han families in Ten Houses are excluded.

Na, Rek'ua, Gami, and Naxi. In a 1982 marriage survey of the Naxi of the township of Eya in the southwestern corner of Muli, Liu Longchu has registered 46 households of a total of 130, or 35.4 percent, that practice fraternal polyandry (1986). Polyandry has also been widely documented throughout Tibet and among Tibetan communities in adjacent areas such as Nepal (see, e.g., Peter 1963; Goldstein 1971, 1976; Aziz 1978; Levine 1988; Ma Rong 2001). In recent years, the practice has seen a revival in some rural areas of central Tibet (Benjor 2001; Fjeld 2007).

Most studies of polyandry in Tibetan areas base their explanations for this rather rare form of marriage on economic and social causes. Fraternal polyandry is seen as a peculiar adaptation to specific ecological circumstances. In the highlands of Tibet, the area suitable for agriculture is strictly limited and cannot sustain an increasing population. All the sons in a family are entitled to inherit a share of the family land. In order to avoid having to partition this land into smaller and smaller shares, and because they are unable to open up new arable land, Tibetans practiced what Goldstein termed the "monomarital" marriage principle, by which there can be only one marriage that produces heirs for each generation

(1978: 208). This would in most cases be fraternal polyandry, but there are also other possibilities. For example, when there are no sons in the family, daughters can inherit by marrying uxorilocally. If there are several unmarried daughters, they can marry one husband in sororal polygyny. Such factors must be seen in combination with other factors such as the tax system and prevailing political structures, according to Goldstein. He also shows that on a larger scale, fraternal polyandry significantly decreases fertility and functions as a mechanism for reducing population growth (1976).

In her study of the Nyinba in Nepal, who are of Tibetan origin, Levine argues that polyandry cannot be explained by economic and demographic factors alone. To a certain extent, her findings support Goldstein, and she demonstrates how fraternal polyandry makes it possible for Nyinba households to engage in both trade and agriculture and therefore be more prosperous then their Nepali neighbors, who do not practice polyandry. At the same time, Levine also shows that culture is involved as an explanatory factor, and indeed, if socioeconomic factors were the only determinant, we would expect to find more communities around the globe choosing this special form of marriage. There are other strategies available for dealing with the socioeconomic constraints. For the Nyinba, kinship is seen as "providing the most reliable basis for trust," and in this way it is an important notion in structuring social relations, including marriages (Levine 1988: 278). The result is the cultural validation of brothers staying together, even at the cost of renouncing sexual exclusivity.

In her rationalization of polyandry among the D'ing-ri Tibetans living in exile in Nepal, Aziz is in line with both Goldstein and Levine: she points to the economic strength of the households based on polyandrous marriages (1978: 134–45). Dividing a household diminishes its prosperity, while well-managed polygamous unions increase prosperity. She also provides an interesting suggestion of how polyandry might have come about, related to the definition of the exogamous group, or *pün*. D'ing-ri Tibetans cannot have sexual relations with or marry anyone to whom they can trace bilateral descent. This excludes a large section of the local population and restricts the choice of marriage and sexual partners. At the same time, it makes anyone who is not kin a potential sexual partner, and casual sexual unions in which one's kin are permitted to share one's spouse are condoned and, according to Aziz, are the first step to polygamous marriages. An ideal that brothers should not be divided further fosters such unions.

The Bustling Township data do not unequivocally underscore this factor of limited access to marriage partners. Among the Premi in Bustling Township, the exogamous unit is established not bilaterally but patrilineally. Clan membership signifies, first of all, a factor of exclusion, determining which categories of people one cannot marry or have sexual relations with. Since exogamy is required only unilineally, and since most villages are made up of several clans, in principle, this provides villagers with enough potential marriage partners. But in reality, several factors limit choice. In one village there is one very large clan, and the other clans are very small. In another village, there are only two clans. Furthermore, Bustling Township marriage data indicate a preference for finding partners close to home, which considerably limits the choices. Of the forty-six marriages I registered in Walnut Grove, fourteen were among the three different clans within the village, and the rest of the marriages were between men from the village and women from outside. Twenty-two of those were with women from the three surrounding villages—one Premi, one Rek'ua, and one Naxi. The other ten women came from nine different Premi villages, all no more than a day's walk away. The majority of this last category of marriages were within three families in Walnut Grove who could not marry locally because they were thought to be possessed by demons (see chapter 4). All of the registered marriages in Uphill and Downhill were between local men and women from nearby villages. Village clusters can therefore be considered basically endogamous. These combined factors might have given rise to an ideology that supports marriages in which same-sex siblings share a single spouse.

The emic argument given for polyandry in Bustling Township is of a materialist nature and tallies with the socioeconomic explanations already mentioned. Asked about the reason for choosing polyandrous marriages for their children, parents explained that when brothers stay together, the land need not to be divided, and polyandrous marriages are a good strategy for maintaining and increasing household wealth. The presence of several men in the house makes it possible for the family to be involved full-time in agriculture as well as to transport goods and find jobs in the market towns of Yongning and Wachang or the county-town. While there were a few older polyandrous and polygynous couples established before the

Cultural Revolution, a substantial number were contracted within the last ten years. This is a remarkable new trend in view of the fact that polygamy is forbidden according to Chinese marriage laws, as discussed in chapter 2. Nevertheless, the trend is apparently not limited to Bustling Township. Recent field studies from rural Tibet and adjacent areas confirm the continued occurrence of fraternal polyandry and sororal polygyny.[11] In a recent study of a rural area in Shigatse Prefecture in central Tibet, the Tibetan anthropologist Benjor describes a strong revival of traditional polyandrous marriages (2001). He demonstrates that the de-collectivization of the early 1980s, which again made households the basic units of rural production, was the catalyst for this revival. Although households did not own the land, they received long-term contracts allowing them to use it.[12] However, since land could be neither sold nor bought and no new land could be opened up, there were no means of providing enough land for an expanding population. The traditional practice of polyandry then became a compensatory strategy for keeping the family land together and facilitating the sending of household members to engage in nonagricultural wage labor (ibid.: 195). Why people would choose precisely these strategies instead of other possibilities, Benjor leaves unanswered, overlooking the workings of cultural variables in his socioeconomic analysis.

Heidi Fjeld, who conducted fieldwork in Panam in rural central Tibet, confirms the findings of Benjor and also notes a strong increase in polyandric marriages, making it a preferred form of marriage among the studied population. But unlike Benjor, Fjeld goes beyond one-dimensional economic and ecological perspectives by placing her results in a larger context of sociocultural change. The practice of polyandry was traditionally limited to the leading classes of local landholders and government representatives. Fjeld suggests that polyandry today has become part of a process of social transformation and upward social mobility for common farmers: families view the adoption of the customs of the old upper classes as a means to both social and economic success (2007).

Many of Benjor's findings are directly applicable to the Bustling Township situation. After de-collectivization, Bustling Township households were given land according to a formula of 1.1–1.3 *mu* per person in the household. Although, because of the lower altitude and more humid climate, Bustling Township does not face the same constraints on agriculture as does central Tibet, there is little level land available for an expanding population. Those mountain slopes that have not yet been brought into production are very steep and difficult to access. Constructing terraces and providing adequate irrigation would be very labor-intensive tasks in themselves. However, the major constraint is government policies on land use. First of all, many of the areas that could be opened up are forest-covered and cannot be exploited because of the Tianbao policy of 1998. Second, on the local level, the township government carries out a very strict land use policy aimed at upgrading the environment in order to avoid further erosion of formerly deforested areas. Land that is deemed at risk of being washed away by the summer rains can no longer be used for agriculture and must be planted with fruit trees or reforested. Consequently, there are several socioeconomic incentives for keeping the population as constant as possible and avoiding division of the land allocated to the family. The traditional practice of polyandry answers both needs; however, this explanation does not fully answer the question of why polyandry has become one of the acceptable remedies. There are other possible solutions that would enable villagers to keep the land in one piece, used by some of the neighboring ethnic groups of the Premi, including, for example, the custom of primogeniture, by which the firstborn son inherits all the land.

As with monogamous marriages, polyandrous marriages in Bustling Township are always virilocal or neolocal, and an in-marrying woman becomes part of her husbands' clan. This implies that her children can marry the children of her brothers and of her sisters, if the sisters married into a different clan. Uxorilocality exists in a few exceptional cases, when a family has no male descendants: after the other daughters have married out to other houses, the husband of the remaining daughter will move into her house but will continue his own patriline. Extramarital sexual relations also strictly observe the rules of clan exogamy. Therefore, when a child is born out of wedlock and when the mother does not want to disclose the father, her child should preferably marry someone from the mother's paternal clan, since this is the only clan that the child's father could not belong to. In this way, the rules of clan exogamy continue to be observed.

In Uphill and Downhill, the thirty-five houses (out of forty) for which I registered *jhü-mè*, or clan names, were divided into seven different exogamous clans; the forty-three houses of Walnut Grove belonged to three different clans; and in one of the neighboring villages of Walnut

Grove, Five Nut Trees, the fourteen families were divided into only two clans (see table 3.2).

Clan genealogies are orally transmitted, but those of the larger clans are also written down by the *anji*, using Tibetan script. The oldest living member of the Ak'ua clan in Walnut Grove could easily recite from memory the agnatic ancestors of twenty generations, not only of his own patriline but also of related lineages. The longest genealogies go back thirty-seven generations to Jiuwu Jiuda^{n}hsi, the common ancestor of the different ethnic groups, followed in the thirty-sixth generation by the first Premi, Hsidi^n.

Several of the Premi clans trace their local origins across ethnic borders. Although the Ak'ua clan had a remembered history of more than twenty generations, its history in Walnut Grove began only six generations ago, when a young man from the neighboring Naxi village moved to Walnut Grove and married two Premi women, one from the Mesé clan in

TABLE 3.2 Clan Affiliation of Houses in Three Villages in Bustling Township

Village	Clan name	Number of houses
Uphill and Downhill	Ts'uop'i clan	19
	Lyim clan	7
	T'aba clan	4
	Ak'ua clan	3
	Mesé clan	1
	Mosiè clan	1
	Lama Guze clan	1
Walnut Grove	Mesé clan	24
	Ak'ua clan	15
	Bot'a clan	4
Five Nut Trees	Sho^n clan	8
	Gonga clan	6

Walnut Grove and one from a third village farther away. Over the years, the Ak'ua clan became culturally assimilated into the Premi, but its Naxi origins were remembered and solidified through its existence as a separate clan in the village. The Ak'ua and Mesé were each the other's most important exogamous group: of the forty-six registered marriages in Walnut Grove, nine marriages, or about 20 percent, were between these two clans. The third clan in the village, the Bot'a clan, also had Naxi origins, and its history in Walnut Grove started just four generations ago. The four houses of this clan were much less culturally assimilated into the Premi than was the Ak'ua: people still spoke Naxi at home, there was a larger degree of intermarriage between the Bot'a men and women from the Naxi village, their genealogies were kept by the Naxi *dtô-mbà* religious expert from that village, and this expert, rather than one of the *anji* from Walnut Grove, also performed the ceremonies at the New Year celebration.

One of the two clans in the village of Five Nut Trees also had a non-Premi origin. The village was established only three generations ago, when Nadjo^n arrived from Yongning and built a house on a small stretch of sloping land on the mountainside facing Walnut Grove. He married a Premi woman from the Sho^n clan. This became the first house of the Gonga clan. The Gonga obtained their clan name because their ancestors originated from Shuiluo, an area in the west of Muli where the famous Gonga Mountain (Gongaling) is situated. They were of Gami origin, a local designation for Kham-speaking Tibetans in Muli. The story of how Nadjo^n ended up in what became the village of Five Nut Trees contains a theme common to Tibetan and Tibeto-Burman stories that are told to explain village or kin origins when brothers leave their ancestral home in search of a new home (Levine 1988: 30; Wellens 1998: 28). Nadjo^n's nephew, Gonga Anna, told me the story:

> Seven generations ago, there were five brothers in Shuiluo. As was customary among the Gami, the oldest brother inherited everything, and consequently the four other brothers had no place to live after their father died. As a result, they left Shuiluo and spread to different areas. One of those four was Dadre P'intsu, the ancestor of Gonga Anna. In the beginning, the brothers came back to Shuiluo once a year at the time of the New Year. But after some time, Dadre P'intsu stopped going, so it is not known what happened to the other brothers. Dadre P'intsu moved to Yongning

in Yunnan. Five generations later, Nadjo^n, Dadre P'intsu's descendant and Gonga Anna's uncle, moved to Five Nut Trees.

It probably did not take long before Nadjo^n's descendants were neatly fitted into the Premi system of exogamous clans in Five Nut Trees. Women from the Gonga clan married into the different clans of Walnut Tree and villages in the surrounding area, and several women from Walnut Tree married into the Gonga clan of Five Nut Trees.

There is some degree of segmentation, and segments cannot intermarry. The Mesé clan is actually a localized segment in Walnut Grove of the larger Ts'uop'i clan. The segmentation of the Mesé out of the Ts'uop'i is, at least according to local stories, closely tied to the origins of the village of Walnut Grove. The word *me-sé* literally means "people-kill," and this connotation of "murderer" is explained in a story that not many people in Walnut Grove were happy to recount. In fact, people in the first houses I visited in Walnut Grove told me that they belonged to the Ts'uop'i clan; only after my local assistant made it clear that I knew the story of Mesé origins did they tell me that they belonged to the Mesé clan. According to the story, it all started in the village of Jiaze in Yunnan, not far from Ts'uop'i Mountain, the sacred mountain of the Ts'uop'i clan:

> A long time ago, there were two brothers in Jiaze belonging to the Ts'uop'i clan. After partitioning the house, the youngest brother, Mo^{n}mo^n, did very well and had many animals. The oldest one was not that smart and was therefore very poor. Every night, he went out to steal some animals from his younger brother. Mo^{n}mo^n could not find out who the thief was, so one night he hid himself among his sheep, carrying a big knife. When the thief finally came, it was already pitch-dark, and therefore Mo^{n}mo^n did not see whom he killed. When the father found out Mo^{n}mo^n had killed his own brother, he became so angry that he chased his son out of the house and out of the clan. That is how Mo^{n}mo^n came here and started the first house in Walnut Grove, and out of shame, he kept the clan name Mesé.

The story does not correspond entirely with the genealogies I recorded, according to which the break between Ts'uop'i and Mesé happened nineteen generations ago, whereas the first house in Walnut Grove was established only six generations ago. There are also variations of the story, in which Ts'uop'i and Mesé are the names not of clans but of two brothers. Whether myth or historical fact, the story functions today as a rationalization of why two clans with different names cannot intermarry.

In addition to acting as a marker of the exogamous group, clans become visible as ritual units when one of their members dies. In Uphill and Downhill, the Ts'uop'i clan has its own place for cremation, called *bu-dzu*, while the other clans share another spot near the village. In Walnut Grove, each of the three clans has its own cremation place. There was no fixed place for cremating the body in North Village; instead, a ritual specialist had to help find a spot for each occasion. The cremation ceremony lasts up to three days and is the major ritual event in Bustling Township. As many ritual specialists as the family can afford will recite almost uninterruptedly and perform numerous rituals. Finally, after the corpse has been cremated, the ashes are collected in an urn together with pieces of certain bones: a piece of the skull, the hand, the hipbone, and the foot. This action of collecting the bones is an important element of Premi ontology in that it has a direct connection with understandings of relatedness and clan identity. *Raka*, or bones, is the substance that is transmitted through the male line, in contrast to *na* or *she*, or flesh, the other constituting part of a human being, which comes from the female side. Small parts of the *raka*, the substance of the male line, are all that is left in recognizable condition after cremation and will be cared for by those who also share this substance in their bodies, that is, the surviving male clan members. On several occasions, Premi living in the vicinity of Nuosu people (who also cremate their deceased) stressed that the Nuosu did not collect bone remains. It was viewed as a sign of incomprehensible lack of respect for the ancestors and an overall marker of a less developed ethnic group. After the pieces of bone have been placed in the urn with the ashes, the older members of the clan carry the urn to the mountain cave belonging to the clan.[13] If the deceased was a woman, seven female clan members accompany the urn; nine men perform this task if the deceased was a man.[14]

Death is one of the few events—apart from choosing marriage partners for one's children—when clan membership becomes salient, and this is reflected in ritual practices. According to local sayings, when a person dies, the bones become stones, the hair becomes trees, the flesh becomes earth, but the *me-drö*, or soul, remains. In addition to taking care of the tangible remains of the deceased after cremation, someone must look after this intangible substance, the *me-drö*. The *me-drö* may be understood as the soul of the deceased (*me* means "person," and *drö* was rendered into Chinese as *lingwu*, corresponding to "soul"). This *me-drö* has to be guided by the *anji* to a place where all the souls of the clan's ancestors reside. This place, which is called Jewopöjeda^n, is said to be an actual place far to the north of Muli where the Premi originated. A ritual expert, the *anji* or the *yèma*, or what might be termed a Buddhist lay priest, recites the *hsip'u* text for the "opening of the road" ceremony, or *drwashu*, for the *me-drö*; like a real guidebook, it contains place-names and descriptions of the route to be followed.[15]

This whole process during which the *me-drö* has to find its proper place among the clan's other ancestral souls is a risky time for all the living clan members. Correct rituals have to be performed so that the *me-drö* will not turn into a wandering spirit or, in the worst case, an evil wandering spirit, a *shep'a*. Furthermore, from this point onward, surviving kin residing in the house where the deceased lived will have to bring offerings every day and on special ritual occasions to his or her *me-drö*, in order to prevent it from turning into a *shep'a* who will cause afflictions among the survivors. It is *shep'a* who cause people to die, and one of the tasks of the *anji* is to figure out what kind of *shep'a* has been responsible for the death. By carrying out the appropriate ritual, the *anji* can chase the *shep'a* away and prevent it from taking the *me-drö* with it. He does this by invoking powerful deities, such as Hlada^n So^{n}ma (see next chapter). But more must be done: in all houses belonging to the clan of the deceased, a small thread-cross, a *nungk'e*, is placed somewhere high on the walls (see fig. 3.3).[16] It is used to prevent the *me-drö* of the deceased from enticing the *me-drö* of its surviving clan members into joining it on its journey to the place of the ancestors. The *nungk'e* stays on the wall for one or two years.

The idea that deceased kin interfere with surviving descendants who do not behave appropriately is found all over the globe. The villagers of Bustling Township conceive of the *me-drö*'s effect on their lives in a way that is strikingly similar to the African Ndembu's view of the influence of their ancestral spirits. Turner conceptualized these spirits by borrowing the term "shades" from Monica Wilson's study of African societies,[17] expressing both the immaterial character of these beings and their relationship to the more tangible manifestation of the ancestors as human beings (Turner 1977: 11). The shades of the Ndembu are "the uneasy inhabitants of the 'unquiet grave,'" and they leave the grave to plague their kinsfolk because they have been "forgotten" or their kinsfolk have acted in a way of which the shades disapprove, such as neglecting to make offerings, quarreling with other members of the kin group, disobeying a wish expressed by the deceased in his or her lifetime, or moving away from the village of the deceased. The afflictions brought on by the shades include causing diseases and infertility or spoiling the hunting (Turner 1967: 9–11). Although *me-drö* seem to be more easily handled by correct ritual behavior than are the shades of the Ndembu, as explained later in this chapter, the mechanism whereby fear and respect for the ancestral spirits influence social behavior and thereby are part of the process of establishing social morality is similar in both cultures.

While showing respect to the *me-drö* is—other than at the time of the cremation—mainly a matter for close descendants of the deceased, there are a few ritual activities for worshipping the common ancestors of the whole clan. Today, only the larger clans such as the T'aba and the Ts'uop'i hold yearly clan meetings on the fifteenth of the seventh month of the lunar calendar. Ideally, one male representative of each house of the clan attends the meetings, which take place near the mountain cave with the urns containing the ashes of deceased clan members. In the case of the Ts'uop'i, a large clan that originated in Yunnan, these yearly meetings are sizable events with more than fifty people participating and are reported on by the local newspaper. The meeting takes place in Yunnan at Cuopidian, near Chabulang in Labai Township. I have been told that during these meetings, ritual specialists hold ceremonies to worship and propitiate the different lines of the clan—up to the earliest common ancestors—and ask all the ancestors to protect their living descendants and bring prosperity to them.

In daily life, however, and in the organization of social life, the role played by clan membership, or descent in general, is not immediately obvious. In Walnut Grove, an often-used alternative expression for *jhü*, the standard word for clan, is *arè dazeze*, "we of the same descent." This points to an awareness of common descent as a factor of common identity, but this is not reflected in social organization. Except for when a person dies, there are very few ritual occasions centered on the clan. Neither is the clan a corporate unit with economic or status connotations: the clan does not manage any property, and, at least in Bustling Township, descent does not seem to have any correlation with class. In Muli, there was one ruling clan, the Bar clan, which provided the ruling elite and kept slaves at its estate in southeastern Muli. But no Bar lived in the Bustling Township area, and there was no significant internal stratification within the majority of Premi commoners. In fact, there are a number of folk sayings expressing the idea of social equality, such as "Just as all eggs are equal in size, so are all Premi equally high" (Yin 1989: 28). Traditional systems dividing society into descent-based classes did exist among several of the neighboring peoples of the Premi. To the west, the Tibetans discerned four classes: aristocrats, priests, commoners, and outcasts.[18] The extent to which these classes are related to the four Hindu castes is a topic of discussion within the field of Tibetan studies (Aziz 1978: 52). But among populations even farther away from India, like the Na of Yongning or the Nuosu of Liangshan, sharp social divisions vested in descent were also prevalent at the time of the Communist takeover. According to Yan Ruxian, the Premi living among the stratified Na of Yongning under the rule of a *tusi*, the hereditary native chieftain, were all considered commoners. While Na society was divided into *sipei* (aristocracy), *zeka* (commoners), and *e* (slaves), the Premi were all considered to be outer-*zeka*, signaling their position as commoners not to be enslaved as well as distancing them from the Na class system. The Premi enjoyed a privileged position under the *tusi* system in Yongning and had a special right to rise in protest against the *tusi* (Yan and Chen 1986: 16–18). One of the stories told among the Premi explaining their privileged position is related to the Ts'uop'i clan, according to which a member of the Ts'uop'i clan from Tuodian, Ts'uop'i Nyima Gyatse, once saved the *tusi* of Yongning during a battle against the Naxi Mu *tusi* from Lijiang by hiding him in a leather bag. Out of gratitude, the *tusi* made Nyima Gyatse an uncle. From then on, there has been a close tie between the Ts'uop'i clan and the *tusi*, as expressed in the participation of the Ts'uop'i in special rituals held at each succession of the *tusi* in Yongning (see also *Ninglang Yizu zizhixian zhi* 1993: 223; Yan and Chen 1986: 16).[19]

While there are clearly differences regarding traditional social stratification between the Na of Yongning and the Premi of both Yongning and Muli, the system of matrilineal descent groups among the Na, called *sizi*, bears some resemblance, at least on the functional level, to the Premi patrilineal clans. Shih Chuan-kang describes the *sizi* of the Na as comprising several *yidu*, or domestic groups, formed by descendants of an ancestress three generations removed from the eldest living member (1993: 116). Shih notes that this *sizi* is not corporate in an economic sense since it does not have any common property or economic activity (117). The corporate character of the *sizi* is apparent only in terms of its members' collective obligation to worship the common ancestors and in defining the outer limit of the incest taboo. When Shih questioned his informants on the meaning of the *sizi*, their answer provides a poignant illustration: "to conduct funerals together, nothing more" (119). The clan system of the patrilineal Bustling Township Premi seems to be more elaborate than that of the matrilineal Na of Yongning: Premi genealogies are traced back much longer than three generations, and the Premi hold yearly clan meetings. But this discrepancy may only be a more recent development: Shih's older informants mention annual worship ceremonies for common ancestors for the whole *sizi* (119).

When larger ritual activities take place in Bustling Township, the whole village is involved, not just one clan. For example, during the festival that occurs in the second month of the lunar calendar, the whole village spends two days out in the open, and everyone participates in propitiating the water and mountain deities. Larger rituals are also held occasionally in times of severe drought, when the *anji* leads the village in praying and making offerings to the water deities, the *lwéjabu*, in the hope that they will make it rain. Furthermore, the larger nonritual activities involving people from several houses, such as construction of a new house or maintenance and repair of the common irrigation and water supply systems, are never organized on the basis of clan membership. Group mobilization for such activities is often based on temporary recruitment of people with specific skills, regardless of kin relationship to the mobilizing individual, household, or village. Otherwise, the kindred of the head of a house (that is, those people considered to be closely related through both descent and alliance) are called upon to assist. As several anthropologists have pointed out (see, e.g., Holy 1996), such assemblies of close kin and affines are temporary, and, in Bustling Township, they do not form any stable culturally recognized units. They constitute, to use Bourdieu's distinction, practical kin as opposed to official kin (1977: 33–38).

The basic entity of ritual activity and at the same time the most visible unit of social organization is then neither the clan nor the practical kinship unit but a unit based, first of all, on common residence, namely, all the inhabitants of a single house. Societies as diverse as the Zulu in southern Africa or the Kayapo of central Brazil have been found to have "houses" as a central principle for structuring societies. In such a context, the term "house" does not refer to the architectural space in itself but to an analytical category for understanding social relations in a given society or community. Rather than framing empirical data collected in Bustling Township within any master theory of "houses," taking a brief look into some of the discussions of houses in anthropological writing can assist in conceptualizing Premi $dzè^n$ and the role they play in the organization of Bustling Township society and the performance of ritual practice.

$DZÈ^N$, THE PREMI HOUSE

As in the case of the D'ing-ri and Dechen Tibetans, Premi houses have names, $dzè^n$-mè (the more commonly used term) or k'a-mè. Mè means "name," and $dzè^n$ refers to the built structure. The word k'a (or ga) specifically designates the people living in a house, the domestic unit. For example, during the fieldwork for this study, I frequently asked the question: "How many people are there in the village?" (Ni-er jiù me chedze re?). Often, the interviewees did not know the exact number and would give replies such as "Our village consists of twenty-five domestic units" (Er jiù nóno-gwa k'a re).

The compound words $dzè^n$-mè and k'a-mè are used completely synonymously. When asking a person about his house name, one could ask either: "You (suffix) what domestic unit name?" (Niè bi miè k'a-mè?) or "You (suffix) what house name?" (Niè bi miè $dzè^n$-mè?). This is not without importance: the house equals the domestic unit as a major marker of a person's belonging in society. House names are an integral part of the names of all the people living in the house.[20] Within a village in Bustling Township, a person is addressed first by his house name, then by his personal name: Jia^{n}hsi Dudjits'er and Jia^{n}hsi Druma are man and wife and live in the Jia^{n}hsi house. Dudjits'er and Druma are rather common names in Bustling Township, but as Premi have no family names, one of the functions of house names is to make a further distinction. The origin of a house name is usually the name of the one who built the house or, if there has been a house on the same location before, the one who built the original house. Few houses in Bustling Township are more than thirty years old; therefore, this name most often refers to a close agnatic ancestor.

When it comes to "splitting the house," or *dzè^n-p'o*—namely, when one of the sons moves out of the house to start a neolocal residence with his wife and children (if any)—a son can either use his own first name for the new house or keep the name of his ancestral home and add *dzè^n-hsi* or *ga-shi* (new house), as in the case of the Azha Dzè^{n}hsi house. The name of the ancestral home is often such an integral part of a person's name that a new house might carry both the former house name (the name of the builder) and the son's personal name. For example, Galo^n's grandfather, Yowji, built a house carrying his name. Galo^n's two youngest sons, Dadre and Drala, shared one wife and kept living in the Yowji house. They had two daughters and five sons in all. One daughter married into another house in a neighboring village; the other daughter married into a house in the village. The youngest son, Pema, stayed at his paternal house after marriage. The other four, including Galo^n, moved out and established new houses in the village: Yowji Galo^n, Yowji Yongjong, Yowji Ashi, and Yowji Yangtsu. In the other four Yowji houses, the ancestral house was then often referred to as Yowji Pema.

House names are thus straightforward references to the person who built the house, the personal name of either a man in the house or one of his agnatic ancestors. They might in addition carry a reference to an agnatic ancestor, by combining the name of the ancestor with the name of the builder[21] or by adding the word for "new house."

Property is inherited in the male line. The land is divided when a brother leaves the house, and the house itself is usually taken over by the brother who marries last, often the youngest brother. Women do not normally inherit, except when a household has no male heirs; in that case, the unmarried daughter takes over the house and the land rights, and when she marries, the husband can move into the house of his wife or wives (most cases of sororal polygyny involve two sisters taking in a husband). Although he continues his own patriline and the children are part of the clan of their father, the house and its inhabitants continue to carry the original house name. This special case makes clear the principle that the named residential unit is not considered a symbol of the patrilineage but is instead an independent category. Moreover, the house name—which all people in a house share, whether or not they are linked by descent or alliance—is not shared with close patrilineal kin living in other houses. Therefore, from an emic point of view, the *dzè^n-mè* links people together and expresses relatedness on the basis of common residence first, even though co-residence is most likely the result of common descent and alliance.

There are also traces of another type of house name. Several villages in Bustling Township have house names that hint at a more complex way of conceptualizing houses. The houses of three brothers all start their names with the word *besé*, which means "village leader." Before the Communist takeover, *besé* was the name of the house of a village leader. The rhetoric of the Communist campaigns and the attendant political indoctrinations not only effectively erased this institution but, unfortunately, also make it difficult to investigate. It is possible that *besé* might be a local pronunciation of an institution that is rendered in Chinese as *maise*. The *maise* was an administrator, appointed by the office of the *tusi* or head lama, responsible for a population that ranged in size from a few households to several tens of households. His job consisted of transmitting orders and pressing tenants to pay rent and provide horses and corvée labor. Unlike the position of village chief, which was hereditary, or that of *rongban*—the dispatched monk bureaucrat working at the village level—which was limited to three years, there was no fixed period of office for the *maise*. If the administration of the head lama found it convenient to do so, it could extend the term. It is unclear whether the position of village leader could become hereditary, and several informers maintained that individuals were chosen for such a position because of what could be termed their moral prestige and social competence, such as a demonstrated ability to lead and mediate. But different villages offered different explanations. According to Besé Nima of Walnut Grove, village leaders were appointed by the *bo^n* (T: *pön[po]*)—or the head lama, as he was also called locally—and if they did a good job, the position could become hereditary. This was the case with the family of Besé Nima, who had been village leaders for many generations.

Besé did not receive any payment from the Muli monastic government and supposedly had no special privileges. One of their major tasks was to divide the burden among the villagers when representatives from the government visited the region, either just traveling through or collecting taxes. It proved impossible to verify whether "village democracy" was merely the origin of an institution that later developed into a hereditary position, or whether this was a way of presenting a pre-Communist institution in a more acceptable light. The fact that the *besé* were only mildly criticized and did not suffer much under the Cultural Revolution points to the former explanation.

There are not one but three houses in Walnut Grove that carry the word *besé* in their names. After the traditional village leader system was abolished during the Democratic Reforms campaign in 1956, the original meaning of the name Besé lost its politico-legal connotations and today functions like any other house name. When the sons moved out of their parental house, they incorporated the Besé name into their new house names. The original Besé house does not differ from the other houses in architectural style, but there are other potential traces of what might have been a local elite. The Besé family had produced several *anji* and is now the house of Besé Nima, or Nima Anji, one of the most knowledgeable *anji* of the village and a very influential figure, instrumental in the flowering of *anji* practice in Bustling Township and beyond. Nima Anji had been educated as a health worker, and his brother was a teacher. Interestingly, one of the points Lévi-Strauss made about the "house" institution is its intermediate position between a kin- and a class-based society and how it "naturalizes" rank differences through the terminology of kinship (1983: 187). It is unclear whether the *besé* institution is reminiscent of the traditional chiefs of the Kachin, or whether the Besé house name is comparable to what Aziz has called "quasi-housenames." These are found among families in D'ing-ri who are in the process of moving up in the social hierarchy and are derived from the profession or rank of a household head, such as the above-mentioned house name U-lag, meaning "Master Craftsman" (Aziz 1978: 123). Unlike the stratified Na of Yongning, Premi society in Muli is not very stratified. As mentioned previously, the head lama and many other leading religious-political figures come from the Bar clan. The manorial estate of the Bar clan is situated in southeastern Muli, and no member of this elite was present in Bustling Township, so this stratification presumably did not affect the local ranking of houses. Perhaps ethnographic data collected on other Premi villages in the future can shed light on the institution of village leaders and their houses.

3 ～ The Premi House

The inhabitants of a Premi house in Bustling Township are usually of two or three agnatically linked generations: an older married couple with their youngest son and his wife and their children. In case of polyandrous marriages, the household might count two or more brothers married to a single wife. Sometimes an unmarried sister of the father or the son might live there as well. Each house has a "housemaster," or (*dzè^n*) *dap'u*, usually the oldest man, if he is still capable of doing all of the work that is expected of him, or he might have relinquished the post to his married son. When there is a polyandrous union in the house, the oldest brother has the role of *dap'u*. He makes all major decisions relating to the house and its inhabitants, and he represents the house in its interactions with the outside world, for example, at clan meetings and cremation ceremonies. Also, some of the ritual practice in the house can be performed only by the *dap'u*. But the *dap'u* is not alone in making decisions. At his side is the *damu*, the female leader of the house, usually his wife or, when she is deceased, his daughter or daughter-in-law. While the *dap'u* decides on the "male" aspects of the house, often related to relations with the outside, the *damu* decides on the "female" side, which includes all internal matters of the house, such as disposition of some of the house income, marriage agreements, or whether to send daughters to school. In some cases, after the *dap'u* dies, the *damu*, not the *dap'u*'s son, takes over the role.

When splitting the house, the oldest son is usually the one who moves out first, either when he marries or, if he is already married, when one of his younger brothers marries. People denied that there were rules about this but pointed to lack of living space resulting from a growing family as the reason for splitting the house. Although land was allocated to households in 1982, it was done on a per capita basis. When sons want to leave the parental house to set up their own, they are entitled to their share of the land, but the average of 1.2 *mu* per person is not enough to sustain a new family. Sons may obtain more if the parental house can do without some land, or they may, for example, take other family members with them. In a few houses, one of the parents had moved into the departing son's house. When daughters leave the house to get married, they do not receive any land, even though in 1982 their presence entitled the household to a share for them as well. It is unclear as yet how land will be divided now that a generation of men is coming of age who were born after the original allocation took place. Since 1982, there have been no major rounds of readjustments, as is the practice in many areas of rural China.

As in traditional Tibetan societies (Levine 1988: 121), splitting the house is culturally condemned, and it is preferable for brothers to stay together. The recorded data do not make it possible to conclude on the possible role of this ideology and how it interacts with the practice of polyandry. In Walnut Grove, brothers who were married to unrelated wives rarely lived in the same house, and it was often jokingly stated that two wives of the same generation could not live under the same roof. Although polyandry is practiced extensively in the surrounding villages and is generally recommended in the village as an ideal means of keeping the land together and protecting the prosperity of the house, at the time I conducted the fieldwork for this study, there were only three recently established polyandrous households in the village. The average number of people per house was 5.5, and many of the houses had been built within the last ten years. So in spite of a positive assessment of polyandry (many of the women born in the village had been married out into polyandrous marriages in the neighboring villages), polyandry was not practiced very much in Walnut Grove. At least four of the recently split houses were brothers who had moved out of polyandrous marriages, married again monogamously, and established their own houses. One reason for this might be the sudden return of men from the village who had been working in lumber-related jobs until 1999, some of whom had engaged in polyandrous marriages. On their return, they were not able to glide into well-established and, in practice, functioning monogamous marriages and, having brought some capital with them, preferred to take their chances and split the house. The situation was markedly different in Uphill and Downhill, where houses tended to be larger and could more easily accommodate an extended household; the average number of people per household is 7.1. No new polyandrous marriages have been established in recent years, but it is much more socially accepted in Uphill and Downhill that brothers married to different wives live together in the same house. Premi "houses" are then manifestations of what Elisabeth Hsu has called a "hearth-oriented" ideology with a focus on household harmony (1998: 71, 90).

The house is also a corporate unit in the sense that it "owns" property and makes up an economic unit: the land is divided between the different houses, and the inhabitants share the tasks of working it. Many of the tasks are strictly divided according to gender and age. Only men can plow the land, and even when no man is available, women are not permitted to use the plow. Killing animals, hunting, and playing the flute are also exclusively male domains. The women perform most of the tasks at home and feed the domestic animals, while herding is done mostly by the smaller children or the younger unmarried girls. Everyone in the house helps with the harvest. The products of the land as well as any other income generated by members of the house belong to all the inhabitants. The head of the household makes all major decisions regarding the house, concerning, for example, selling and purchasing domestic animals, renovating the house, finding suitable marriage partners for the children, and so on. Chinese authorities register and tax based on "single households" (*hu*), and since this measurement largely corresponds to the inhabitants of a house, the system does not interfere with Premi social organization.

HOUSES AND RITUAL PRACTICE

The most important contribution of the notion of the "house" is that it makes it possible to link the architectural, social, and symbolic aspects of a single institution and treat them as being closely related. The house as a principle of social organization cannot be seen detached from its role in religious practice. The Premi of Bustling Township have no temples in which to worship their deities or their common clan ancestors, but every house constitutes its own sacred space. It enables the residents to establish and maintain relations with their ancestors and deities as well as among themselves through the practice of rituals.

The house's centrality as a cornerstone of Premi society is expressed through its prominence in ritual activity in Bustling Township. Ritual in this context is not limited to special sacral activities that are markedly different from everyday actions such as funerals or large communal offerings to the gods. In order to pinpoint some of the dimensions of ritual activity, Catherine Bell looks at how cultures ritualize human activity. She discerns different attributes of "ritual-like" action, such as formalism, traditionalism, disciplined invariance, rule-governance, sacral symbolism, and performance (1997: 138). Several daily, often recurring, activities that take place in the Premi house are highly symbolic acts. They are tightly connected to the way Premi in Bustling Township interact with ancestral souls, deities, and evil spirits. Nevertheless, they are only to a limited extent rule-governed or formal. Regular rituals vary from house to house and are subject to the creativity of the performers in the house.

In daily life as well as on special occasions, the hearth and fireplace with its iron tripod, or *hsin-drwè*,[22] make up the locus of worshipping the "ancestors" (*bap'u*) and divine beings of the mountains, water, wind, heaven, and earth. Close ancestors are worshipped over large areas of Asia, but the available ethnographies of Tibetan communities mention few such cases. In many areas of Tibet, people worship territorial deities that are recognized as ancestors of local communities and apply kin terminology to them.[23] Hildegard Diemberger mentions rituals (*lha-bsangs*) in southern Tibet centered on mountain and clan deities. According to her study, among border communities that have retained a certain degree of autonomy from the state, such rituals constitute a vital part of the sacred relation between the territory and the community's self-definition (1994: 144). Being focused mainly on close agnatic ancestors of the people living in the house, Premi ancestral worship does not have this extended aspect of larger communal self-definition. The persistence of some concepts of ancestral worship combined with the dearth of reported instances of close-ancestor worship in present-day Tibetan communities could be linked to the adoption of Buddhist teachings on rebirth and reincarnation. These conceptual notions do seem incompatible with a belief that ancestral souls exist eternally as immaterial spirits. But then again, it is unclear whether Tibetans ever had a well-developed system of worshipping close ancestors. Matthew Kapstein argues that the relative ease with which Tibetans adopted the concepts of rebirth and reincarnation might point to the fact that rebirth was considered possible under certain conditions even in pre-Buddhist Tibetan beliefs (2000: 43–44). In this context, he refers to an article by Anne-Marie Blondeau on the rebirth of children who died at a very young age (Blondeau 1997).

Some studies have tried to establish a link between kinship organization and ancestor worship. In a comparative study of 114 societies, Dean Sheils finds a clear correlation between descent type and ancestor worship: ancestor worship is absent in most cognatic societies, while a clear majority of unilineally organized societies are supportive of it. Relying on the Human Relations Area Files, Sheils classifies Tibetans as cognatic and without ancestor worship (1975: 434).

Such generalizations of both the category of Tibetans and Tibetan religious practice lack a sound empirical basis. To complicate matters even further, ethnographic evidence clearly points to the existence of worship of close lineage ancestors among at least some Tibetan communities. Eva Dargyay describes how—among the Tibetans of Zanskar—members of the same patriline, or *rus-pa*, worship a particular god that protects the family and their property. Such a family god is called *pha-lha*, or "god of our fathers" (1988: 127). Worship of the *pha-lha* has been integrated locally into Buddhism in different ways: one patriline, after its ancestral shrine was destroyed, started to worship its *pha-lha* in the local Buddhist temple, while another patriline identified its *pha-lha* as the six-armed Mahākāla (ibid.: 129–31).

The combination of Buddhist concepts such as reincarnation and rebirth with ancestor worship has also been described among the Shuhi^n people of Shuiluo in Muli. According to Swiss ethnobotanist Caroline Weckerle, the Shuhi^n people make offerings to the souls of their ancestors, believing that such a soul is immortal and that, after the person has died, it spends some time in a "world of souls" (Welt der Ahnen) before it finally reincarnates. An important component of Shuhi^n funerary ritual focuses on driving the souls of the dead out of the house and into this "world of souls" so that they will not cause harm to the surviving family members (1997: 36).

In traditional Chinese society, ancestor worship is the most important aspect of religious practice and is inherently connected to the centrality of the patrilineal family. The family makes offerings to close ancestors in the house as well as in clan temples that the larger community has dedicated to more distant common clan ancestors. Certain ancestral spirits of famous persons or other humans sometimes gain even wider recognition and become veritable deities worshipped throughout a larger region. Ultimately, Chinese ancestor worship and the hierarchical clan system are part of the system legitimizing the rule of the emperor and the state (see, e.g., Paper 1994: 78–80; Faure 2007; Feuchtwang 2001).

But while Chinese ancestor worship is strongly rooted in the existence of a common clan and a focus on the patrilineal family, as exemplified in the importance attached to family names, Premi ancestor worship is largely limited to the house, as expressed in the status of the house name as the most important indicator of a person's belonging, and through the daily offerings made to ancestors who died in the house rather than to those of the whole patriline.

The Buddhist influence on Premi society can be seen in the *za^{n}bala*, a Tibetan Buddhist–inspired picture or relief placed in the corner of many houses where Buddhist deities are worshipped. In addition, the whole process of establishing a new house—starting with the ritual of splitting the house, then finding a suitable place to built a new house, constructing it, and finally consecrating the hearth—is steered by highly ritualized practices. With the exception of life-cycle ceremonies, these are the most ritualized practices in Premi society, and many involve religious ceremonies performed by *anji* or *yèma*. The head of the house-to-be must also carefully carry out several ritual tasks during the house-building process. Because of the sacral dimension of the house, small mistakes in the process can ruin prospects for prosperity and jeopardize the lives of members of the new house unit.

Before construction can begin, a suitable place must be found. In order to find such a spot, the man who plans to establish a new house collects several stones from different locations on the land the state has given his parental house the right to use, which will be divided when the new house is ready. The stones must be strongly connected to the location and the spirits who reside there. In order to avoid taking stones that people have placed there or that have been deposited recently by natural means like water, the stones must be dug up from at least thirty centimeters underground. They will then be shown to a person presumed to have a good sense of the invisible dimension of the natural world. Such a person need not be the *anji* or *yèma* but may also be a locally recognized—Buddhist-inspired—reincarnation or a *soma*, a medium through whom spirits and divinities communicate with the human world. These matters are not taken lightly, since choosing the wrong location could have grave consequences, as my host family in Walnut Grove experienced. Forty-seven-year-old Galo^n explains:

> This house is situated on the location of my grandfather's house. This is quite a steep place though, and when the house had to be renovated, my father decided to build a new house farther down the slope on a place that

was more level and closer to our fields. This turned out to be a very bad idea: my father, my mother, and my uncle, one after another, all died of disease at the new house. So I decided to rebuild the house on the location of my grandfather's house, which had proved to be a good location. Since the moment we moved in, we have not been struck by disaster again.

After the best spot has been selected, an *anji* or *yèma* uses traditional Tibetan almanacs to divine the most beneficial dates for performing important parts of the house construction. The first date the ritual specialist must fix is for cutting down the trees; the *anji* or *yèma* also participates in picking the right trees. The next date is for the start of digging to make the ground wall and the floor. The porch and the main door are constructed on a separate date. The final two dates are for moving in and for starting to use the iron tripod.

Even at the height of the Maoist period, people chose to risk being criticized for "old thinking" rather than face the dangers of not following the traditional procedures for constructing and consecrating a new house. Campaigns to wipe out "superstition" were more likely to drive these newly vilified practices underground than to produce a heartfelt acceptance of the official ideology. K'enbuzo of the Naxi Bot'a clan of Walnut Grove, who was sixty years old in 2001, still lived in one of the few houses built during the Cultural Revolution:

> This house is one of the older ones here. Because we are a poor family, we have not been able to built a new house like many of the other families here [Walnut Grove]. The house was built in 1970, entirely according to the rules. But during the Democratic Reform period and the Cultural Revolution, everything had to be done in secret, otherwise we would be criticized. At that time we also were expected to go to the doctor when we were sick, but we would first secretly ask the *anji* to find out whether it was evil spirits who caused the disease or whether is was something the doctor might be able to cure.

The person who builds the house—the future head of the house—mobilizes his close kindred. For a few tasks that demand specialized competence, such as woodcarving or smithery, he calls in craftsmen and compensates them with *arje* or dried pork. A house-building team

FIG. 3.3. Part of the *gujhi-jhata^n*, or central pillar, with a small *nungk'e*, or thread-cross.

usually consists of five to eight people, and it will take about a month to build the house. The ritual specialists who together spend a great deal of time reciting and performing rituals also receive gifts such as dried pork.

In Walnut Grove, all main doors must face east, and the main roof beams must run east to west. East is the location of the river that cut the steep slope on which the village and its surrounding fields are situated. The village of Five Nut Trees is on the opposite slope. Here the roof beams follow the same east-west direction, but the main doors look out toward the west, facing the river. The *gujhi-jhata^n*, the central pillar or post in the house, must be constructed and placed very carefully, so that it follows the direction of growth of the tree it was cut from. Placed in this way, it says that the house is living and growing. During my fieldwork, I heard terrible stories about what happened to houses in which the *gujhi-jhata^n* was placed upside down by mistake: this misalignment causes misfortune and death.[24] It is said, furthermore, that the *gujhi-jhata^n* connects the earth with the house and, further, with heaven and the deities.

Such beliefs are not limited to Bustling Township. Claes Corlin writes that in Gyelthang, a two to three days' walk southwest of Bustling Township, the central pillar of a house, or *bekha*, is a symbolic representation of the world-tree, "the centre of the universe, and the communication channel between the middle world of men, the upper world of gods and beings, and the subterranean world of the *kLu* serpent spirits" (1980: 87). In Bustling Township, the central pillar forms one of the major supports for the platform, called *drè^n* in Walnut Grove, and represents the connection of the inhabitants of the house with the earth and heaven. Although the style may differ slightly from village to village, every house in Bustling Township contained such a platform, including the houses of the Naxi and Rek'ua (figure 3.4 illustrates the main room of a house in Walnut Grove). The platform is elevated about fifty centimeters above the earthen floor and covers about a third of a Premi living room or *jima*. There are basically two styles of platform. The elevated version shown in figure 3.4 is found in the south of Bustling Township and is called *drè^n*. In the northern villages, *drè^n* means "bed"; here platforms are called *goli*, are only about ten centimeters above the floor, are rectangular in shape, and fill roughly half the main room. The main hearth is also on this platform, which is where Premi spend most of their time in the house; it is where they eat, talk, entertain guests, perform rituals, and—at least for some family members—sleep. Therefore the platform has to be connected to the *gujhi-jhata^n*.

When people are not working in the field or herding their animals, they spend almost all of their time on the platform. Being so important, the platform is also one of the places where social and ritual positions are expressed: in Walnut Grove and Uphill and Downhill, the oldest men sit closest to the fireplace, while women sit on the perimeter because they are considered ritually polluted. Children are farthest away from the fireplace. In some of the villages, the men sit on the right side of the hearth, and the women on the left, with the oldest people or guests closest to the hearth. The most important place is always the place on the left, closest to the hearth. In the middle of the hearth, or *hualip'e*, is the iron tripod, and in one corner of the hearth is the offering stone, or *drwama*. Both iron tripod and offering stone are the most important loci of worship and offering in Premi houses. Before each meal or before drinking, people place offerings of food or wine, *che-drö* (lit., "food for the souls"), on top of the iron tripod, specifically on the three places where its feet join the upper ring. Food and drink offerings are also placed on the offering stone. When an animal has been slaughtered, its head is placed on the offering stone during the meal. While some people told me this was an offering to the ancestors, I was also told on several occasions—note the clear Buddhist influence—that the divine powers of the offering stone would cause the soul of the animal to be reborn in another animal far away, so that it would not be killed again. The offering stone links the house, the ancestors, and the mountain, water, and other deities to the inhabitants of the house.

The offering to the *me-drö*, or souls, of the ancestors, is strongly related to the house and the patriline. Food is offered to the *me-drö* of male ancestors who have died in the house, not to the entire patriline. It invites them to join the family in eating and drinking. Anyone in the family can make such offerings, which are part of the ritual reaffirmation of the house as a unit, linking present co-residents to previous residents. As mentioned before, the Kachin term for "house," *htinggaw*, has the sense of "the people who worship the same set of household spirits" (Leach 1970: 126), and although the Premi word *dzè^n* does not explicitly carry this meaning, it certainly has this connotation. Ancestor worship and the belief that ancestors, or their souls, influence the world of the living are the most central aspects of religious beliefs and cosmological understanding of the Bustling Township Premi. Besides strengthening the relations of those who share a common residence, ancestor worship also provides a powerful basis for morality in Premi society. The ancestors will protect their living descendants, if these descendants behave in an appropriate way. This of course involves performing all the required ceremonies at the time of death as well as making the regular ritual offerings in the house. But the ancestors are also keeping an eye on the general behavior of their descendants and can punish them if the harmony of the house is disturbed, for example, by a matrimonial dispute.

The offering stone and iron tripod are also involved when members of the house make prayers and offerings to the divine beings: to the mountain deities, or *rèdzeng rèda*; the water deities, or lwéjabu; Lama Yida^n, the deity of heaven; and several others (see next chapter). The head of the house asks these divinities and the ancestors to protect the residents of the house. In Walnut Grove, this is done every morning in every house by burning some branches of a bush called *sanske* or *dzajhi*. It is a very informal form of prayer and can be improvised to fit special needs or the personal style of the one who prays. As one head of a house explained: "Praying can be about many different things: protecting the people of the house, paying respects to the ancestors who died in the house, and so on. The real words are not that important; it's the meaning or the thoughts that count. You can make it up yourself and say something like 'Oh, this or that *hla* [deity], I ask you: please protect the members of this house!'"

In Uphill and Downhill, praying is not done regularly by all families and is more common on special occasions, such as before someone from the house sets out on a journey or the day a pig will be slaughtered. Before the prayer, it is not permitted to pollute the air by smoking or drinking. When the head of the house is away, another male household member conducts the morning prayer, but women are excluded because they are considered ritually polluted.

During the construction of a new house, making the offering stone is one of the important tasks of its future head. He must cut it from a large stone that comes from a ritually cleansed place in the mountains. On the underside of the offering stone is a small cavity where the builder places some silver or gold (depending on the financial situation of the builder) as well as a few grains of maize, highland barley, wheat, and rice. Only these grains can be placed there. This is to assure the future prosperity of the house. People deny that this is an offering to any divinity or ancestors, which implies that the house, in addition to being a medium for worshipping ancestors and divinities, possesses an animistic quality in itself. It can provide its inhabitants with good harvests and material wealth. This aspect is very important during times when maintaining and increasing prosperity seem increasingly unpredictable and when villagers can no longer count on outside support in case of adversities. Even families who are less "religious" and, for example, do not normally invite *anji* when someone gets sick will have an offering stone that conforms to the rules.

In the corner of the platform, behind the hearth, is the *sarra*, a small bench, with an incense burner. Behind it is the *set'u*, a cupboard or chest, usually the most beautifully carved piece of furniture in the house. Both are dedicated to the Buddhist deities worshipped by the house's residents as well as to the ancestors. Here, on fixed dates, and especially during the New Year period, the family presents offerings such as fruit or spirits. Pictures of famous lamas, such as the Panchen Lama or Dalai Lama, as well as highly revered heroes of the Communist Party, including Mao Zedong or Zhou Enlai, are often placed in this corner. On the wall behind the cupboard is a painting or a relief with a motif taken from Tibetan Buddhist iconography, most often the "precious jewel," or *norbu rimpoche*. This is the *za^{n}bala*, and it is found in the houses of many Tibetans, Na, Naxi, Premi, and other ethnic groups in this corner of Southwest China. Zambala (or Dzambala) is the wealth-granting or wealth-restoring deity

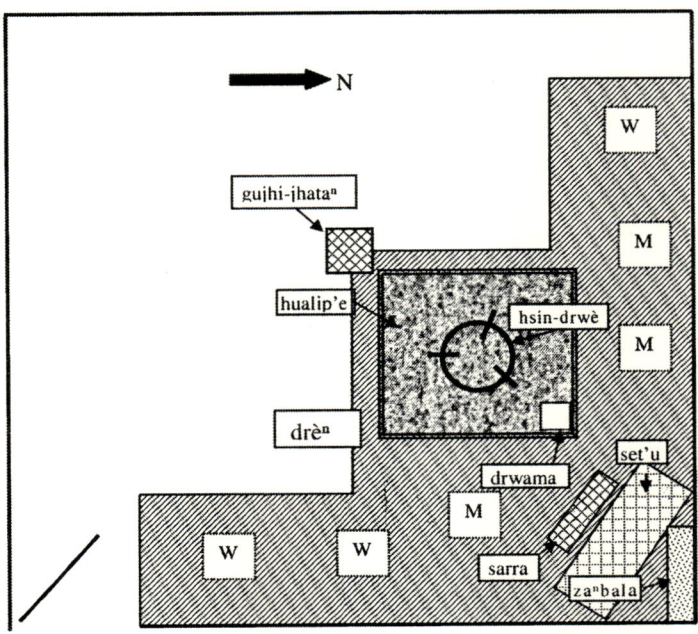

FIG. 3.4. Main room or *jima* as found in Walnut Grove, with fixed sitting places for men (M) and women (W).

FIG. 3.5. The family burns pine branches as an offering in the morning. The iron tripod with offering stone to the right of it are in the foreground, and the *gujhi-jhata^n*, or central pillar, is visible in the back.

of Tibetan Buddhism. Few *za"bala* actually depict this deity, and even fewer people understand the origins of their *za"bala*, but it likely started as an altar for worshipping the deity of wealth (in the hope of bringing prosperity to the house), not unlike the practice of putting gold or silver and grain into the offering stone.

In many houses, the *za"bala*, the *set'u*, and the *sarra* constitute an alternative means of worshipping the same ancestors and deities worshipped by means of the iron tripod and the offering stone, rather than being a shrine to a different divine being. In some houses in Uphill and Downhill with a stronger Buddhist connection—such as having, or having had, a monk in the family—the *za"bala* forms a more prominent presence in the house and is considered the central place of religious activity. Several of the families who seldom pray and make offerings in the morning regularly burn incense on the *sarra*. Because of the clear association with Buddhist religion, most of the *za"bala* were destroyed during the Cultural

FIG. 3.6. *Sarra* and *set'u*, the small bench and chest, with incense burners and other paraphernalia used in ancestor worship. The inhabitants of this house had not yet repaired their *za"bala*, the Buddhist picture or relief, which was destroyed during the Cultural Revolution. Until then, Chairman Mao would have to suffice.

Revolution, and not all houses have replaced or rebuilt theirs, although many plan to do so. The placement of the *set'u*, *sarra*, and *za^{n}bala* in the corner of the platform testifies to its important position in Premi households: it is close to the offering stone and the hearth with the iron tripod, and the imaginary line from the *set'u* and *sarra* to the *gujhi-jhata^n*, or central pillar, creates a sacred alignment that cannot be transgressed. In Walnut Grove, this prohibition is strictly observed, and no one would ever pass behind the hearth to get to another part of the platform, no matter how inconvenient the resulting detour.

Many of the houses of the northern villages have a room that is used exclusively for worshipping deities and in which monks may stay, called *ch'ako^n* or *hlije^n*. This room is always the most luxurious place in the house, sumptuously adorned with Buddhist iconography, and is most often found in the houses of families with strong Buddhist connections, such as those with a son at the monastery. The *ch'ako^n* is the place where the son sleeps when visiting his family. In North Village, the biggest house had a very nice *ch'ako^n* especially prepared for the visits of an important lama who lived in the next township. In Walnut Grove, every house with an *anji* also had a *ch'ako^n*. The head of the house must put two more items in place before the house is finished. On the flat part of the roof there must be a small offering oven, which is used once a year on the ninth day of the first month, when pine branches are burned in all the ovens as an offering to the mountain deities, the *rèdzeng rèda*. Finally, on top of the roof, an iron trident must be fixed. This is the *kadra^n*, and its function is to protect the houses from the *zyè*, or wind demons. The master of the house must place the *kadra^n*, but it must be consecrated by an *anji* or *yèma*, who touches the *kadra^n* with a rooster, the *zyè-ro*, or wind-demon rooster. The *zyè-ro* is viewed as a temporary help lent by the mountain gods. As such, it does not belong to humans and can never be killed; when it dies a natural death, it has to be taken into the mountains and left there so that it is returned to the mountain deity.

When construction is finished, an auspicious day must be chosen for starting to use the iron tripod. First, the head of the household makes an offering of a sheep, to ask for the protection of the different deities. Then, either an *anji*, *yèma*, or other person with special powers, such as one of the living deities, recites prayers and, most important, touches the iron tripod to consecrate it. Until it is touched by such a person, it remains just an ordinary piece of iron. The ceremony, which lasts half a day, is called *jalaso^n*. In all the Premi, Rek'ua, and Naxi households in Bustling Township I visited, the iron tripod had been consecrated. In the Naxi and Rek'ua villages, this was done either by an *anji* or a *dtô-mbà*, but the custom was said to be Premi in origin. The fire can be lit for the first time only on the date after it has been consecrated, but this is ritually regulated: first the pot is put on the iron tripod, next clean water is poured into the pot, and finally firewood is placed under the pot; only then is the fire lit. Some houses wait until the Premi New Year to use the iron tripod for the first time, because this is an auspicious period in general. It is also the only period when the iron tripod may be cleaned.

4 ∾ PREMI COSMOLOGY

Ritual and the State

At the beginning of the millennium, religious life among the Premi of Bustling Township is focused largely on maintaining the relationship of the members of the *dzè^n*, or "house," with the ancestors and thereby strengthening its unity. This is achieved for the most part through daily prayers and offerings of food on the iron tripod and the offering stone. But the prosperity of the *dzè^n* and the well-being of its members also depend on ritual activity directed at beings other than *me-drö*, or souls, in their afterlife manifestation of ancestral souls.

THE INVISIBLE DIMENSION OF THE NATURAL WORLD

In Premi cosmological understanding, the natural world is inhabited not only by humans, animals, and ancestral souls but also by countless beings that may be described as spirits, ghosts, and deities. These beings are present almost anywhere, and their categorization is as natural as that of the different animals or ethnic groups. They are found in what I call the "invisible dimension of the natural world," a term that avoids words such as "supernatural," which implies an out-of-the-ordinary quality.

Many spirits in Premi cosmology are not considered to be of a fundamentally different character than, for example, poisonous snakes or blood-sucking eels. When asked what makes *shep'a* and *hla*, wandering evil spirits and deities, fundamentally different from humans and animals, many Premi answer that they cannot be seen or touched by most people. That makes them more difficult to relate to. Turner has used the modifiers "mystical" and "nonempirical" to describe similar categories of beings or powers found in other cultures (1967: 19). However, from an emic point of view, their existence is established empirically almost daily. Living among the villagers and taking in their conception of, for example, the disease-causing evil spirits, I was struck by the analogy with everyday modern perceptions of bacteria and viruses: we cannot see or feel them, but we accept their existence and understand that they can make us sick; if we are careful, we can often avoid their harmful effects, and if the affliction is too serious to be a handled on our own, we go to an expert. In this sense, day-to-day religious practice in Bustling Township contains a significant element of pragmatism and centers largely on the immediate concerns of protecting one's livelihood and that of one's *dzè^n*.

The following sections introduce some of the most important categories of these beings, inhabitants of the invisible dimension of the natural world, and describe how they affect people's lives and how villagers relate to them through ritual practice. The *anji* of Walnut Grove, Hill Village, and North Village provided the information. The principal source was undoubtedly Nima Anji of Walnut Grove (the most knowledgeable of all *anji* in Bustling Township), and consequently cosmological and ritual details apply mostly to Walnut Grove practices and conceptions. *Anji* did not always agree on the precise nature, power, and formal classification of these deities and evil spirits, and villagers also often held different opinions. In Uphill and North Village, some individuals—mostly educated people such as schoolteachers, members of the government, or Party cadres—denied the existence of evil spirits and some of the local deities, although they still expressed belief in deities considered to be part of the Tibetan Buddhist pantheon and participated in house rituals dedicated to the ancestral spirits. Nevertheless, none of the people I interviewed in Walnut Grove and the other southern villages denied the existence of evil spirits. All were very concerned about acting in an appropriate way in order to obtain the protection of benevolent deities and avoid becoming targets of interference from ancestral souls or the evil tricks of malevolent spirits.

The whole community shared cosmological beliefs and traditional values, but the exact details and precise categorizations were left to the specialists, the *anji* and the *yèma*, or Buddhist lay priest. Villagers needed specialized knowledge to identify the causes of ill fortune, consecutive bad harvests, persistent ailments, and dying livestock, and they needed this knowledge so that they could perform the correct rituals, which would help them avoid or remedy recurrent adversities. While cosmological beliefs and ritual practice were grounded in remembered tradition and enduring cultural structures, they were also shaped by the recent experiences of the Mao period and concerns regarding current government policies. Practice theorists have pointed to the mediating role of ritual in the dynamic two-way relationship between cultural structures and the current situation. Catherine Bell, in her summary of practice theories on ritual such as those of Comaroff and Ortner, states that "it is through ritual practice that culture molds consciousness in terms of underlying structures and patterns . . . current realities simultaneously instigate transformations of those very structures and patterns as well" (1997: 79).

HLA: THE BENEVOLENT DEITIES

The connection of the word *hla* ("hl" is an aspirated "l") to the Tibetan word for "deity," *lha* (as in *yüllha*, the god of the locality), seems evident. But as is the case for several other words and concepts in this nonwritten Tibeto-Burman language, it is not possible at this time to determine whether *hla* is a recent loanword that replaced a Premi term after Buddhism was introduced in the region or whether *hla* might also be related to the Tibetan word *la* (*bla*). Jäschke gives the following meanings for *la*: soul, life, strength; blessing; and an object with which a person's life is ominously connected, such as *bla-shing*, a tree of fate planted at a child's birth (1998). Samuel identifies *la* as a major concept of Tibetan folk religion, connected to the cult of local deities, and links it to the term *lha* as well (1993). He stresses the non-Buddhist meaning of *la*, through its connection with worldly good fortune rather than rebirth and salvation. At the same time, he notes that it is closely connected with the individual: "The *la* is a spirit-essence or life-principle, residing in the body, and, particularly in the earlier period, it was seen as connected also with one or more external objects. Such external objects or resting-places of the *la* might be hills, lakes, or groves of trees" (ibid.: 187). Indeed, these are the three major loci associated with the Premi *hla*, and it may be that the Premi word for "deity" is related to this Tibetan pre-Buddhist principle. The analogy is less certain with regard to the idea of *la* as a life essence or soul that can leave the body. This concept has its own specific term, *drö*, in Bustling Township, translated here as "soul."

According to all the *anji* consulted, the *hla* category was made up mainly of mountain deities, or *rèdzeng rèda*, and water deities, or *lwéjabu*. Unlike in Tibetan areas, where local mountain deities are male and water deities are female,[1] in Bustling Township, the two categories include both male and female deities. There are, however, some elements of local worship that ascribe male attributes to mountain deities and female attributes to water deities. Along with these two major categories, which both villagers and *anji* in Bustling Township clearly and unanimously acknowledge, several other classes of divine beings are recognized and named, although mainly by the different *anji* rather than by the villagers. The most important in this category are Hlada^n So^{n}ma and Yida^n So^{n}ma. As the names might suggest, it is possible that these deities—or at least their appellations—entered the Premi pantheon as a result of Tibetan or Buddhist influence, and those familiar with Tibetan religion will find many striking analogies to Tibetan beliefs and practices in this chapter. Although some of these resemblances may be the result of the many elements of a pre-Buddhist religion very similar to that of the Premi that are contained in Tibetan religious practices and beliefs, most similarities arguably are relatively recent borrowings from Buddhism. Finally, the term *hla* also designates humans who are regarded as embodiments or reincarnations of divine beings, here called "living deities."

WATER DEITIES

Water deities, or *lwéjabu*, are worshipped near springs, rivers, and lakes. They are classified into five different categories, each associated with one of the five "directions" (*ch'ü*): *lwéjabu* Tso^{n}nanrènyi ch'ü, in the center; *lwéjabu* Syè ch'ü, in the east; *lwéjabu* Fu ch'ü, in the south; *lwéjabu* Ngo^n ch'ü, in the west; *lwéjabu* Ch'o^n ch'ü, in the north.

FIGURES. 4.1–4.5. The five water deities, or *lwéjabu*, painted by Nima Anji.

FIG. 4.1 Tso^{n}nanrènyi, water deity of the center

FIG. 4.2. Syè ch'ü, water deity of the east

FIG. 4.3. Fu ch'ü, water deity of the south

FIG. 4.4. Ngo[n] ch'ü, water deity of the west

FIG. 4.5. Ch'oⁿ ch'ü, water deity of the north

These deities are very powerful because they control water, which manifests itself through their ability to both cause and heal diseases and their power over the weather. They reside near places with water, especially lakes or places where water wells up from the soil or from between the rocks. Such places are called *tirè* and are held to be sacred. Trees and other plants cannot be disturbed in the neighborhood of the *tirè*. The help of the water deities is solicited in cases of "watery" diseases, for example, ailments of the eyes or "women's diseases" such as menstrual disorders, infertility, or the absence of male children (mostly—but not exclusively—ascribed to a deficiency in the woman).

The practice of praying to the water deities for male offspring is a recent development brought about by stricter birth control policies, an interesting example of how recent concerns may shape the remembering and (re)construction of religious practices and beliefs. Limiting the number of children to three, in communities where male heirs are very important in continuing the *raka*, or bone, line of the *jhü* and worshipping the ancestors in the *dzè^n*, has shifted one of the main functions of the water deities from curers of diseases to providers of male offspring. In the early years of the People's Republic of China, ethnographic descriptions among Premi in other areas mention water deities. In these descriptions, people worship and propitiate water deities, not as potential providers of male children, but as an element in a well-developed system of curing different kinds of disease, only some of which were related to so-called women's diseases. Better health care and the eradication of many deadly diseases such as pulmonary tuberculosis and bubonic plague have reshaped needs for divine assistance.

In order to summon the water deities, the *anji* or *yèma* uses a *nida*, a specially constructed implement made of a branch with effigies of the deities hanging from it. During such rituals, outsiders are not allowed to talk within hearing distance of the spring, in order to avoid disturbing the process of summoning the deities. People pray and make offerings at the village springs, which are easily recognized because of the little groves that surround them and the many *nida* placed around them. In the neighborhood of North Village, there is a place where a whole river bursts out of a mountain cave. Although it is rather difficult to reach, this place is an important spot for worshipping the water deities, and, interestingly, most of the people who make offerings there are those who want daughters.

More important even than the role the water deities play in the health of the people is their influence on agriculture, through their control over water. They are able to help the villagers by making it rain during a drought, yet they are also seen as the cause of flooding and waterlogging, which are considered reprisals for the villagers' offensive behavior, such as cutting down certain trees or hunting an animal favored by the deities. Consequently, ritual activities must be performed on a very regular basis. This concept of causality, in which adversities are attributed to divine retribution for all kinds of rather "normal" human actions, such as hunting or cutting trees, and have to be addressed by ritual action, has been observed in other border areas of Tibet. In Tsari, in the southeastern border region of central Tibet, these beliefs have been syncretized into the maṇḍala world system of Tibetan Buddhism, in which it formed the basis for general state concerns about maintaining large-scale restrictions on the exploitation of natural resources (Huber 1998). In Walnut Grove, when the water deities have been displeased, small rituals do not suffice, and they must be appeased through large-scale activities involving constant prayer and countless offerings:

> In 1998, there was a period of terrible rain. It just did not stop raining for weeks, and the fields were flooded with water. Because this endangered the spring planting, we asked Tenzin Droma [a living deity] and the *soma* [medium] to pray to the water deities in order to appease them. The whole village accompanied the living deity and the *soma* to the mountains to a place with clean water, where we burned incense for a very long time. Soon afterward, the rain stopped.

Another time in 1999, Main Crossing had the opposite problem, and the young *anji* led a ceremony praying to the water deities to make it rain. This ceremony lasted three days and three nights, and it took place at a spot in the mountains with much water, making it an appropriate place from which to ask the deities for rain. People agreed that the practice of worshipping the water deities in order to obtain good weather for agriculture had become more prevalent because of renewed reliance on subsistence farming resulting from the 1999 ban on logging and decreasing government compensation for bad harvests.

MOUNTAIN DEITIES

Mountain deities, or *rèdzeng rèda*, are most often worshipped on mountaintops but are also often included in prayers in the house. As with the water deities, they are both male and female, and they also both protect and punish. Much like the local deities of Tibetan folk religion, mountain deities often are named local deities related to specific mountains, but unlike the Tibetan *yüllha*, the god of a locality, they are in a more diffuse category, and the term *rèdzeng rèda* also designates the throng of uncountable, nameless minor divinities living in trees in the mountain forests. Some mountains do get divine status and a cult somewhat comparable to that of the Tibetan *neri* (*gnas-ri*), or "mountain abodes," which means that the mountain is worshipped not only for being the place where the deity or deities reside but also for being a deity in itself (Huber 1998:

22). One illustrious mountain god in the north of Bustling Township is Gwèⁿbu, who lends his name to a famous sacred cave near North Village. Gwèⁿbu is the mountain deity who is said to have created the mountain and its cave. People from the surrounding villages visit the cave and make offerings to Gwèⁿbu in order to solicit his help. In the past, the cave was also a refuge for Buddhist recluses.

Since mountain deities usually reside in mountain forests, they are closely connected with the proper use of forest resources. Wanton destruction of trees or indiscriminate hunting incurs their displeasure. Premi villages are often recognizable from a distance because the forests are so close to the villages. People try to limit forest destruction in their immediate surroundings so that they will stay on good terms with their closest divine neighbors and are less worried about those farther away. Mountain deities can, like water deities, influence the weather and cause diseases. According to villagers, the ability to identify the kind of deities or spirits that are responsible for problems is precisely what distinguishes a good religious expert. After three consecutive years during which hail and snowstorms destroyed a considerable part of the crops, Walnut Grove held a large ceremony for the mountain deities, led by Nima Anji and involving all the *anji* of the village.

During the New Year's period, every *dzèⁿ* must make one trip into the mountains with the *anji* and offer three chickens to the mountain deities. This is done in order to ask for protection against the evil spirits and to show respect so that the deities will not turn against any member of the house or its animals. The ceremony is called *yizèⁿgu*, which is also the name of the scripture read by the *anji*. Smaller ceremonies may be held, if necessary, on the fifth, fifteenth, or twenty-fifth of every lunar month.

NAMED DIVINE BEINGS

Lama Yidaⁿ is a deity of the sky. It is worshipped especially to protect people from the *zyè*, or wind demons.

Hladaⁿ Soⁿma is one of the mightiest deities, summoned during funerary rites to protect the *me-drö* against the evil spirits. Many deities, including the mountain deities, might manifest themselves during the recitation of scriptures at the cremation ceremony, but all the minor deities disappear as soon as an *anji* or *yèma* manages to summon Hlada^n So^{n}ma. There was some disagreement among *anji* in Walnut Grove as to whether this major deity had a particular connection to certain clans. According to Nima Anji, himself from the Mesé clan, Hlada^n So^{n}ma was originally the protecting deity of the Mesé clan of Walnut Grove, but since the Ak'ua and Bot'a clans had moved into the village, it had become possible to invoke this deity upon the death of one of their clan members as well.

Yida^n So^{n}ma has particular connections with one *anji* line and functions as a personal divine helper and protector for the line. An *anji* can receive his *so^{n}ma* from his teacher, often his father, but this does not have to be the case. In fighting evil spirits, an *anji* can invoke his personal *so^{n}ma*, for example, by offering a chicken. If the *anji* does not worship his *so^{n}ma* in a fitting manner, he may become sick, or the *so^{n}ma* may leave the *anji* altogether, causing him to lose his powers. The Yida^n So^{n}ma is probably related to the Buddhist meditational or tantric deities, or *yidam*, both in name and in the concept of a deity that is strongly connected to personal practice (see, e.g., Samuel 1993). It is no coincidence that Yida^n So^{n}ma was very prominent in the pantheon, as explained by Nima Anji, probably the only *anji* in Bustling Township whose Tibetan-language skills enabled him to grasp some of the semantics of the texts in his possession. Indeed, several of the other *anji* denied the existence of a personally invoked deity. Nevertheless, through the offering of a chicken and connection to the *anji* lineage, this original Buddhist concept has been firmly "naturalized" into local practice and cosmology.

SHEP'A AND BRÖ DEMONS: THE MALEVOLENT BEINGS

While deities can make life hard for humans when they are not properly respected and worshipped, they are mainly benign in nature. If deities become displeased because of human actions, it is possible to propitiate them through rituals conducted by an *anji*. The actions of *shep'a*, cunning and irate spirits, present a more constant nuisance.

Shep'a or *sheba* (Uphill and Downhill pronunciations) is a collective appellation for many different kinds of evil spirits. Some *shep'a* are wandering souls of people who did not have descendants to perform the funerary rites or take care of them by worshipping the ancestral spirits or of people who died a violent death. These evil spirits are a constant menace and are the cause of most diseases. The task of the *anji* or *yèma* is to identify which kind of *shep'a* is responsible for the disease or the death so that he may apply appropriate remedies. Diseases are categorized into types, and the types often correspond to the kind of *shep'a* that causes the disease. One type of *shep'a* causes colds, another kidney problems, and so on. One especially vicious kind of *shep'a* can snatch a person's *me-drö* away. This may happen in special circumstances when the *me-drö* is not that closely connected to the body, as when dreaming or when one is startled. If the *anji* does not quickly manage to convince the *me-drö* to leave the world of the *shep'a* and return to the body of the afflicted person, the person in question will die or lead a terribly reduced life.

The help of a deity is often necessary in combating and subduing the evil spirits. The *anji* and the *yèma* use different techniques: the *anji* will try to chase the *shep'a* away in a violent way, while the *yèma* will try to gently entice the *shep'a* to leave, for example, by setting out some food as bait. Many houses have spells written in Tibetan above the entrance door to keep these spirits out; the spells are often combined with magical charms blessed by a religious expert. *Shep'a* are also believed to be able to find their way to the village by following travelers. Therefore, at all the major paths entering a Premi village in Bustling Township, there is a wooden gate with a threatening or confusing message addressed to the *shep'a* painted on top of it, in the hope that this will keep them out of the village.

Stories about the *shep'a* and their actions permeate the local oral tradition. Dingba Shenro is one of the great mythical heroes with divine status, not only among the Premi but also among some of the neighboring peoples such as the Na.[2] He is said to be the founder of *anji* religion and is famed for his heroic battles with the *shep'a* (as indicated by one of his other titles, Ya^{n}ge Dingba Shenro, in which Ya^{n}ge means "suppressor of *shep'a*"). Nima Anji, who said that the content was confirmed by writings in ancient Bön texts, told the following story:

> Before, there were a lot of *shep'a* on Earth. They had almost devoured all humans. This was noticed by Heaven. Subsequently, a large convention of all the deities was held to find a way to subdue the *shep'a*. None of the

deities was willing to go down to Earth. So there was no alternative but to resort to election. Finally Dingba Shenro was chosen to go down to Earth and subdue the *shep'a*. Unfortunately, the news that a deity would come to fight the *shep'a* had reached the ears of the king of the *shep'a*, Zènbuma. Zènbuma changed himself into a beautiful girl and asked Dingba Shenro to marry him.³ The girl was so beautiful that Dingba Shenro succumbed and agreed to the marriage and settled down. One day, Dingba Shenro suddenly remembered why he had come to Earth. Through magical implements, he managed to subdue the *shep'a*, helped the suffering people, and received gold, silver, and other valuables in payment. But when he returned home, his *shep'a* wife was very ill, and he did not understand why. She made him go out again and perform magic, insisting that he should not accept gold, silver, and valuables in return for helping the people. The second time Dingba Shenro went out, he did not accept gold, silver, and valuables but just performed magic. The people nevertheless wanted to pay him and hid some valuables in his bag. When he came back, his wife was even more ill. Then, Dingba Shenro found out about the valuables in his bag and finally became suspicious. He performed magic while his wife slept, and the *shep'a* king returned to his original shape and was immediately killed by Dingba Shenro. After completing his task, on the way back to Heaven, he met a *mu* [a wild fowl living in the forest in Bustling Township, whitish in color with a black crest and red feet]. He said to the *mu*: "I have completed my task in a satisfactory way, and now I return home." The *mu* answered: "You came to subdue the *shep'a*, but you were fooled by them into marrying their king. Your magical powers are too shallow." Dingba Shenro felt very embarrassed and gave his black hat and red shoes to the *mu*. That is why in paintings, Dingba Shenro has no shoes and hat, and why the *mu* has a black crest and red feet.⁴

Nima Anji assessed the story as demonstrating that it is possible to subdue the evil spirits, but one has to outwit them and use magical powers. Nevertheless, a recurring underlying theme of many such stories is that *anji*, either as mythical first ancestors or cultural heroes, somehow do not completely live up to their elevated status. This might be related to local conceptualizations of the coexistence of *anji* religious practice with that of Tibetan Buddhism.

Shep'a are the most common evil spirits, but they are far from the only malevolent beings. One of the most serious afflictions that can beset a person or a whole house is possession by *brö* demons. A house may become possessed by *brö* demons through marriage relations. A woman from one of the northern villages of Bustling Township brought *brö* demons to Walnut Grove when she married a Walnut Grove villager. Her family had been infected through marriage with a woman from a village close to Yongning.[5] At the time, *brö* demons had been in Walnut Grove for three generations, and four houses were affected. *Brö* demons do not immediately infect those who visit an affected house, but they can make the callers sick.[6] According to the villagers, everyone who ate at one of these houses swelled up in the stomach and vomited. People possessed by *brö* demons will frequently feel bad or sick and die young. The villagers saw the large spot of pigmentation on the eyelid of an allegedly possessed person as a symptom and proof of affliction. People affected by *brö* demons can also practice magic and cause others to be sick or, most threateningly, be possessed by *brö* demons. It took a lot of persuasion before my local assistants were willing to let me visit the four affected houses, and even then, I had to conduct the interviews outside. The young Nuosu policeman who first took me to Walnut Grove was more than a little shaken when, upon calling on one of the possessed families to have a serious talk with an unruly young man in their midst, the house residents threatened him with *brö* demons. Although he had not grown up in the area, the otherwise brave policeman had spent enough time in Bustling Township to share the villagers' fear.

The most certain way to become possessed, however, is through establishing the stable sexual relations of marriage, and beliefs in *brö* demons might be related to uncertainty and fears about establishing affinal relations with families from more remote and unfamiliar villages.[7] Casual sexual contact is not necessarily sufficient to cause possession by *brö* demons. Once a new house is possessed, communication lines are opened, and *brö* demons are able to travel freely among the infected houses. The *ditsyèp'o* ritual cures diseases caused by *brö* demons but cannot end the spiritual possession. In fact, there is currently no cure for banishing these ghosts. As a result, the infected families in Walnut Grove were completely ostracized, could not find marriage partners in the village, received no visits, and could not participate in common village ceremonies and celebrations. Their social network was limited to the houses in some of the northern villages that also were affected by *brö* demons. These villages were a day's walk from Walnut Grove, so contacts were limited. Each time the affected Walnut Grove families needed the services of an *anji*, they had to fetch one from these northern villages because none of the local *anji* dared to help them. One of the few people in the village who was not too afraid to show some compassion was the living deity Tenzin Droma, who did not discriminate against these families when extending her yearly blessings to all families in the village.

The family situation of two brothers illustrates what it means to be considered a possessed house in Walnut Grove. Duji is forty-six. He is not married. He does not know who his father is. His two unmarried sisters, forty-two and thirty-nine, also live in the house. Tsésomo, the older of the two, has two children by two different fathers: a boy of twenty-one and a girl of thirteen. The father of the boy lives in the village but is married to someone else [it is unclear whether he married Tsésomo and divorced her or whether the boy is the result of premarital or extramarital relations]. The father of the girl is from Yongning, whence he hastily returned when he became aware that the house he had married into was possessed by *brö* demons. Duji's brother is fifty-three and lives in the neighboring house with his family. His wife is from the northern villages. He has five children: two daughters are married to men from the northern villages, one daughter is not married, one son has married uxorilocally to a woman from the northern villages, and one son is living at the parental home with his wife, who is also from the northern villages.

I did not observe negative attitudes toward the people of these four houses. The other villagers talked with them in a friendly manner, but preferably from a safe distance. Nevertheless, the lack of a local affinal network and the difficulty in establishing a "normal" family made these families among the poorest in the village, and they were extremely vulnerable to natural adversities such as bad harvests or illness among house residents or their domestic animals. The chaotic period of the Cultural Revolution, when many of the local traditions and beliefs came under attack, offered these families a brief reprieve.

RITUAL EXPERTS AND OTHER RELIGIOUS PRACTITIONERS

In neutralizing the actions of the evil spirits, which can make them sick, or in seeking to avoid the anger of deities or ancestral souls, the villagers regularly pray and make offerings. Fortunately, they can solicit the assistance of different kinds of religious experts and other people who have special relationships with the inhabitants of the invisible dimension.

Anji *and* Yèma: *Premi Ritual Experts*

On my first visit to Walnut Grove, I stayed at the house of Galo^n, the Party chairman of the administrative village to which Walnut Grove belonged. After dinner we continued talking around the hearth and were joined by Galo^n's thirty-four-year-old cousin. Galo^n made us drink several cups of *arje*, complaining he could not drink the strong spirits because of a recurring stomachache. Reacting to this complaint, his cousin matter-of-factly stood up and went to fetch a wooden plank standing in the corner of the room. He placed the plank in such a way that one end pointed to our host and the other to the hearth. On the end closest to Galo^n, he laid out a bit of charcoal from the hearth in the form of a circle. He fished two small pieces of wood out of his pocket and placed them on top of the circle with a few grains of maize. Then he sprinkled some drops of *arje* on this little mound. Breaking the silence, Galo^n's cousin began reciting in Premi, repeating in a very monotonous way the same invocation addressed to the water deities for help in getting rid of *shep'a*. After a few minutes, he winked at Galo^n's teenage son, who apparently knew what he was supposed to do: he took the plank, carefully made two circling movements with it above the head of his father, and then went out to empty it. He then returned the plank to Galo^n's cousin, and the whole ritual was repeated several times.

Categorizing the different ritual experts is not a straightforward task. Some villages had one or more practicing *anji*, such as the cousin of the Party chairman in Walnut Grove; in other villages such as Uphill and Seven Houses, there was a *yèma*. The word *yèma* is undoubtedly a Premi rendering of the Tibetan word "lama." While "lama" in Tibetan originally meant "spiritual teacher," its meaning has been extended to refer to senior monks or *tulku*, monks who are reincarnations or emanations of important deities or previous lamas, so-called incarnate lamas (Samuel 1993: 280). In Premi, the word *yèma* also designates any monk or novice living in a Buddhist monastery. To complicate matters, in North Village, the Buddhist lay priest was also called *anji*.[8] The village of Walnut Grove could boast the presence of a *soma*, or medium, through whom the deities communicated with the villagers. Furthermore, people all over the township solicited the help of the two living deities. These individuals were considered in some way to be in the same category as the *tulku* residing at the Buddhist monasteries but were not recognized as such by any of these monasteries.

Some families with affinal relations to Naxi or Rek'ua, such as the Bot'a clan in Walnut Grove, might also call on the *dtô-mbà* religious specialists of Battleground or Gaku. People of those villages might also request the services of the *anji* or living deities in addition to inviting the *dtô-mbà*. The religious specialists are all men, but *soma* and living deities may be women because, according to Nima Anji's explanation, deities, not humans, select these people for their positions.

The tasks of *anji* and *yèma* are very similar. They read scriptures and perform ritual acts such as making offerings at cremation ceremonies, weddings, and name-giving ceremonies; when called on by villagers in cases of disease ascribed to evil spirits; or in response to disasters ascribed to the actions of water or mountain deities. They also perform the larger ceremonies of the Premi calendar: the most important of these is the New Year purification ceremony, or *wu-hsi*, when every house, especially its hearth, in the entire village has to have its annual cleansing of evil spirits. Other ceremonies are related to agriculture, including those performed at the time of sowing and of harvesting. Furthermore, both *anji* and *yèma* carry out divination in connection with the different aspects of house construction (described in chapter 3) or to ascertain important dates related to agriculture (e.g., when to sow), travel, weddings, and the like. They are also responsible for consecrating the iron tripod, and the *kadra^n*, the iron trident on top of the house.

Although the religious and ritual tasks *anji* and *yèma* perform seem very much alike, the way in which they carry out these rituals and cere-

FIG. 4.6. An *anji* in full ceremonial dress, usually worn only at cremation ceremonies.

monies are not always the same. This difference in ritual practice between *anji* and *yèma*, especially in relation to treating afflictions brought on by *shep'a*, is related to their background. An *anji* acquires his knowledge in the village from his teacher, another *anji*, often his father. He has developed the expertise to conduct many different rituals and can recite a large corpus of oral texts from memory as well as recite Tibetan Buddhist texts. *Yèma*, in contrast, are people who have spent time in a Tibetan Gelugpa monastery, where they learned to recite Tibetan Buddhist scriptures;

depending on the length of time spent there, they may have acquired some minimal understanding of the content of these texts and perhaps a few general concepts of Buddhist learning, such as the precept that one should avoid killing. Consequently, the practice of the *yèma* is limited to the recitation of Buddhist scriptures accompanied by the performance of ritual offerings, the burning of incense, and the use of prayer sticks, drums, and bells. This practice is an inherent part of local Buddhist practice in many Tibetan areas. Certain "classical" Buddhist texts are incorporated into a larger manual, complete with practical instructions on how to conduct relevant rituals. One of the important reasons for performing these rituals is to exorcise all kinds of evil believed to be brought about by malevolent forces. The Heart Sutra (Sherab Nyipo) is one such classical text. According to Lopez, the use of this text is extremely widespread throughout Tibet because of its brevity and "because of its potency (as the quintessence of the Buddha's wisdom)" (1997: 511).[9]

The best way to characterize the *yèma* is as a sort of Buddhist lay priest, a person who acquired a certain level of knowledge by spending some time as a monk at the monastery—which he uses to perform rituals for the villagers—but who no longer lives at the monastery.[10] In Bustling Township, especially in the northern villages, a distinction is made between two different kinds of Buddhist lay priests. *Jabyè* are monks who have left the monastery but continue to lead an existence considered to be that of true monks: spending a lot of time praying and reciting, abstaining from eating red meat, avoiding productive labor, and, most important, abstaining from marrying and establishing a family. *Jabyè* is possibly the Premi rendering of "trapa,"[11] the Tibetan word designating the ordinary celibate monk. In some Gelugpa areas of Muli and in the area around Yongning, there are very few resident monks at the monasteries; instead, most monks live at home and visit the monastery only for religious celebrations. The other category of Buddhist lay priests are *sa^{n}roa*. They also have a certain knowledge of Buddhist learning acquired at the monastery and are able to recite some scriptures. But unlike *jabyè*, they have broken their vows by marrying and taking up the lives of ordinary villagers after leaving the monastery. This distinction is made in the northern villages in particular, and there is a clear perception of status difference between *jabyè* and *sa^{n}roa*. Most *yèma* in Bustling Township belonged to the latter category.

The most visible difference between *anji* and Buddhist lay priests is in the choice of ritual garments. At most ritual performances, such as the one to cure the stomachache of the Walnut Grove Party chairman, both *anji* and *yèma* wear their normal clothes, but at important ceremonies, such as for cremations, the two kinds of ritualists are easily distinguished by their garments. If the *yèma* has a Buddhist monk's habit from his time at the monastery, he is likely to wear it on such occasions. *Anji* present quite a contrast to this outfit, with their colorful red or pink gowns and crownlike hats with five adorned sides.

Table 4.1 shows that villages with an *anji* never concurrently have an active *yèma*. Furthermore, there are clearly more *anji* in the southern villages, and more people participate in monasticism in the northern villages. The rather large village of Ten Houses, where one-third of the residents are Na, has no *anji*, *yèma*, or other ritual specialists, because in the past everyone who studied to become a ritualist died prematurely, so no one in this village wanted to take the risk.

The *anji* recites from two differently transmitted sources: written and oral texts. Orally transmitted texts are all in the Premi language. One such text is the *hsip'u* text recited at the "opening of the road" ceremony, a kind of travel guide for the souls of the deceased, to help them find their ancestral lands, and a central aspect of the ancestral cult of the Premi. The written *anji* texts are recited from Tibetan Buddhist and Bön scriptures, which, over the centuries, found their way to the Premi villages. Here they have been integrated into local practice and transmitted from one *anji* generation to the next, some of them meticulously copied. These Tibetan texts are used not for their specific content but to fulfill the various purposes of summoning deities, exorcising *shep'a*, or bringing magical powers to the one who recites them. A few are used for divination. Nima Anji and his students frequently use a text consisting of invocations of the Bön deity Welchen Meri and the Bön sages Drenpa Namkha and Tsewang Rigzin.[12]

Most *anji* or *yèma* I interviewed do not understand the actual content of these texts but can pronounce the Tibetan letters. The *anji* generally have no knowledge of Tibetan language, and the *yèma* have not spent sufficient time in the monastery to have acquired a thorough knowledge of written Tibetan. In view of the traditional teaching methods of the monasteries, where the focus is on recitation, monks must study many years before they acquire any real understanding of the content of the texts and of Buddhist doctrine in general. As the seventy-five-year-old *yèma* from Spring Rain explained: "I can recite Tibetan OK, but even after four years at Muli Gompa, I could understand only very little [of the content of the texts]. Nowadays at school, these kids, they learn to both read and write! The Party clearly does a better job than the monastery did!"

The titles of the texts used in rituals in Bustling Township are related not to the titles of the Tibetan originals but to their specific function in local practice. So, in addition to learning how to recite the texts, *anji* possess the knowledge of how to use them, even without understanding their exact content. The text becomes a form of magic spell with a

TABLE 4.1. Ritual Specialists in the Premi Villages of Bustling Township, 1999

Village (village group)	Number of full anji and number of apprentices in ( )	Number of Buddhist lay priests (yèma, sanroa, jabyè)	Number of monks at Muli Gompa	Number of inhabitants (approx.)
Northern villages (North Village, White Stone, Rocky Outcrop)	2	at least 1	4	200
Spring Rain	0	1	0	350
Uphill, Downhill	0	1	2	280
Hill Village	3	0	0	170
Main Crossing	1 (5)	0	0	130
Ten Houses	0	0	0	230
Walnut Grove	7 (4)*	0	1	220
Five Nut Trees	0	0	0	90
Total	15 (9)*	at least 3	7	1,670

*Two of these apprentices come from villages outside Bustling Township.
Data in this table are based on my field notes and are not the outcome of a systematic survey.

specific power to invoke a deity or drive out an evil spirit. There are a few texts written in Premi language using Tibetan letters. Although it was often rumored that such texts contained ritual and historiographical writings, all the texts I saw were genealogies in which Premi names had been recorded in Tibetan script. Learning the oral tradition and becoming fluent in reciting scriptures is a long process, and various *anji* have widely varying levels of knowledge. It may easily take up to five years of almost daily classes to reach an acceptable level of knowledge of the texts. At this stage, an *anji* is able to recite five or six scriptures, perform some of the less complicated ceremonies, and assist full-fledged *anji* in larger ceremonies such as cremations. These ceremonies last several days and often require the services of at least five *anji* and *yèma*. Learning to perform all of the necessary rituals may require as much as ten years of study. The position of *anji* is normally transmitted from father to son, and this is also how the texts are handed down. If the *anji* has several sons, those who demonstrate the most talent for the difficult task of memorizing the long rituals take on the position. The *anji* line of Nima Anji in Walnut Grove stretched over nineteen generations. But one does not have to belong to an *anji* lineage to become an *anji*. Most of the older *anji* taught several students in addition to their own sons or grandsons. Many of these students go on to become the first *anji* in their patriline. In all probability, accepting students from outside the family was a form of cultural flexibility meant to remedy an acute lack of *anji* caused by the recent substantial population growth in Bustling Township combined with the loss of a whole generation of *anji* during the Cultural Revolution, when fathers dared not teach their sons.

The *anji* of Walnut Grove divide the ritual texts into twelve categories, with the following seven being the most important:

1. The *ts'ère* summon the water deities, or *lwéjabu*.
2. The *hsip'u* guide *me-drö* in finding their place among the ancestors.
3. The *drahala* call on the help of all the *me-drö* of the ancestors.
4. The *ji^{n}jü* solicit the assistance of a specific kind of deity.
5. The *yizè^{n}gu* is read especially to honor the mountain deities, or *rèdzeng rèda*, while burning incense.
6. The *ditsyèp'ö* is read to placate the spirits who cause *brö* demons and *dzè*, another type of disease-causing demon.

7. The *ninjyop'é* is recited at a ritual for people who are born under an unlucky constellation in the twelve-animal-cycle Premi calendar, which resembles the Tibetan and Chinese calendars. These people have difficult lives and are prone to disease and all kinds of disasters. The ritual must be performed every eleventh year. It makes the *me-drö* of the affected person temporarily leave the body and join the ancestors. This process will make life better during the next cycle.

Except for illness suffered by this last category of people, disease is understood to be caused mainly by *shep'a* or other evil spirits, displeased deities or neglected ancestral souls, and *brö* demons. *Anji* or *yèma*, however, are not the only people who have dealings with the invisible dimension of the natural world.

Soma, *or Mediums*

The *soma* of Walnut Grove was an important figure in relating to the inhabitants of this invisible dimension and thereby played a key role in curing disease and avoiding or remedying disasters. He was the only *soma* in Bustling Township, and people from all over the township, and occasionally even from farther away, came to visit him. The term *soma* is probably related to *sungma*, the word for Tibetan mediums. Such mediums were found in several of the monasteries in the region, and Joseph Rock noted their presence in the Gelugpa monastery of Yongning (where monks were mostly Na and Premi) in 1928 (Rock 1959).[13] He also described two female *sungma* from the ruling Bar clan of Muli, one of whom became possessed by the spirit of a murdered ancestor who was seeking revenge (ibid.: 816–17). One common feature of the *soma* and the *sungma*, as Rock pointed out, is that they serve as mediums for one particular spirit, deity, or category of deities. After being possessed or used as the medium for one deity, they are not used by other deities and most likely will be connected with this deity for the rest of their lives.

For Galizega, the sixty-six-year-old *soma* in Walnut Grove, the realization that he had become a medium was a gradual process, which began several years before, when his health was not good, and he started to have dreams. These were pleasant dreams. He dreamed about flowers and about deities who gave him nice clothes to wear. This kind of dream came again and again, and for a while he had them every night. In one of the dreams, he saw a deity coming down from a rainbow. He decided to consult Nima Anji and ask him to carry out a divination. After Galizega told Nima Anji about his dreams, the *anji* concluded that he had become a medium. Galizega's health improved, and he was able to tell fortunes. When he drank a bit of spirits or when he went to sleep and closed his eyes, he saw the deity. One day, Nima Anji took him into the mountains; they made an offering of some *tsamba*, a bread made from highland barley, and recited scriptures. That was when the *anji* became convinced that the water deities had made Galizega into a *soma*.

From that time, Galizega received many visitors inquiring about what was wrong with them, what to do in order to conceive a son, on which day to build a house, and so on. In the beginning, he felt as though the deities told him what to tell the people who sought his advice, but after some time, he knew by himself what he should say. He was no longer self-conscious about the deities communicating through him. This power made it possible for him to diagnose all diseases related to the water deities, and he was often able to provide a cure as well. If necessary, he sent sick visitors to an *anji* who could carry out the required rituals. Many of the visitors' requests were not specifically related to disease but rather were aimed at acquiring knowledge about the deities' intentions so that they might obtain better control over the uncertainties of life.

On one occasion, a visitor from another village wanted to know whether his family would be safe in the future. The *soma* first asked for more information, including which animal of the calendar the person had been born under and the precise location of his family's house. Then the *soma* sat still for two or three minutes while his legs shook slightly. He asked some more questions about the place where the house was situated. "Is there water close by?" The visitor replied that there was a small pond next to the house. After a short pause, the *soma* answered very slowly, his voice markedly different from when he had been asking questions. If the family managed to keep the water in the pond free from pollution, he said, all would be well, and there was no reason to worry.

Once a year, at the time of the New Year, the *anji* and *soma* go into the mountains to a place near a lake, where they make offerings and read scriptures to the water deities. Upon their return, the *soma* is able to tell the villagers what they should and should not do in order to avoid offending the deities, noting, for example, which trees they must not cut down.

Living Deities

Finally, two personages with important roles in ritual and religious life in Bustling Township are the living deities, also called *hla*. In Chinese, they are called *huofo* (lit., "living Buddhas"), and the same Chinese term is used as the translation of the Tibetan word *tulku*. One living deity is a government cadre in a neighboring township; the other is a young woman in Walnut Grove. Both are greatly revered by the local villagers and are called upon to receive yearly blessings and *sungdü*, the knotted red threads worn around the wrist or neck for luck and protection. Although their divine status places them among the company of deities and spirits, they also fulfill an important role as religious experts and perform many of the ritual functions of *anji* and *yèma*. Living deities are also shown stones from potential sites for houses, recite Buddhist scriptures and burn incense at larger ceremonies to worship the water deities or some of the other deities, and—if they happen to be in the neighborhood at the right time—consecrate a new iron tripod.

The concept of the *tulku* is a traditional Tibetan institution whereby individuals are recognized as rebirths of previous lamas or as an emanation of deities such as Avalokiteśvara or Mañjuśrī, or both (see, e.g., Samuel 1993: 281–82). This system was also used as a means to regulate the succession for monastic thrones, especially among the Gelugpa, since monks or abbots were supposed to be celibate, and as such it also enabled certain aristocratic families to maintain their hold on power by ensuring that rebirth took place in the right families. New *tulku* were recognized through certain tests and by prophecies, and in view of its importance for local power structures, the process was usually not taken lightly (Aris 1992: 118). The Muli monastic domain counts one official *tulku*, Guzyo Pema Rinchin. The term *guzyo* is a Premi honorific;

it was used to designate the *tusi* but today is reserved for the officially recognized reincarnation.

The living deities in Bustling Township and in the neighboring township were not part of this Gelugpa monastic succession system and were not recognized by either the monastery or the Provincial Religious Affairs Bureau (Sheng Zongjiao Shiwuju).

The female living deity of Walnut Grove, Tenzin Droma, went by the name Tadrema before she was recognized as a living deity. She came from a village family who was very poor because her father died when she, her younger sister, and her brother were very young. Her youth was difficult, and her brother had to work as hard as a grown-up from a very young age to support his two sisters and his mother. Their house became a model of tenacity and hard work in the village.

Then strange things started to happen to Tadrema. Every fifteenth day of the lunar month, she saw the silhouette of the Buddha in the sun, and at night, she saw the Buddha in the moon. After three years had passed in this way, she started seeing the Buddha in the palm of her hand. She consulted Nima Anji and felt an inexplicable urge to study Tibetan scriptures. Nima Anji then saw that she had white stripes all over her body and a strangely colored stripe on her chest in the form of a seal. Each fifteenth day of the month, this line would take all possible shapes and colors. After practicing some divination, the *anji* found out that Tadrema was a living deity, and she took the name Tenzin Droma.

This revelation came at the age of sixteen, and after that, she became even more eager to study Tibetan. She stopped eating beef, chicken, fish, garlic, and other spices. Her reputation as a living deity grew quickly, and more and more people came to seek her blessing. She went on pilgrimages to Muli Gompa and Lhasa and circumambulated Gonga Mountain. Some of these activities were financed by loans and contributions from the people who sought her blessing. In 1994, the villagers donated labor and building materials and constructed a small house for her in the neighborhood of her family's house. The aim was to provide her with a place to study, worship the Buddha, and receive visitors. Out of gratitude for this support and with the aim of returning part of the contributions to the community, her brother purchased a video machine and a generator and showed videos for free in his house every evening. Tenzin Droma became more and more engrossed in Buddhism and spent long periods of time in textual study and meditation. On one of my visits, I was not able to call on her because she was completing a sixty-day period of silence. Such feats greatly awed the villagers but, at the same time, created increasing distance between her and them. One villager complained that while the living deity from the neighboring township still had time to listen to the people, Tenzin Droma was "too much occupied with the Buddha." For the villagers, her role as a resource in dealing with beings of the invisible dimension became less and less important.

There was also another aspect to Tenzin Droma that added to the high regard in which she was held, and that was her self-imposed celibacy. The villagers considered her to be a good-looking and capable young woman, and it would not have been difficult for her to be married out. As the only woman playing a religious role in Bustling Township, her position was unique, and she enjoyed a high social status. People in Bustling Township were very conscious of her gender and always mentioned that she was a *female* living deity, "something that had never happened before," and in Walnut Grove, the villagers seemed to be very proud of this. It really was remarkable in view of the fact that there was no tradition in Bustling Township—or in other places in Muli, as far as I could verify—of women studying Buddhism. Unlike many other Tibetan Buddhist areas, Muli and adjacent areas in Yunnan also have no Buddhist nuns or nunneries. Given that being a deity is a position that one can only be recognized in, rather than one that a person chooses, it would be an exaggeration to state that Tenzin Droma was a role model for the girls and women in the village. Nevertheless, in male-centered Bustling Township, she appeared to contribute to increased self-confidence about gender identity among women, especially those who had not had much schooling and outside experience. Although I did not focus specifically on the gender aspects of religious practice, in going through my notes, I was struck by the fact that women spoke significantly more often to me about Tenzin Droma. Women of all ages also constituted the clear majority of the steady stream of visitors she received in Walnut Grove. And since people often visit religious personages, such as an *anji, yèma,* or living deity, because they are experiencing various personal problems, it would seem that she also played an important role as a resource for women, in a function that in a modernized urban context would be defined as a psychosocial service.

Anji *Survival after Mao*

According to Nima Anji of Walnut Grove, Bustling Township had never before had the good fortune of having a living deity, and the *soma* was a new phenomenon. Without Nima Anji, these personages would most likely not have existed in Walnut Grove. Their roles were widely accepted and respected, underscoring the fact that Nima Anji did not just invent them in a vacuum. Rather, they emerged out of a shared cosmological understanding in Bustling Township and the acceptance among the villagers that Nima Anji was an expert endowed with the knowledge necessary to recognize people with a divine nature or special powers. But Nima Anji was just one of seven practicing *anji* ritualists in Walnut Grove at the start of the new millennium, and the village counted even more apprentices who would soon strengthen their ranks even more.

This was a remarkable development in view of the recent past. Starting from the period of the Democratic Reforms in 1956, and especially during the Cultural Revolution, the Communists did their utmost to eradicate *anji* practice. Members of the local "revolutionary organizations" (*geming zuzhi*) burned a large part of the *anji* texts. The texts of Nima Anji's father were all burned, but another *anji* in Walnut Grove hid many of his texts; even when he was beaten by the local Red Guard brigade, he did not reveal their hiding place. Several *anji* handed in some of their texts to be destroyed and hid the rest to await better times. In many houses, people were too afraid to pray or make offerings, and most *anji* ritualists stopped practicing—at least openly.

Almost a generation removed from the Cultural Revolution, it was hard to assess the effect this virtual disappearance of traditional practices from the public sphere and the Party's relentless ideological indoctrination had on beliefs and cosmological understanding in Bustling Township. People's memories were shaped by their individual experiences both during and after this tumultuous period. Families with bad class labels or who had other reasons for wanting to present a "progressive" outlook were much more cautious about being associated with traditional practices. It was, for example, no coincidence that all the texts of the *anji* of the prominent Besé house—Nima Anji's house—were burned. Several people said that Mao had been really good for the minorities, but the Red Guards had made a mess of it. As an outsider, I had a difficult time trying to make people remember what they had believed and practiced at that time, but it was even more difficult to draw general conclusions in view of the many conflicting views expressed. Some of the elderly people were very clear that most of the practices related to evil spirits, ancestral spirits, and the deities had ended. When, in 1999, I asked sixty-nine-year-old Shenggi from Uphill whether his family had invited the local *yèma* to conduct ceremonies in the house to exorcise *shep'a*, he shook his head vigorously and exclaimed: "Aphuuuuu [No way]! During the Cultural Revolution, this was out of the question! At that time, we did not believe! Nobody dared! There was no reciting, no *za^{n}bala*, no food offerings on the offering stone, nothing!"

Sixty-one-year-old Rinchin of Downhill also recalled that they did make food offerings to the ancestors during that time, but when they became ill, they did not dare ask the *yèma* to recite and instead went to the local state health station that had been established next to the township government building. Others, mainly in more remote Walnut Grove, insisted that they not only continued to practice—albeit discreetly—throughout the whole Cultural Revolution but even found a few *anji* willing to conduct rituals. As K'enbuzo, who built his house in 1970, tells in chapter 3, when people were sick they secretly visited the *anji* to find out whether they had to go and see a doctor at the health station or have a ritual conducted. Rituals had to be simple, though, and for the most part people did not dare to slaughter animals. Moreover, when people died, their families were unable to slaughter cows or yaks as had been the custom, because these animals were collectively owned. And none of the *anji* dared teach his knowledge for fear of being accused of spreading counterrevolutionary ideas.

On more than one occasion, villagers also said that they firmly believed at the time that Mao and the Communist Party would protect them from bad harvests and diseases. At the end of the 1950s, a government building was raised in Uphill along with a state shop and health station. Once in a while, occasional work teams arrived, admonishing the villagers to adapt their traditional way of life, be it cultivation techniques, hygiene, or marriage customs. Later, Red Guards from bigger towns such as Xichang visited, mobilizing local youths to attack the traditional *anji* ritual system and the beliefs associated with it. Even local dress and hairstyle had to be abandoned as a sign of total devotion to Mao and his teachings. It is tempting to think that Mao, and in particular the more ritualistic aspects of the Mao cult, somehow *replaced* traditional Premi religious practices and beliefs. Nevertheless, people in Bustling Township assessed their beliefs during the period from the late 1950s to the late 1970s in too many different ways to allow definitive conclusions on the depth of the impact Mao and Maoism had on local beliefs or even whether they actually had an effect. The relative speed and intensity of the post-Maoist revival of traditional practices at least suggests that the underlying beliefs and cosmological understandings these practices served never really disappeared. Intense ideological indoctrination surely influenced these understandings, at least temporarily, and in many cases caused considerable confusion. It might be safer to propose that Mao, as a mythical figure, managed to forcefully claim a space in local cosmology rather than to conclude that his ideology destroyed and replaced it. As such, the imprint of Mao and Maoism is similar in nature to that of the Buddha and Tibetan Buddhism: certain aspects of Tibetan Buddhism—such as ritual implements and iconographic elements—found their way into the local religion and did not in any way replace it. Today, the most visible trace of Maoism is the picture of the Chairman found in many houses throughout Bustling Township, next to the za^nbala, a representation of the Tibetan Buddhist god of wealth.

Ironically, most za^nbala and offering stones were destroyed in the heyday of Maoism. One of the most zealous destroyers of za^nbala in Walnut Grove was a young man from one of the families said to be possessed with *brö* demons. For these families, the new ideology presented a welcome opportunity to improve their social and, consequently, economic situations. They became convinced that they could benefit from the destruction of local beliefs and "old" practices, and this young man joined the most radical Red Guard group in Muli. One cannot simply eradicate the spirits and deities by destroying their representations, however, and, as Yaoji Galo^n, a forty-three-year-old *anji* from Walnut Grove, put it in 2001, "If one goes against the deities and offends them, one will have to face the consequences!" That was the most common explanation for why, at the end of the Cultural Revolution, the young man became mentally disturbed. Traditional perceptions of the functioning of the natural world regained the upper hand, and "possessed" families were again ostracized in their local community and clearly poorer than the rest of the village.

Indeed, the Communists' attempt to eradicate "feudal superstition" proved unsuccessful, and after having survived centuries of Buddhist hegemony, *anji* beliefs and practices proved too deep-rooted and adaptable to be demolished by this ideological storm. Furthermore, during the de-collectivization period of the late 1970s and early 1980s, the single house assumed responsibility for livelihood and prosperity while the supporting collective of the Maoist state gradually disappeared: marked mechanisms replaced work points, bad harvests condemned the entire village to poverty, and a sick family member ruined a house. With the local health station crumbling and services and medicines no longer free, *anji* remedies became attractive again, and their use no longer involved any risk. Moreover, *anji* ceremonies provided potential remedies for other adversities threatening the subsistence farmers of Bustling Township, such as hail storms and floods.

The process of recovering traditional practices was nevertheless slow in the first years of the Reform Period. Although Yaoji Galo^n and his brother were the descendants of a famous *anji* line, their father had not dared to teach them anything during the entire Cultural Revolution. It was only after two of their uncles dug out their hidden texts and ritual instruments and started to perform small-scale rituals in the early 1980s that the brothers managed to convince their reluctant father to start teaching them. But it was especially Nima Anji from the Besé house, the descendant of a long *anji* line, who became instrumental in making Walnut Grove the major center of *anji* practice in the post-Mao period. A central element of *anji* practice is combating disease, so the local people saw Nima's education as a basic health worker as an extra asset: it was a combination that provided the broadest possible competence in treating their ailments. Rather than being viewed as two competing knowledge systems, *anji* practices and modern medicine became conceptualized as part of the same system. This view was also shared in other villages of Bustling Township. In Uphill, which is outside Nima's main field of operation, I asked all households this question: The last time somebody in the family was sick, did you invite the health worker in the village, the *yèma* (also from the village), or the *anji* from Hill Village (a neighboring village)? There were no clear winners here, and, as mentioned earlier, people often invited all three experts, again, without a clear preference as to whom they would ask first. The financial situation of a house or its relatedness to an expert was the only clear variable that could be positively linked to choice.

The Besé house to which Nima Anji belonged was not only the house of a long *anji* line but also one that had played an important role in the village before the Communist takeover. Available information suggests that the position of the Besé as village leaders under the *tusi* system was vested in their moral prestige. The reestablishment of *anji* practice could certainly be conceived as a means for Nima Anji to reclaim or reassert a leading moral role for himself and his house. Several studies of religious revival in China have pointed specifically to the central role in religious revival of local leaders who wield authority because of their moral strength (Chau 2005; Jun Jing 1996). Rebuilding temples or reestablishing traditional practices gives people with traditional knowledge an opportunity to "reclaim the roles as moral leaders denied to them in the previous era." According to Chau these are often older men "interested in reviving or maintaining traditional values in what they perceive as a society in moral decline" (2005: 250). It was very obvious that Nima Anji's new position of moral authority was related to his endeavor of reviving *anji* practice, but it was difficult to tell the extent to which his efforts had been motivated by the quest for such a position. He did not seem to have personal ambitions other than to work continuously at spreading the *anji* tradition. Other factors contributing to his success were surely related to his personal qualities: he combined a humble and friendly personality with a clear intellect that he used to study everything he could about traditional practices. As one of the few *anji*, he was also capable of understanding a substantial part of the Tibetan-language texts used in *anji* rituals. Gradually, his reputation not only reached Premi villages at a considerable distance from Walnut Grove but traveled as far as the neighboring province of Yunnan, where in 2000 he became a teacher of ritual practice in a veritable *anji* school (see chapter 5).

When the revival became successful beyond the local villages of Bustling Township, *anji* religion also became an element in larger discourses on Premi religion and ethnic identity. Its relation to another important religion in the region, Tibetan Buddhism, became a prominent issue that greatly engaged local elites, whether they were monks at the local Gelugpa monastery or Premi teachers and government cadres. Like the *anji* ritual system, Buddhism had also fallen victim to the radical policies of the

Democratic Reforms and the Cultural Revolution. However, in contrast to *anji* practice in Bustling Township, it would be an exaggeration to speak of a revival of Buddhism in Muli in the late 1990s and early 2000s.

MULI GOMPA: RELIGION AND POWER RELATIONS IN POST–CULTURAL REVOLUTION TIMES

Perched on a forested mountain slope high above the narrow gorge of the Muli River lies the monastery of Muli; its full name is Ganden Shedrub Namgyel Ling, but it is usually called Muli Gompa. Farther down the slope, about forty minutes' walk distant, lies the small town of Wachang, the administrative center of the first of the three districts, or *qu*, into which Muli County is divided. The long circular white wall that sets the area apart from the surrounding forest and fields is a reminder of the monastery's former grandeur. Inside the wall, at the southern end, is the *tshokhang*, or main assembly hall, which today consists of a three-story Tibetan-style building covered in glazed yellow tiles; there is a small courtyard in front of it, and it is flanked by a row of prayer wheels. The rest of the compound consists of a few smaller buildings scattered across a chaotic landscape of vegetable gardens, overgrown spaces, and the ruins of numerous constructions large and small. On the northern end is a small scripture hall, one of the few buildings that was not destroyed during the Cultural Revolution. Some of the walls of the former main hall are still standing, together with a tower several stories high, giving some idea of the size of the giant bronze Maitreya Buddha statue it once housed. The statue was built in 1711 and was 27.5 meters high. The only piece left is a loaf-size fragment of one of the Buddha's fingers, now on display in a glass box in the rebuilt main hall.

Construction of the monastery began in 1656, and its outline was modeled on Drepung Monastery in Lhasa (see *Muli chöchung* 1993). All the major halls were constructed in the thirty years that followed, but new buildings were added continuously, until the monastery reached its maximum size in the mid-nineteenth century. At that time, the monastery counted more than one thousand monks living in more than three hundred *khang*, or abodes for monks (*Muli Zangzu zizhixian zhi* 1995). From the beginning of the twentieth century, the number of monks began

FIG. 4.7. Muli Gompa. The new main building and the ruins of the old one.

to decline, and in 1919, two outbreaks of plague decimated the monk population. Around the time of the Communist takeover, the number was probably around six hundred.[14] Muli Gompa continued to be active in the 1950s, but during the Democratic Reforms campaign of 1956, the Communists abolished the rule that every third and fourth brother had to enter the monastery. In July 1959, during the Four Antis movement (anti-uprising, anti-lawbreaking, anti-privileges, and anti-oppression), all the monasteries in Muli were closed down, and most monks were sent back to their villages of origin, with only a few staying on as caretakers. In subsequent years, a small proportion of the monks continued to visit the monastery regularly to participate in religious celebrations, but like all monks, they were forced to reside at home and participate in agricultural labor. At the start of the Cultural Revolution, in 1966, all monasteries in the county were razed, and most religious items such as texts, statues, and *thangka*, or religious paintings, were destroyed. Muli Gompa did not escape the destruction, and even large parts of its surrounding wall were torn down. The small scripture hall was the only hall that survived. Reconstruction began here in 1982, when the county government allowed its restoration and contributed ¥40,000. The following year, Muli Gompa began to admit monks again. Between 1989 and 1991, the *tshokhang* was rebuilt, funded by a major commitment of ¥446,000 from the Sichuan provincial government (*Muli Zangzu zizhixian zhi* 1995). However, the present temple is considerably smaller than the original. No major halls were rebuilt after 1991, and between 1999 and 2004, only a few new dwellings were built for the monks and some repairs were made to the wall.

In 1999, forty-one monks were residing at Muli Gompa.[15] Almost all of them came from the First District, and half were from the township of Shuiluo, one of its seven townships. The three districts of Muli correspond to the three subdivisions of the pre-Communist monastic domain, which were administered by a large monastery. Muli Gompa administered the area of what is now the First District. This area includes five smaller monasteries subordinate to Muli Gompa. Three of those have only a few resident monks, one in Shuiluo counts fifty nonresident monks, and Renjiang Monastery, in the township of Wujiao, has more than fifty resident monks. In addition to these five, two monasteries outside Muli are also subordinate to Muli Gompa: Zhamei Monastery in Yongning, Yunnan, and Qiansuo Monastery, in neighboring Yanyuan County. In 1999, the official tally of monks in the three major and ten lesser monasteries of Muli County was 253.[16]

Roughly one-fourth of the monks in Muli Gompa belonged to the pre–Cultural Revolution generation, and in 1999, they were all over sixty years of age. The remaining monks were considerably younger, with some novices as young as twelve. Chinese legislation on education and religious practice prohibits organized religious teaching for children under the age of eighteen. But as with some other ethnic minority regions with a tradition of recruiting monks at a very young age—such as the Theravada novices among the Dai in Sipsong Panna—local authorities display a certain degree of laissez-faire (see, e.g., Hansen 1999). In order to comply with the law on education, children were supposed to have finished elementary school before being allowed into the monastery. The local authorities also demanded that monasteries provide children with a general education along with their religious training.[17] The younger monks in Muli Gompa therefore received regular visits from a Han teacher living in Wachang. He went to the monastery two or three times a week and conducted courses in subjects such as Chinese, English, and mathematics. Nevertheless, most of the time at the monastery is spent on reciting sutras, and consequently literacy is limited mainly to the ability to pronounce Tibetan texts with not much understanding of the content. A fifteen-year-old monk who had been in Muli Gompa since he was twelve admitted in an interview that he still had not reached a level of Tibetan or Chinese that made it possible for him to read or write in either language.

Since it is an aspect of the five recognized religions in China,[18] the practice of Buddhism is guaranteed in principle by Article 36 of the PRC constitution, which stipulates that citizens have the right to participate in "normal religious practice" (*zhengchang de zongjiao huodong*). This vague formulation has been repeatedly amended and made more specific through various documents issued by the Chinese Communist Party and the State Council. CCP Document 19 of 1982 states, for example, that CCP members are forbidden to profess any religion and that the CCP must promote atheism (see, e.g., Potter 2003: 320). The strict limitations that apply to religious practice became increasingly visible during the 1980s and 1990s through a series of State Council documents.[19] Nonetheless, these and other official publications simultaneously convey the message that the Chinese government and the Party do not intend to suppress religious practice altogether as long as they are able to control such practice.[20] Other legislation also mentions religious practice. Article 147 of the revised Civil Code mandates punishment for state officials who unlawfully deprive citizens of their freedom of religious belief and infringe upon the customs and habits of national minorities.

In 1994, the State Council issued Regulations on Managing Places for Religious Activities. This was an attempt at collecting and standardizing regulations, official documents, and laws pertaining to religious practice. A revised and more comprehensive version was issued in 2005, Regulations on Religious Affairs (Zongjiao Shiwu Tiaoli). While these regulations do not contain many significant new elements, they make it more difficult for local officials to act arbitrarily in regulating religion.[21]

Two types of bodies constitute the main instruments for the administration of religions. First, the State Administration of Religious Affairs (Guojia Zongjiao Shiwuju) is responsible for implementing and supervising policy relevant to religion. This bureau exists at all levels of the state administration, down to the county level, and its employees are cadres of the administrative system. At the local level, this bureau also administers ethnic affairs and is in that case known as the Ethnic and Religious Affairs Bureau (Minzu Zongjiao Shiwuju). Tasks include everything from registering religious activities, sites, and clerics, to propagating new policies, supervising patriotic education campaigns at religious sites, and administering the number of monks at monasteries. Second, each of the five recognized religions is represented by an organ that is responsible for administering that religion's so-called internal affairs. Such affairs might be related to religious education, organization of religious festivals, publication of religious texts, management of religious sites, service as a host organization for visitors from abroad, and the like. Its members are often clerics and lay believers. For Buddhism, for example, this function is performed by the Buddhist Association (Fojiao Xiehui). In addition to accepting this double system of administration and control, religious institutions have been forced by the Chinese government to establish their own administrative body: the Democratic Management Committee (Minzhu Guanli Weiyuanhui). In Tibetan Buddhist monasteries, the committee is composed of monk-representatives who are elected by all the monks of the monastery. In many monasteries since the late 1990s, the committees have been extended to include nonreligious government-employed bureaucrats. The committee is responsible for administering the day-to-day affairs of the monastery, implementing government policies, and reporting and informing the government about issues and events at the monastery.[22]

As mentioned, one of the religious administration's most important tasks is to set quotas for the number of monks at each monastery. It does this through a fixed procedure, characterized by Wang Yangzhong, the head of Muli County's Religious Affairs Bureau, as "reporting upward, approving downward" (*shang bao, xia bi*). After consulting with the Democratic Management Committee at the monastery, the county government sends a recommendation to the prefectural government. The prefectural government then adds its own comments and forwards the application to the provincial government. Only after the provincial-level religious authorities approve the recommendation is the number of monks at a certain location determined. In 1999, the number of forty-one monks at Muli Gompa was well below the quota of fifty. A discrepancy in this direction is rare in Tibetan areas in China and might suggest that the quota was set unrealistically high.[23] Furthermore, the county bureau is required to approve and recommend all reopenings and reconstructions of monasteries that were closed and destroyed during the Cultural Revolution. Recommendations to higher administrative levels are also important in that they may result in the monastery receiving a share of the subsidies for reconstruction of cultural and religious sites available at the provincial level.

An interesting case of how the Chinese government has meddled in Buddhist affairs is the modern institution of the *tulku*, or incarnate lama (known as a "living Buddha" in Chinese). The Chinese secular state has accepted the existence of an institution based, in the case of the Muli Guzyo Pema Rinchin, on the presumption that a person is the embodiment of Mañjuśrī and a reincarnation of one of Sakyamuni's disciples. Rather than trying to abolish a system that leaves the power to appoint religious leaders outside its domain, the Chinese state chose to exercise its control in other ways.[24] Admittedly, the Religious Affairs Bureau does not directly interfere in the process of finding a new reincarnation of the *tulku*. Government cadres do not go out and select a child, but the bureau has to endorse each step of the process that leads to the choice. The search for the tenth reincarnation of the Muli *tulku* is a case in point. In 1973, the ninth *tulku* passed away, but due to the political climate at the time and the resulting uncertainties about the status of living Buddhas, efforts to identify a new incarnation were not made until 1992. In that year, the Communist Party of Muli, several government institutions, and the Chinese People's Political Consultative Conference—which in Muli includes several higher monks and some members of the old elite—invited the vice chairman of the Sichuan Buddhist Association, a *tulku* himself, to come to Muli and organize the search for the tenth Muli *tulku* (*Muli Zangzu zizhixian zhi* 1995: 111–12, 906). In order to leave no doubt about the role of the government and Party, an official document was issued publicizing the decision. Each step of the process followed the same procedure, such as selecting the members of the search party or compiling a short list of possible candidates. Official documents were issued at the prefectural level as well. The stamp of official government approval could be observed in many other aspects of the process, from small details such as announcing government sponsorship of expenses monks incurred during the search process to the government and Party cadres being highly visible at the inauguration ceremony. As many as five thousand religious, government, and Party personalities—including representatives from the prefectural level—were reported to have attended the ceremony at which Guzyo Pema Rinchin was issued an official "living Buddha certificate" (*huofo zhengshu*) and thereby officially endorsed as the tenth Muli *tulku* (ibid.: 112).

But government control extends significantly further: in view of their important role in Tibetan communities, *tulku* receive a fully sponsored, mandatory education of two years at the Chinese Higher Institute of Tibetan Buddhism (Zhongguo Zangyuxi Gaoji Foxueyuan) in the Huang Temple in Beijing. The government set up this institute in 1987 in response to a petition from, among others, the tenth Panchen Lama, who also became its first director. According to vice director Li Guoqin (pers. com., June 2004), its main purpose is to provide *tulku* and other high-ranking lamas from the Tibetan Buddhist tradition with high-level Buddhist studies as well as an understanding of Chinese government policies on religion and basic laws.[25] The hope is that these religious figures from Tibetan and Mongolian areas of China will come to identify more closely with the Chinese state through staying in the capital and learning the Chinese language. This hope may be realized, once these people from mountainous, often remote areas get over their initial culture shock. Guzyo Pema Rinchin said in an interview that it had been hard to adapt to life in a big city when he left Muli to study at the institute in Beijing in 1999.

As a result of this close administration of Buddhism in Muli, the leading monks and the government and Party cadres have to work together closely. They often hold meetings together, participate in the same events, and travel together. During my first visit to Muli Gompa in 1999, during a *ch'am* festival, I was struck by the cordial interactions between the monks of the Muli Gompa Democratic Management Committee and the people from the county Religious Affairs Bureau. The level of agreement on most of the issues discussed during an interview with both parties present was also striking. While I had expected leading monks to display total support of government policies on religion, I was surprised by their unrestrained enthusiasm for these policies. For their part, the government cadres expressed a clearly positive attitude toward Buddhism. Not only did they show obvious respect for the monks, but several of them also participated in religious activities such as lighting butter lamps, making offerings, and prostrating themselves in front of the statue of the Buddha. They were very keen to present the monastery and its festival as an example of well-managed religious policy. At the same time, they were somewhat unhappy that the quota for monks had not yet been filled and were obviously hoping that more men would want to become monks.[26] They proudly pointed out that the monastery had the only officially recognized living Buddha in the county. When I mentioned that there was a "female living Buddha" (C: *nü huofo*) in Bustling Township, one of the leading monks (and member of the Democratic Management Committee) reacted very strongly: "There is only one living Buddha in Muli! We know these so-called living Buddhas in the villages. Just because this or that person is perceived to be a good person [*shi ge hao ren*], the villagers have no right to declare him [or her] a living Buddha!" In addition, the monks frowned on much of the practice of the *yèma*, or Buddhist lay priests, called *anch'ui* by the monks, which they deemed to be an aberration of Buddhism. Obviously, the Chinese state and the Gelug monastic system in Muli have a mutual interest in controlling religious practice. The alliance of institutionalized religion with the Party-state is not new or limited to this corner of China. As has been shown in relation to organized Buddhism elsewhere in China, there was a clear consensus between the leading monks and the bureaucrats of Muli government on issues such as the Buddhist-inspired Falungong religious movement or the several millenarian cults that reached Muli from other parts of the country. Organized Buddhism saw practices and beliefs inspired by but deviating from Buddhist teaching as both a threat to orthodoxy and a form of religious competition (Penny 2005: 39). They found a natural ally in the State Administration of Religious Affairs, which implemented policies grounded in the Communist Party's fear that uncontrollable and seemingly murky cults were a genuine threat to its power.

How then did the monastery attend to the religious and spiritual needs of the villagers? In general, it was acknowledged, there was not much contact between the monastery and the villagers. Monks were allowed to leave the monastery for three days—exclusive of the time spent traveling—to conduct cremation ceremonies in the villages, but this happened only infrequently. In contrast to practices in other regions such as Yongning, where the monks of the Gelug monastery live at home and go to the monastery only for major religious celebrations, the monks of Muli Gompa live very separate lives from the villagers. The advantage, according to the leading monks and government cadres, was that monks could concentrate on learning and maintain a strict practice. It also meant, however, that they did not interfere with village-level practice and that, as a result, "heresy" could flourish. This does not mean that Buddhism in Muli had entirely dropped the concept of compassion for the suffering of living beings, or, to put it more mundanely, a sense of social obligation. After remarking that people in Muli were too poor and should not have to pay for medical expenses and schooling, Guzyo Pema Rinchin also explained what he sees as a potential role for Buddhism in an increasingly materialistic society: it can teach people to be content with what they have. In other words, once basic needs are met, they will not always want more. As he put it: "You leave this life with no more than what you had when you were born!"

In practice, villagers had no other way to get in touch with established Buddhism than to visit the monastery. And indeed, on each of my visits to the monastery, I met a few people from Bustling Township who had come to be blessed by the monks or, preferably, the *guzyo*, burn incense, circumambulate the main hall, and turn the prayer wheels. Sometimes a small group of villagers would come to the monastery to acquire a large amount of red thread or cloth, blessed by the *guzyo*, which they would take back to their fellow villagers for use in making *sungdü*, the luck-bringing charms bound around the neck or wrist. On one occasion, a private driver had the monks perform a ceremony to bless his newly acquired Beijing Jeep. Most people, however, visited the monastery only during one of the major festivals, such as the *ch'am*. Such celebrations, in which monks danced in colorful costumes, enacting in a very visual way the victory of Buddhism over demons and evil spirits, attracted crowds of people and was one of the very few occasions when the monastery could establish its spiritual authority in the larger community.

Direct ties between the villagers from Bustling Township and Muli Gompa were limited. As shown in table 4.1, in 1999 there were only seven people from Premi villages in Bustling Township at Muli Gompa. This figure had risen to eight in 2004 but cannot be interpreted as a trend. In addition to these seven young men and boys who had entered the monastery in recent times, there was one old Rek'ua monk from the village of Gaku who had been a monk before the monastery closed in 1960. Four of the seven monks were from the northern villages, two from the central part (Uphill and Downhill), and only one from one of the southern

Premi villages (Walnut Grove). This was the son of a retired district cadre who had spent most of his life in the district-town of Wachang, near Muli Gompa. The people of Bustling Township who visit the monastery go only to see their relatives, to participate in religious festivals, or to perform other religious activities. They are also mainly from the northern villages, or from Uphill and Downhill; in these villages, most houses had at least one member who had visited Muli Gompa. The situation was different in the southern villages such as Walnut Grove and Five Nut Trees, where significantly fewer people had been to the monastery, yet when villagers were asked about the difference between what the *anji* does, what the *yèma* does, and what the monks in Muli Gompa do, the question seemed to be not entirely meaningful. Although it would be possible to suggest—as some villagers do—that the northern villages were Buddhists and the rest of Bustling Township were *anji* practitioners, in day-to-day life, matters are more complicated. What should one make of an *anji* in Walnut Grove who discovers a living deity who consequently immerses herself in Buddhist studies, and of an *anji* in North Village who sends his son to become a monk at Muli Gompa? How should the relationship between Buddhism and *anji* religious practice be interpreted?

BUDDHISM AND *ANJI*: TWO CONTENDING RELIGIONS?

When posing the question of how the two seemingly disparate traditions of Buddhism and *anji* religious practice relate to each other, it is necessary to bear in mind that these categories mean different things to different people. Not only is the boundary between the two vague and contested, but for some actors in Muli, the binary nature of religious beliefs or practice is nonexistent or irrelevant. It is the foreign researcher who formulates the question of the possible coexistence of two different religious traditions and presupposes a duality that is not necessarily experienced by all members of the community. At the same time, contradictions and dualities also exist *within* the large category of Tibetan Buddhism itself, as evidenced in the coexistence of different traditions, schools, and lineages involving many differences in teaching, interpretation, and practice. And even within one local tradition of Tibetan Buddhism, certain ritual practices may also be the subject of controversy and antagonism.[27] Neverthe-

174   4 ∾ *Premi Cosmology*

FIG. 4.8. Procession around Muli Gompa during the annual *ch'am* festival.

less, asking questions about the distinction between the two categories proved a very fruitful analytical strategy. The different answers provided different coexisting perspectives from which to view religious practice in Bustling Township or Muli. These perspectives were not static attitudes held by social actors; rather, they could change through time as a result of interaction between the different actors or, for example, as a result of social mobility, thereby providing an understanding of the dynamics of religious practice—or praxis—in Muli.

From the historian's point of view, the presence of two different religious traditions in the villages may be reduced to a historical accident: this is the simplest answer—and also the least thought-provoking—and is related to the local effects of the larger political events of the early PRC period. With the closure of the monasteries in 1959, many Premi villages counted one or more people, in addition to the *anji*, who had acquired ritual expertise in Gelug Buddhist monasteries. These monks and novices often married and became integrated again into their home villages. The degree to which they had been imbued with Buddhist concepts varied greatly, depending on the number of years they had spent in the monasteries. After their return, they continued to be called *yèma*, the Premi designation for monks and novices. Some had been very young, such as the brother of Anna Yèma, who became the practicing *yèma* in Uphill. He had entered Muli Gompa at eight and returned to the village when he was ten. Unlike his brother, who had spent twelve years at the monastery, he was no longer able to read or write Tibetan. When religious practice was again officially tolerated at the beginning of the 1980s, many of the older, more knowledgeable monks had died, taking with them the main source of Buddhist influence in the villages. In some cases, Buddhism was literally burned along with the deceased *yèma*, as in the case of Duji P'intsu from Five Nut Trees:

> His [the informant's] father, Duji P'intsu, was also a *yèma*. He came back in 1959 when Muli Gompa was closed. He had to go to the monastery because he was the middle of the three brothers in his family. His monastic name was Jia^{n}yo^n. After he came back, he married [polyandrously] the wife of his brother. When he died in 1992, he had only a few books left [which had survived the Cultural Revolution].... He was only a low *yèma*, looking after the horses, and therefore he was not criticized. After the Reform and Opening Up [Gaige Kaifang] policies of the 1980s, he wrote a few things about Buddhism, but since his family had no use for his books and writings, they were burned with him at his cremation. After his death, they invited an *anji* when people were sick and when performing the rituals at the New Year.

The case of Duji P'intsu is also instructive on another point. After 1983, when religious and ritual practice were again permitted, there was a real lack of ritual experts. Many old *anji* had died, and none had dared to teach the tradition to the younger generation. The few who were left started the tough task of educating a whole new generation of *anji*. But many years would be required before these young pupils would be able to conduct all the necessary ceremonies. In the meantime, villagers turned to the few surviving *yèma* living in their midst, hoping to use their knowledge of reciting scriptures to help in propitiating the deities, to combat the evil spirits, and to perform the necessary ceremonies for taking proper care of *me-drö*, or the souls of the deceased. Not all of these practices were acceptable to orthodox Gelug monks, but since the surviving *yèma* had spent only short periods of time in the monasteries, they may have become localized again in their thinking and readjusted easily to the cosmological beliefs of their fellow villagers. Moreover, these *yèma* were most likely to have broken their vows of celibacy and were therefore not allowed to reenter the monastery. They accepted the role the villagers wanted them to play and took pride in being able to use their knowledge of scriptures. In some villages, such as Spring Rain and Uphill and Downhill, the old *yèma* were the only ritual experts.

However, such a historical explanation is not entirely satisfactory. It says very little about the relationship between *anji* and *yèma* practices and local cosmology. How was it possible for these *yèma* to re-localize so easily?

Distinguishing different coexisting traditions in local religious practice is not limited to empirical observations in Muli. How different traditions meet and become syncretized or combined, or how one religious system replaces another constitute some of the central debates in the historical and anthropological study of religion.[28] The encounter between a large organized religious system and traditional local beliefs and practices has been conceived as a recurring historical process observed in many other parts of the world, where the more rationalized religious system slowly replaces what Geertz has called "the 'little' religion of clan, tribe, village or folk" (1973: 172). In his study of Balinese religion—a complex amalgamation of Hinduism and pre-Hindu elements—Geertz draws on the work of Max Weber. In his *The Sociology of Religion*, Weber distinguished between two idealized polar types of religions in world history: the "traditional" and the "rationalized." Traditional religious concepts relate all aspects of human activity to the "circle of symbolic magic." They are an unorganized collection of rituals and animistic images that meets "the perennial concerns of religion, what Weber called the 'problems of meaning'—evil, suffering, frustration, bafflement, and so on—piecemeal" (Weber 1964, in Geertz 1973: 172). Rationalized religious concepts deal to a much lesser extent with details of everyday life. They are more abstract, more logically coherent, and phrased more generally. They address the "universal and inherent qualities of human existence." Throughout history, Weber discerns a process of rationalization in which the more amorphous traditional religions slowly develop into or give way to world religions characterized by "a greater conceptual generalization, tighter formal integration, and a more explicit sense of doctrine" (Geertz 1973: 172).

The people who are most likely to subscribe to this perspective on religious practice in Muli are the members of what could be termed the local elites among those classified as Tibetans, or Zangzu (and, to a lesser extent, among those classified as Mongolians and Naxi, the Mengguzu and the Naxizu). They are the leading monks and abbots, the local intellectuals such as the teachers at the township school, the government cadres, and even the Party bureaucrats in the county-town. Minority elites and their hegemonic role in defining issues related to ethnic minority culture have been discussed in studies on other places in China as well. In his study, Litzinger defines Yao elites as follows:

> I use the term elite to refer to minority intellectuals, scholars, government officials, Communist Party cadres, and local tour guides, all of whom claimed to be in a position to know and speak for the Yao. These individuals came from a range of social and class backgrounds and occupied differential positions of authority and influence in minority studies. (2000: 21)

Using the term "elites" makes it possible, in the case of Muli, to understand that there are different views as to what constitutes religious practice among the people classified as Tibetans.

> The term elite, therefore, allows us to avoid a totalizing or homogenizing view of minority consciousness, as though all Yao think and behave in the same way. It allows us to ask how different social actors have critically engaged, negotiated, and even authorized the various discourses of historical progress, modernity, tradition, and political emancipation that have been at the centre of Chinese socialist and postsocialist national imagining. (ibid.: 21)

According to the Zangzu elites, the practices of the traditional ritualists and the content of local beliefs are just poorly understood corruptions of Buddhism created by ignorant villagers. Describing these practices, government cadres used the Chinese term *mixin*, "superstition" (the literal translation, "confused beliefs," is even more evocative). Buddhists and Communists have reached a remarkable entente cordiale in Muli. State and religion have a long history of being closely linked in Muli, and it was precisely through their close association with the Tibetan monastic system that the local elite legitimated its hold on worldly power. Several members of this elite were co-opted by the Communists, and even in recent years, some members of the government maintain close ties to this former elite. They take pride in Muli's past glory as a "Lama Kingdom" and have a certain sympathy for organized Buddhism.

Furthermore, the relationship between the state and Buddhism changed dramatically after the demise of the monastic system in the late 1950s. The revived Buddhism of the post-Mao reform period was stripped of its political role. It could not force every third son to enter the monastery, and it reemerged in the 1980s at a very slow pace. In consequence, Buddhism in Muli did not present any real challenge to the power of the state and the Party, and with its transparent organizational structure and rationalized religious doctrines, clerical Buddhism proved easy to control. At the same time, the recovering monastic elite was clearly aware of the need for state support in reviving Buddhism in Muli. Although its members could not reclaim a *political* role for Buddhism, they could claim a *cultural* role by allying themselves with the state. The conception of Muli as a primarily Buddhist region was legitimated and supported through the Party's creation of a Tibetan autonomous county, where Buddhism and Tibetan ethnicity were equated most naturally.

This official discourse has not found much resonance in the Premi villages, but it has been easily absorbed by local intellectuals through sources such as the school system, an important cornerstone of the elite's ideological hegemony. Litzinger, inspired by the work of Gramsci, defines such an ideological hegemony in the Chinese context as referring "to the capacity of dominant classes with their affiliated elite to get the general population to internalize the values and ideas of the ruling class. The masses would then become the very agents for the reproduction of a social system. A ruling elite draws on the state, its laws and procedures, as well as the educational systems and the mass media to mould both participation and consent" (2000: 17).

Many of the educated Premi in Muli expressed a strong interest in Buddhism, and several stated that they were practicing Buddhists. Buddhism in Muli as such has become a modernized religion, with people becoming Buddhists not because they are born into it but because they are persuaded through acquired knowledge. Although awareness of being classified as Tibetans certainly strengthens interest in Buddhism, a person still has to make a conscious choice in order to become a believer.

Moreover, the elites look down on the seemingly unstructured religious practices in the villages and dismiss them as irrational. From the perspective of the state, the existence of unorganized religion in the villages becomes a nuisance not only because it is very hard to control but also because its very existence implicitly questions the official discourse. It is interesting to note that the *Annals of Muli Tibetan Autonomous County*—the polished official version of Muli's history and current conditions—dedicates only four sentences to *anji/hangui* while providing a twenty-page exposé of Buddhism (*Muli Zangzu zizhixian zhi* 1995: 908). The local elites have no doubt that, after the setbacks of the Cultural Revolution and its slow return during the 1980s, the rationalized religion of Buddhism will gradually replace the hazy beliefs of the villagers and the heretical practices of *anji*. But until they disappear, these practices—with their frequent offerings of animals, their female living deities, and their ancestral spirits—continue to provide the monks of Muli Gompa with a vilified Other, with Buddhism presenting in comparison a more civilized alternative.

It remains to be seen whether Buddhism will displace *anji* practice in the long term. In the meantime, at the turn of the millennium, the number of *anji* ritual specialists in Bustling Township continues to increase, while the number of monks in Muli Gompa who come from Bustling Township remains stable. This might suggest that the deterministic vision of the elites does not represent the entire story. But does the duality of religious practice matter in the villages? How is it conceived? Nima Anji, the most knowledgeable *anji* of Bustling Township, tells the following story about the relationship between Buddhism and *anji* religion:

> When Buddhism entered Tibet, it met with tough resistance from the traditional *anji* religion, and a battle erupted between the followers of the

two religions. The *anji* religion won the struggle, and in despair the followers of Buddhism asked Herba Rimpoche, a deity, for help. He was able to unite both sides because he also had a high position in the *anji* religion. He asked the followers of the *anji* religion to make a concession and let Buddhism enter Tibet. Herba Rimpoche also demanded that the adherents of the *anji* religion stop making blood offerings. After this arbitration, the two religions coexisted peacefully for some time, but after some lifetimes, the followers of the *anji* religion started to kill and make offerings of animals again. They therefore lost many followers, and Buddhism gained strength. This is the reason Buddhism thrives and Buddhists are in a higher position today.

Versions of these archetypal stories of the battle for religious hegemony are told in Tibetan and Tibeto-Burman communities as far west as Nepal.[29] They function as an explanation for the apparent coexistence of seemingly disparate religious traditions, and all the stories center on religions that meet and compete. The basic difference between the antagonists boils down to two basic oppositions: one advocates making blood offerings, and the other opposes it, or one possesses written texts, while the other is based on orally transmitted rituals.[30] All *anji* in Bustling Township agree on the existence of two different systems of rituals, those with and those without blood offerings. But the distinction between the two systems does not necessarily coincide with *anji* understandings of the difference between Buddhism and *anji* practices. Those with a certain knowledge of Tibetan, like Nima Anji, use the word *chö* (from Tibetan *chos*, meaning the dharma, the teachings of the Buddha) for "Buddhism." An often heard Premi expression for designating Buddhism or Buddhist practice is *ch'wi-p'ö*. It refers to the practices and concepts learned at the monastery or to texts identified with the monastery. *Ch'wi-p'ö* literally means "[doing] good things." In daily language, this stands in contrast to *dedrwè-p'ö*, meaning "[doing] bad/evil things," something that is said, for example, to naughty children in the expression "Don't do bad things!" (Dedrwè-p'ö ma ha!). *Ch'wi-p'ö* might be related to the idea of cultivating good karma, but unlike this Buddhist concept, which is one of the major aims of all Buddhist practitioners, both monks and laypeople, the term *ch'wi-p'ö* is used mainly to identify practices by a special category of people: monks, Buddhist lay priests, or living deities. It is difficult to combine *ch'wi-p'ö* with a "normal" lifestyle, as Rinchin from North Village explains. Rinchin was twenty-six in 2004 and made a living by transporting people and goods in his Beijing Jeep, mostly in the district-town of Wachang. This gave him some limited opportunities to *ch'wi-p'ö*:

> Before 1991, I believed only in science, but then my father became ill and no doctor could cure him. In the course of one month, he consulted several but without any result. Then he met a *yèma* who did not much else than read some scriptures and advise him to drink boiled water. After one week, he was better! This made me change my view on religion. So now, once in a while, I also try to do good things [*ch'wi-p'ö*]: I sometimes drive people around for no money at all, especially to and from Muli Gompa.

The concept and practices of *ch'wi-p'ö* and those of the *anji* are seen as belonging to different categories, different in nature but not necessarily opposed. Eva Dargyay has characterized a very similar duality of *mi chos* (people's religion) and *lha chos* (divine or royal religion) among the Zanskar Tibetans as two complementary sides of one religion, even though the two concepts in the past defined opposing religious systems: "One is the supramundane, which corresponds to *lha chos*, where the aspiration for attaining nirvana is the focus of all religious effort; the other is the mundane level, corresponding to the *mi chos*, where the continuation of the individual family and of one's own group, here in terms of one's *rus pa*, and their well-being and prosperity are the essential values" (1988: 133).

Binary opposition is found *within* the *anji* practice, between two systems of rituals: Bompo Anji and another set variously known as Nyima Anji, Lama Anji, or Yida^n Anji. There is no consensus on the exact content of the two categories, except that the last category does not involve making blood offerings and many of the texts recited in its rituals are Buddhist texts. This category of rituals is also identified by some *anji* as the one used by the *yèma*. It therefore makes sense to say that Buddhism, in the sense of a ritual system, is also translated into Premi as Nyima Anji, Lama Anji, or Yida^n Anji. Consequently, *anji* may mean "religion" (or rather, "ritual system") and does not necessarily express a binary opposition to Buddhism.

Another perspective on the duality of religious practice is that of the

Bustling Township subsistence farmers, conceptualized in connection with this discussion as "consumers" of ritual and religious services. They depend on the performance of such rituals in order to keep their $dzè^n$, or "houses," in order and check the workings of the powers that provide their livelihood. To a certain extent, they share the views and understanding of *anji* ritualists. Time and again, when asked the difference between *yèma*, Buddhist lay priests, and *anji* or living deity, the villagers answered that there was no difference. As one of the villagers, exasperated by my slow comprehension, expressed in Chinese: "They are all in the same work unit!" (Tamen shi yige danwei de!). Both the *anji* and the *yèma* are viewed as specialists whose role was to take care of the villagers' immediate religious needs; if they want a ritual performed, they call on the specialist who is available. In Spring Rain, this would almost certainly be a *yèma*, since the closest *anji* lives several hours' walk away. In Walnut Grove, villagers would be more likely to request help from an *anji*. In other villages, people might first consult or invite one kind of ritual specialist, and if that specialist did not solve the problem, they would ask the other kind for assistance. When I insisted that this indicated an awareness of some difference between the two types of specialists, they would say that the working methods these specialists used in relating to the beings of the invisible dimension were not the same. On the one hand, an *anji*, for example, would kill a chicken and use violent means to drive the *shep'a* away. A *yèma*, on the other hand, would patiently try to convince these evil spirits to leave the house and stop bothering its inhabitants; instead of frightening and threatening them, he might try to entice them out of the house by putting some food outside the door and hoping that they would leave.

When discussing these different working methods, people in Bustling Township did not agree on which methods were most effective. Some insisted that *anji* were better at getting rid of *shep'a*, while *yèma* were slightly more effective in worshipping the deities. Nevertheless, most people in Bustling Township mentioned that *yèma*, monks, and *anji* ritualists were arranged in a certain hierarchy. The *yèma* and certainly the monks at Muli Gompa and the living deities were more highly respected and considered generally to be on a higher moral plane: they refrained from eating fresh meat, they did not demand material compensation for their services, and they did not kill. The villagers generally believed that *yèma* conducted rituals to deal with the deities, the souls of the ancestors, and the evil spirits out of a genuine wish to help them, in contrast to *anji*, who were thought more likely to be "just doing their jobs."

At the same time, those who were most respected in this way—both the older monks who lived at the monastery and the living deity—were viewed as being mainly preoccupied with reading scriptures. An underlying but rarely expressed critique was that these persons were preoccupied with their own salvation. Often a living deity would be meditating or reading (and therefore could not be disturbed), or he or she would be on pilgrimage. Add to this the moral obligation to offer a sum of money when visiting living deities, and it is clear that the threshold for obtaining their help was high. As mentioned earlier in this chapter, Tenzin Droma, the female living deity of Walnut Grove, once did not speak for sixty days. It may be the case, however, that these difficulties in obtaining the living deity's help with performing rituals created a scarcity value for their help and strengthened the sense of hierarchy. People often preferred to wait until a living deity passed through the village to have their iron tripods consecrated rather than to ask the *anji* in the village to do it.

This preference was even more obvious with regard to the naming ceremony. In Bustling Township, newborn children were supposed to be named between five and six days after birth. This is done through divination based on several pieces of information, including the time of birth, the animal sign in effect on the birth date, and the age of the mother. The child receives the name at a ceremony, which is a very important event for the family and the clan, since a fitting name will please the ancestors and bring luck to the newborn clan member. When a child does not thrive and is sick often, these problems may be ascribed to an inauspicious name. In Walnut Grove, both the different *anji* and Tenzin Droma could perform this ceremony and bestow a name. Names given by Tenzin Droma were typical Tibetan names, while those given by the *anji* were more likely to be recognizable as typical Premi names. In recent years in the village, boys tended to be named by Tenzin Droma and girls by an *anji*. Considering the higher value placed on boys in Premi society and the barriers that must be surmounted in order to consult with the living deity, this would support the conclusion that villagers distinguish between the practice of *anji* and that of other religious personages. This does not mean that the villagers conceive of this difference as representing the existence of two different religions standing in opposition to each other; rather, they view it as a difference of degree.

From the villagers' point of view, then, there are notions of difference in ritual methods, but these are not significant in relation to their cosmological beliefs, which center on worshipping ancestors and deities. Differentiation is more significant when the concept of religion is expanded to include ideas of higher morality and personal salvation. Such a differentiation of the various aspects of religion as social practice has been addressed in several studies, in particular on Theravada Buddhism. This form of Buddhism has been shown to coexist with indigenous religions, for example, in Burma. In his study of Burmese religion, Melford Spiro writes that the *nat* cult, a syncretic development of indigenous pre-Buddhist Burmese religion, coexists in uneasy tension with the official state religion of Theravada Buddhism. These two religions exist in parallel and interpenetrate at many points, in such a way that the *nat* cult is both legitimated by and subordinated to Buddhism (Spiro 1967, quoted in Lewis 1996: 129–30). David Gellner distinguishes at least seven different aspects of religion as social practice. According to Gellner, religion provides the following:

1. legitimation and expression of the household or family group
2. legitimation and expression of the locality (or village, caste, etc.)
3. legitimation and expression of the nation or ethnic group
4. sanctification of the stages of the life cycle
5. socialization of the young and a moral code
6. psychological and practical help in case of misfortune, especially illness
7. a path to salvation from all ills, that is, a soteriology

Gellner's point is that some religions, such as Christianity, claim to include all seven aspects, while others, such as Theravada Buddhism, provide only for some aspects (a soteriology and a moral code) and can therefore coexist with some other systems that satisfy the needs Buddhism does not meet (1997: 280–81).

In contrast to Theravada Buddhism, in Tibet, Mahayana Buddhism has developed into a dominant political and cultural system that lays claim to all aspects of religion as social practice. Geoffrey Samuel distinguishes three orientations *within* Buddhist practice in Tibet, each responsible for addressing different aspects of religious needs: the Pragmatic, the Karma, and the Bodhi. He relates the Pragmatic Orientation to folk religion in Tibet, interaction with local gods and spirits, and, to some extent, the pre-Buddhist religion of Tibet, which some researchers refer to as Bön.[31] The Karma Orientation, centering on rebirth, is the realm of clerical Buddhism, while the Bodhi Orientation is concerned with obtaining Enlightenment through tantric practice (1993: 31).

From the point of view of the leading monks of Muli Gompa, there is no room for non-Buddhist activities and beliefs in the villages of the officially recognized Tibetans of Muli.[32] There is only one true religion that can address all the religious needs of the people, and that is Buddhism; the rest is heresy and superstition that should disappear. Buddhism provides for most of the seven aspects, and it covers all three of the orientations Samuel distinguished within Tibetan Buddhism. The monks view the cosmological beliefs of the villagers, which center on ancestor worship and the *dzè^n*, as incompatible with the concepts of karma and reincarnation. This stands in marked contrast to the view of the villagers themselves. They do not see the practices of *anji* and those of *yèma*, monks, or living deities as contradictory. All are able to perform rituals to propitiate the ancestral spirits or the water deities, drive the disease-causing *shep'a* away, consecrate an iron tripod, give a name to a newborn, open up the road for the souls of the deceased, and so on. In the field of morality, the ancestor cult and the worship of water and mountain deities provide for a day-to-day moral code, by which people have to behave appropriately if they are to avoid the wrath of the ancestors and the deities. In the eyes of the villagers, a higher form of moral behavior—the karmic principle or "ideology of merit" (Samuel 1993)—is reserved for those who are chosen by the deities, including living deities and those monks and *yèma* who have gained a deeper understanding of such issues through their study of Buddhism or *ch'wi-p'ö*, or "doing good things."

Conceptions of what constitutes religious practice among Premi in Muli vary substantially. These variations are related to the differences in cosmological beliefs and social contexts of, on the one side, the villages, where life centers on subsistence farming and the *dzè^n* society, and, on the other, the monasteries and the more urbanized Premi living in the district- and county-towns. This is not a rigid state of affairs: young people in Bustling Township who continue their educations beyond the township school significantly change their views on religion after learning about the officially sanctioned conceptualization of Muli as a Tibetan Buddhist territory (at least in regard to the one-third of the population classified as Tibetans). Part of this official picture, which coincides with that of the monks at Muli Gompa, entails a conceptualization of village practice as opposed to Buddhism. But even when these people return to the countryside, for example, as schoolteachers, they seem to have only limited influence in altering village beliefs, in marked contrast to the educated Premi elites, who play a role in the religious revival taking place in villages in neighboring Yunnan. The analogy between the two areas is striking in what it suggests about how official state discourses influence Premi elites in their conceptualization of Premi religious practice. But, as discussed in the next chapter, these elite views have significantly different impacts in the two regions.

When the villagers of Walnut Grove today pray to and propitiate the water deities, they do so because these deities are part of their remembered and shared cosmological beliefs. Generated by their habitus, this practice is a culturally consistent strategy for addressing present-day concerns produced by the forces of modernization and the policies of the Chinese Communist Party. Habitus in this case is not a straitjacket that denies people the possibility of self-conscious, dynamic cultural literacy, as some critics have characterized Bourdieu's concept (Webb, Schirato, and Danaher 2002: 59). As Certeau points out, people (i.e., the Kabyles of Algeria) "'play with all the possibilities offered by traditions,' and make use of one tradition rather than another, compensate for one by means of another" (see Certeau 1984: 54, cited in Webb, Schirato, and Danaher 2002: 59). What is going on, then, in Walnut Grove is a "dynamic cultural process by which human activities reproduce cultural structures in strategically reshaped ways" (Bell 1997: 638, on Sherry B. Ortner). While Nima Anji's interest in traditional ritual practice was to a large extent the product of his being the heir of a long and important *anji* line, his active and creative engagement in reviving the tradition certainly confirmed the villagers' acceptance of the validity of remembered cosmology. In addition, rather than merely trying to reconstitute and take up past practices, the villagers also accepted and supported more nontraditional institutions such as the female living deity and the *soma*. Although these religious personages fitted the religious logic of local beliefs, their existence in Bustling Township was unprecedented. It is furthermore interesting to note that villagers did not choose to actively engage in monastic Gelug Buddhism, an option that would certainly have been culturally acceptable.

5 ⁓ MODERNITY IN YUNNAN

Religion and the Pumizu

While Premi elites of Muli have been engaged in an attempt to define the territory of Muli as Tibetan and, consequently, a large section of its population as Tibetans and therefore adherents of Buddhism, they have not made much impression on the Premi subsistence farmers of Bustling Township. The Premi elites in the neighboring province of Yunnan have been occupied with their own endeavor of constructing a modern ethnic identity based on religious practice, in this case, based not on Buddhism but on the so-called *hangui* religion, *hangui* being a variant pronunciation of *anji*. Although the two projects would seem on the surface to be aiming for very different goals, they are very much alike in that both are produced by state discourses on ethnic categorization, culture, and religion.

THE PUMIZU OF NINGLANG COUNTY

South of Muli, in Yunnan, lies the Yi Autonomous Nationality County of Ninglang. In spite of its name, official statistics reveal that Ninglang is also home to 9,696 Premi, or about one-third of the 32,595 Premi of Yunnan.[1] In contrast to the Premi living in Sichuan, the Premi in Yunnan have been formally recognized as a separate minority *minzu*, the Pumizu.

In Ninglang, they live primarily in the central and northern townships of Xinyingpan, Xichuan, Jinmian, Cuiyu, Hongqiao, Yongning, and Labai (*Ninglang Yizu zizhixian zhi* 1993: 125). These last two townships, which border on Muli, contain about half the Premi population of Ninglang County. Culturally, the Premi in Ninglang and Muli are closely related. The local variations of Premihli, the Premi language, are similar enough that most Premi in these two counties are able to communicate with each other in their mother tongue.

The history of the Premi in Ninglang dates back to at least the year 1253, when Kublai Khan enlisted large numbers of soldiers from Muli in his campaign against the Dali Kingdom in Yunnan. The families of the soldiers followed in the wake of the armies, and after the war, many Premi families settled in locations such as the northwest of Yunnan (see also Yan and Wang 1988: 13). Many folk stories told among the Premi in Yunnan are related to this migration under the Mongols (Wellens 1998: 28). During the centuries that followed, more Premi, who at the time practiced a form of semi-nomadism, moved south. This later migration was to some extent induced by a continuous southward and westward expansion of the Nuosu people, an expansion that has continued into the PRC period, according to some Chinese researchers (Long 1991: 28). Until the Communist takeover, the area of Ninglang consisted of two separate territories ruled by *tusi*, or hereditary native chieftains: Yongning in the north and Langqu in the south. The name "Ninglang" is a PRC construction combining the names of these two former administrations.

Ninglang is also the area where most of the Na people live. In Yunnan, the Na, or Naze, have officially been classified as part of the larger Naxi *minzu*, but in Ninglang County—where all the Na of Yunnan live—they have obtained semiofficial status as Mosuoren, or "Mosuo people." For various reasons, communities of both the Na and the Premi in Ninglang have been the subjects of significantly more ethnographic research than their ethnic brethren in Muli. There is therefore detailed knowledge available about Na and Premi society in Yunnan beginning in the 1950s as well as, more anecdotally, from the 1920s and 1930s through the work of Joseph Rock.

Culturally, the Premi in Ninglang do not distinguish themselves very much from the Na. Each ethnic group speaks its own Tibeto-Burman language, but most Premi in Ninglang County also speak Naru, the language spoken by the Na. In Yongning, the Premi villages are usually situated on the lower ranges of the hillsides, while the Na occupy the valleys. In mountainous Labai, Na and Premi villages are interspersed within the same ecological space. There are also a few villages—mainly in the Yongning plain—where Premi and Na live in the same villages; these include Gala near Yongning Town and Luoshui on the shores of Lugu Lake. The close relationship between the two is expressed in the often used appellation Ba-Na, or Ba-Naze ("Ba" being the ethnonym of the Premi in Naru). As in Bustling Township, where there is frequent intermarriage between the Premi and the culturally closely related Rek'ua, Na, and Nahi^n, the Ninglang Premi and the Na commonly intermarry. Such relations have altered the kinship system in some Premi villages. In Wenquan, near Yongning, the Premi of the villages of Biqi, Tuoqi, Bajia, and Wadu participate in the "walking marriages," or *tisese* of the local Na.[2] These walking marriages are duolocal or natolocal unions, in which men visit their sexual partners at night without establishing a separate household. The two partners continue to live in their respective matrilineal households, and children born of such unions belong to the matriline. In 2004, on a visit to the village of Tuoqi, I was told that the shift in the kinship system in these villages is a relatively recent development. This tallies with the findings of Wang and Yan (1990: 194–98), based on fieldwork carried out in 1963, which found that many Premi families in the four villages studied had changed from a patrilineal to a matrilineal system of descent within the last two or three generations.[3]

In religious practice, there are also many similarities between the Na and the Premi. Today, most Premi and Na in Ninglang are adherents of Tibetan Buddhism. In the north of the county, the local center of this religion is Zhamei Gompa,[4] which is part of the Gelug School and a dependent monastery of Muli Gompa. Unlike Muli Gompa, however, Zhamei Gompa has few resident monks.[5] The monks belonging to this monastery either live at home or study at the Sera or Drepung monasteries in Lhasa. Even though they are away for several years, they are still counted as monks belonging to Zhamei Gompa. On my last visit in 2006, one of the younger monks had just returned from a two-year stay at Sera and had served for one year at the Potala Palace in Lhasa. A few of the monks even study at the Yunnan Nationalities University (Yunnan Minzu Daxue) in Kunming. Traditionally, the monks gathered at the monastery on the first and fifteenth days of each lunar month to recite scriptures together, but at the present time, most monks show up only at major Buddhist festivals such as the Ganden Ngamcho, which is held on the twenty-fifth day of the tenth lunar month to commemorate Tsongkhapa's death. About one-fourth of the 180 monks and novices belonging to the monastery are Premi, and the rest are mainly Na, which approximately reflects the proportion of the two ethnic groups in the total population in the area of Yongning and Labai townships. In the villages in this area, the monks—and to some extent their families—enjoy high social status. In Tuodian, this situation is expressed graphically in the saying "There is no person higher than the *yèma* (monk), just as no tree grows at higher altitudes than the *kwasè^n* tree" (Yèma ganto me ma re, kwasè^n ganto se ma dyé). Close to the town of Yongning, at the foot of Lion Mountain, is the small Zhebo Temple, which belongs to the Sakya School of Tibetan Buddhism. Almost all of its forty-five monks are Na from the surrounding villages, but there are a few Premi as well; all reside at home. South of Hongqiao, in central Ninglang, Premi and Na traditionally adhered to the Sakya sect of Tibetan Buddhism. This was the area ruled by the former Langqu *tusi*, and in pre-Communist times, every second son in a household was required to enter a monastery and become a monk; if a family had four sons, two had to become monks.

Although the Sakya School today has few monks compared to the monasteries of the Gelug School to the north, this form of Buddhism is reclaiming some of its former position. The major Sakya monastery in Ninglang is Samye Gompa, and it was rebuilt in the late 1990s on a small hilltop near Daxingzhen, the capital of Ninglang.[6] The original Samye monastery was situated at Dongfeng, sixteen kilometers to the south of Daxingzhen, but it was completely destroyed during the Cultural Revolution. It is not far-fetched to suppose that rebuilding the monastery close to the developing county capital was a strategic decision. Not only is the location more accessible to a larger number of people, but the visibility of the new building from the center of town is a firm reminder of the existence of Buddhism in Ninglang (not necessarily obvious, given that the Yi, the majority of the Ninglang population and the basis for the establishment of a Yi autonomous county, are not Buddhists). The monastery put a lot of effort into making the premises appealing and in 1998 paid two Tibetan painters from Lhasa almost ¥20,000 to adorn the interior and exterior front wall of the main hall with Buddhist iconography. They spent two months on the job, and the results are impressive. The thirty monks staying at the monastery in 2000 make up a considerably smaller cohort than the seventy to eighty monks connected with the monastery in pre-Communist times, yet there appears to be a tendency toward increase (e.g., on my first visit in 1998, there were only twenty resident monks). After three years at the monastery, many monks return to their home villages, where they continue their study independently while serving their communities by providing ritual services. Like the monks attached to Zhamei Gompa, they usually return to their monastery once a month, and all of the monks (as well as many lay believers) go there for the major annual festivals.

Buddhism is not only a matter of monasteries or the personal practice of monks; indeed, it is part of daily life for many of the local people, as becomes apparent in a Na or Premi house. Many houses have a prayer room—called *hlidzè^n* in Ninglang Premi and *ch'ako^n* in Bustling Township—that is dedicated especially to the recitation of Buddhist texts. If there is a monk in the family, this is where he will reside. Visiting monks also use the room when visiting a family, for example, when invited to perform a ceremony. As in Bustling Township, almost all houses—whether owned by Premi or Na villagers—have a picture or relief behind the fireplace dedicated to the wealth-granting Tibetan Buddhist deity Zambala. In addition, people often place pictures of famous Buddhist monks behind a small house altar where they make offerings to the Buddha or different bodhisattvas.

In Ninglang, as in Bustling Township, religious practice is more complicated than this superficial account seems to imply. In many of the Na villages of Yongning and Labai today, one encounters Na ritualists called *ddaba* in addition to monks who live at home. The *ddaba* base their ritual practice solely on orally transmitted texts. The relatively large amount of ethnography on the Na has focused primarily on their kinship system and sexual practices, and until recently very little research had been done on their religious practices.[7] Christine Mathieu and Shih Chuan-kang both note the coexistence of Tibetan Buddhism and the *ddaba* tradition. Shih concludes that "Ddabaism" and "Lamaism" have reached a form of peaceful coexistence in which the *ddaba* are principally responsible for the death ritual (1998: 106–7). Mathieu argues in contrast that *ddaba* practice has been marginalized by Buddhism and forced out of the Yongning plain into the mountainous regions of Labai; furthermore, she holds that the death ritual has been taken over by Buddhist monks (1998: 210). Mathieu also notes the strong influence of Buddhism on *ddaba* practices themselves: *ddaba* ritualists do not make blood offerings anymore, and they use peaceful means to combat evil spirits rather than the violent methods used by the Naxi *dtô-mbà* ritualists (ibid.: 211, 219). On the one hand, most Na villagers I interviewed in Yongning and Labai did not conceptualize the *ddaba* tradition and Tibetan Buddhism as being contradictory. The monks, on the other hand, held different opinions: a thirty-year-old caretaker monk at Zhamei Gompa did not hesitate to express his assessment of *ddaba* rituals, arguing, "All this is folk superstition!" (Dou shi laoba-ixing de mixin!).

Chinese ethnographies mention that the Premi of Ninglang also have their own non-Buddhist ritualists, called *hangui*. Like the word *anji* (a local pronunciation of *hangui* in Muli), the term *hangui* refers both to a set of ritual practices and to the ritualist performing them. These ethnographies also note the use of Buddhist texts and other Buddhist paraphernalia by *hangui* ritualists. Yang Xuezheng, who wrote a very detailed ethnographic study on *hangui* in Ninglang, states that all *hangui* are supposed to have a certain level of Buddhist knowledge in addition to their knowledge of traditional Premi rituals. He uses the term *haba* to denote those *hangui* who study for several years in a Buddhist monastery and consequently enjoy the highest prestige in Premi society. He argues that at the time of his study in 1991, two-thirds of *hangui* in Ninglang were "lamaist monks and priests" (*lama senglü*) (1991: 208).

The word *haba* is used in somewhat confusing ways: although Chinese research suggests that *hangui* ritualists are all Premi, they are also consulted by the Na, who designate all Premi ritualists as *haba*. Wang and Zhan note that they are consulted in particular by the Na in order to exorcise evil spirits or assist with the worship of mountain deities (1988: 112). It is precisely this Buddhist aspect of *hangui* practice that leads Rock to conclude that the *haba* used by the Na, must be

> sorcerers belonging to the Nyi-ma-pa (rNying-ma-pa) or Red Lama Sect. They are survivors of the adherents of Padmasambhava. They differ from the regular Nyi-ma-pa in that they have no lamaseries and, like the Nda-

pa [*ddaba*], perform their ceremonies out in the open. They are still to be found in Yung-ning and Mu-li. Unlike the Nda-pa they have manuscripts written in Tibetan on very thick paper; whether they chant from them or merely consult them I could not learn. In 1929 there were still a few Ha-pa [*haba*] alive, but with them their rites and ceremonies have come to an end. (1959: 806)

Rock does not mention the Premi origin of the *haba* ritualists, and his prediction of their extinction proved somewhat premature. As the work of Wang and Zhan testifies, *haba* were still an integral part of Na religious practice in the Na village of Zhongshi, on the Yongning plain, at the time of their fieldwork in 1963. Interestingly, while *ddaba* religious practice managed to survive both Buddhism and the havoc of the Cultural Revolution, *hangui* or *haba* had completely disappeared from Ninglang by the mid-1990s. During a 1995 survey of several Premi villages across the county, I could not locate one practicing *hangui* (Wellens 1998: 27–28).[8] But older people were often familiar with the term *hangui* or *haba*, and in two villages, a practicing *hangui* had recently died. In all of these villages, people now invited a *yèma*, a monk from Zhamei Gompa living in his home village, to recite Buddhist scriptures at important ceremonies such as cremations.[9] While there is no doubt that political campaigns through the twenty years from 1956 to 1976 were equally devastating for all religious practice in Ninglang (Zhamei Gompa was completely leveled in one day), it seems that only *hangui* practice had not recovered by the mid-1990s. That a religion such as Buddhism recovered in the politically more relaxed 1980s and 1990s is not so difficult to understand, in view of Gelug Buddhism's status as a large and well-organized religion that could draw on a standard set of widely available ritual texts.

The answer to the question of why *ddaba* were better able to reestablish themselves beside the Buddhist *yèma* than were *hangui* is more obscure, and it is likely that some combination of factors may have played a role. First, there are twice as many Na as Premi in Ninglang and therefore many more active *ddaba* than *hangui*. This provided a larger pool of surviving ritualists capable of reviving the tradition after the Cultural Revolution. Second, *hangui* ritual practice in Ninglang was supposedly based on textual transmission, and I still have not seen any ritually used text among Premi that is not in Tibetan *language*. Nevertheless, Chinese researchers and older Premi people insist that ritual texts using Tibetan *script* to write Premi existed in the past. While this is possible, another explanation could be that *hangui*, imitating the actions of Buddhist monks, looked like they were reciting from the texts while they were in fact reciting from memory. This does not mean they were cheating: the magical power was in the ritual action of turning the pages, ringing bells and other ritual instruments, and reciting the Premi orally transmitted text. Probably it was a combination of reading some of the Tibetan-language syllables constituting the magic formulas and reciting Premi language from memory. This would explain the close connection between scripture and recitation and why *hangui* appeared to the uninitiated to be reciting from the scriptures. In this way, the scripture also functioned as a mnemonic for remembering the orally transmitted part of the ritual. The *ddaba* ritualists, in contrast, did not use texts, and all their rituals were memorized. Since only the texts were destroyed during the Cultural Revolution, and not the people, the *ddaba* had an advantage in this area as well. In several villages, *hangui* texts had been used as fuel, first during the Campaign against Feudal Superstition (Fan Fengjian Mixin Huodong) in 1956 and then again during the Cultural Revolution, and, consequently, when religious policies relaxed in the 1980s, the surviving *hangui* ritualists had no texts left. And regardless of whether they were in Premi or Tibetan language, these texts were a necessary element of the ritual, and without them, the tradition collapsed.

Whatever the reason, by the late 1990s, religious practice among people in Ninglang classified as Pumizu was related solely to Tibetan Buddhism. In the county-town, a few urbanized Premi had turned to Christianity, and in a few villages, the millenarian cult of Mentuhui[10] challenged the hegemonic position of Buddhism for some years before it was suppressed in 2003. In two or three villages adjacent to Muli, people occasionally invited an *anji* from across the provincial border. Nevertheless, by the late 1990s, *hangui* and their rituals were but a faint memory of bygone customs and practices through Ninglang County, victims—along with so many other local cultural practices—of the cultural radicalism of Communism and the forces of modernization.

Various ethnographical descriptions of the area in the 1950s, 1960s, and 1970s testify that *hangui* practices constituted a veritable religious tradition with a relatively widespread and consistent set of beliefs and rituals. Although current *anji* practices in Bustling Township and other places in Muli are strongly connected to the defunct *hangui* religion of Ninglang, it is very difficult merely to equate Bustling Township practices and cosmological beliefs with what is found in these ethnographic descriptions. On the one hand, the rather isolated position of Bustling Township facilitated the survival of nonmainstream religious practices while, on the other hand, producing highly local versions of these practices through a process of constant cultural invention. Today, Bustling Township *anji* practice is to a significant degree molded by the recollections of a few old men and the creativity and charisma of one person, Nima Anji. Against this background, it is interesting to examine one of the more well-informed, detailed, and conscientious descriptions of *hangui* religion in Ninglang.

HANGUI IN CHINESE ETHNOGRAPHY

Yang Xuezheng, a researcher from the Yunnan Institute of Social Sciences and a Tibetan from Yongning, wrote a very informative piece on Premi religion based on his fieldwork in Ninglang County. His essay "Investigation into the Religion of the Pumi of Ninglang" (Ninglang xian Pumizu zongjiao diaocha) was published in a book that appeared in 1991 and was part of the large series of publications that presented the results of extensive ethnographic investigations carried out in the 1950s and 1960s. Yang's essay contains many detailed ethnographic descriptions of rituals, but unfortunately, its value is somewhat diminished because he seldom mentions place-names or the dates of investigation. Only once does he refer to the time and location of data collection, when he notes that the old *hangui* of Lakua Village in Hongqiao, Ninglang, was still alive and in good health at the time of the investigation in 1976. This is a common problem in earlier Chinese ethnographic writing and is connected to the supposition that it is possible to uncover a pure and timeless form of the culture of a specific ethnic group; in connection with this, the task of the ethnographer is to present this essentialized version in a generalized way as the specific culture of the specific group. Yang acknowledges that there are differences in practice between the larger geographic areas of Lanping, Lijiang, and Zhongdian, on the one hand, and Ninglang, Muli, and Yanyuan, on the other. He even mentions occasionally that there are local variations within these regions, but the underlying assumption is that there is a common basis for all Premi religious beliefs and practices, including for Premi who are classified as Tibetans in Muli and Yanyuan in Sichuan. Variations are mostly ascribed to the influence of the cultures of neighboring ethnic groups.

Yang categorizes Premi religious practice in Ninglang as essentially a form of "nature worship" (*ziran chongbai*) and describes in detail large offering ceremonies to heaven, mountains, and springs. He notes that the most complex of the three, ceremonies of offerings to heaven, were already rarely held in the years immediately after Liberation (1991: 199). In these large clan-based ceremonies, people made offerings to the spirits of heaven, including the sun, moon, stars, wind, rain, thunder, lightning, hail, frost, and fog. This involved the sacrifice of large numbers of animals, and several families within a clan therefore pooled resources to provide some of the larger animals such as oxen, pigs, or sheep. In Yang's descriptions, the worship of the deities of mountains and springs are reminiscent of the ceremonies held in Bustling Township at the turn of the millennium to worship the mountain deities, the *rèdzeng rèda*, and the water deities, the *lwéjabu*. Many elements related to the worship of these deities, such as the existence of sacred woods and trees, are very similar. Yang distinguishes two types of ritual activities: those performed at home and centered on the relationship of the family with the deities, with or without the presence of a *hangui*, and large clan-based ceremonies held on fixed dates, which stretch over several days and require the sacrifice of many animals. In Bustling Township, large communal ceremonies to mountain or water deities are also held on specific dates of the calendar but only in case of special need, and the whole village participates, not just the clan. This is significant, since Bustling Township is one of the very few Premi areas where *jhü*, or clan, still plays a role in social life.

According to Yang, the worship of ancestors and totems is among the basic ingredients of Premi religious practice (1991: 202). Totem worship in this case is the practice in which every clan worships a totemic object, usually an animal that it believes is its first ancestor; these are most often the frog, tiger, and dog. Although dogs have a special status and cannot be killed in Bustling Township, as in all other Premi communities I visited, when questioned on the subject, most people denied that there were particular objects of worship related to specific clans. One *anji* in Hill Village remembered a few stories telling that the Ts'uop'i clan originated from a tiger. Yang's description of rituals related to day-to-day ancestor worship could just as easily have been descriptions of what people in Bustling Township currently do; again, however, his description of larger clan-based rituals has no parallel in Bustling Township today. This is also true of the worship of the female deity Badinglamu, which Yang describes as a general feature of Premi religion but is most likely a local cult in the Yongning area originating with the Na people.

A major component of Premi ritual practice in Ninglang at the time of Yang's fieldwork was a very well developed system for curing disease. Yang characterizes this aspect of *hangui* practice as "witchcraft" (*wushu*). He also remarks on the Premi belief that the evil spirits cause most human ailments; as explained in chapter 4, many of the categorizations of these ailments—wet and dry diseases, bad dream diseases, and so on—are used in Bustling Township today. But in Bustling Township, there is now a considerably lower number of categories of diseases, which can to a large extent be attributed to a general improvement in health in the region in the last thirty years.

According to Yang, Premi "witchcraft" is heavily influenced by Tibetan Bön religion (1991: 205). An interesting point is Yang's claim that the texts used at these rituals, in addition to the usual Tibetan Buddhist scriptures, consisted of texts written in Premi language with Tibetan letters, which he designates "*hangui* script" (*hangui wen*). He provides many examples of the content of these texts. Although reminiscent of the few rituals I saw performed in Bustling Township, none of the rituals was based on the kind of texts mentioned by Yang; Bustling Township ritual texts were, except for the occasional recitation of Tibetan Buddhist scriptures, based mainly on orally transmitted texts. It is possible that some *anji* in Bustling Township did possess texts written in Premi language before the destruction of the 1950s and the Cultural Revolution, but by the early 2000s, people in Bustling Township could not remember that these texts had ever existed.

In his account of the "opening of the road" ritual performed at the cremation ceremony—called *drwashu* in Bustling Township—Yang compares the different routes the soul of the deceased must take in order to reach the place where the ancestral souls dwell and concludes that the closest common identifiable place is somewhere in Muli. Yang holds that, in contrast to the cosmological beliefs of Bustling Township villagers, the beliefs of the Premi in Ninglang have been greatly influenced by Buddhist concepts such as reincarnation and transmigration (1991: 210).

In premodern Ninglang, the role of the *hangui* in society was significantly more important than that of the *anji* in Bustling Township today. In addition to being ritual experts, Yang argues, *hangui* also mediated in disputes and passed judgment in criminal cases. This last function was related not only to the *hangui*'s special social position in his local community but also to the belief that he could appeal to the deities for help in deciding whether or not a person was guilty of a crime. One method, in use at least until a 1957 case to which Yang refers, consisted of a *hangui* making the concerned parties grope for one of two stones—a black and a white one—in a pot of boiling oil. The party that grabbed the white stone was judged to be innocent. Yang furthermore observes a close association of ritual practice with other aspects of knowledge transmitted from generation to generation, including genealogies, ceremonial customs, local history, stories, and legends. In addition to teaching about ritual, *hangui* also gave instruction on these aspects of local culture and, in this way, functioned not only as bearers but as transmitters of this local culture (1991: 211). This traditional *hangui* role may contribute to an understanding of how a person such as Nima Anji of Walnut Grove came to play such a pivotal role in the revitalization of *anji* practice in Bustling Township.

Yang distinguishes three major branches, or schools, in *hangui* practice: Geimu, Kuaba, and Yinqu. These are the names of three legendary brothers who were students of the first *hangui*, Yishi Dingba, and who each started his own *hangui* branch. Ritualists of these branches traced their genealogies back to the three brothers. One such genealogy recorded by Yang went back forty-two generations, which, he argues, implies that *hangui* have a history of more than one thousand years. In examining the distinctions in ritual practice among the three branches, some of the recurring dualities and oppositions in religious practice in the border areas of Tibet again present themselves (1991: 212–14). The Geimu branch was concerned specifically with doing good: singing praises to the deities, urging people to do good deeds and avoid doing evil deeds. *Hangui* of this branch did not drive away evil spirits but were called upon mainly to perform ceremonies to worship the deities and to conduct rites of passage. Recollecting that *ch'wi-p'ö*, or "doing good things," is one way of designating Buddhism in Bustling Township, it is not surprising that all the Geimu *hangui* had studied for some years in a Buddhist monastery. In contrast to the small number of practitioners of the Geimu branch, the Kuaba branch included many ritualists. The expertise of the *hangui* of this branch was varied: they performed exorcisms of evil spirits, sacrificed domestic animals, performed magic to harm personal enemies, conducted ceremonies related to the ancestor cult, and performed the "opening of the road" ritual at cremations. *Hangui* of the third branch, the Yinqu, specialized in sacrificing animals as well as performing cremation ceremonies and engaged in activities such as conveying divine judgment. Although there were only a few *hangui* of this branch, Yang recounts that they played an important role because they handled ritual services in cases of "unnatural" death. These events, such as a woman dying in childbirth or a suicide, could have catastrophic consequences for a community, and only a Yinqu *hangui* possessed the necessary magical powers to remedy such events. Because Yinqu *hangui* were associated with magic, monks and *hangui* from the other schools looked down on them.

It is obvious from Yang's study that before the Communist takeover, *hangui* practices were widespread throughout Ninglang and in the two adjacent counties of Muli and Yanyuan in Sichuan. Every family with more than three sons wanted one son to study to become a *hangui*, and, according to Yang, on average, every village had more than ten practicing *hangui*. In Zuosuo in Sichuan, very close to Yongning, the village of Taozi was famed as a "*hangui* village": with a population of forty-two households, it could boast twenty-eight practicing *hangui* (1991: 214). Interestingly, Yang remarks that although *hangui* activities decreased after the 1950s, in recent years—and by this he presumably refers to a period not too remote from his publication date of 1991—young people have again begun to study *hangui*, especially village cadres and people who left school after finishing "junior middle school" (*chuzhong*). The survey I undertook in the mid-and-late 1990s did not really support this claim for Ninglang County; then again, Yang himself does not make clear whether he is referring only to this county in this context or whether he also includes the areas of Muli and Yanyuan.

THE *HANGUI* SCHOOL OF CHICKEN FOOT VILLAGE

Chicken Foot is a Premi village of about eight hundred people, situated no more than half an hour by bus from the county capital of Ninglang, Daxingzhen. Houses in Chicken Foot Village resemble those in many other traditional agricultural villages in northwestern Yunnan because of their construction method, which combines the pressed earth technique for the ground floor with a wooden structure for the first floor. At first glance, the most noticeable difference between the houses of Chicken Foot Village and the log houses in Bustling Township is not their construction method but the strikingly larger size and better condition of the houses. Many houses in Chicken Foot Village have glass windows and concrete courtyards, and all the roofs are tile covered. This last feature contrasts markedly with the shabby-looking roofs in Bustling Township, which consist of loose planks held in place by heavy stones.

As with all the villages in Bustling Township, Chicken Foot Village is also an agricultural village. Most families still work on the plot of land, averaging ten *mu*, that they have contracted from the collective. In contrast to Bustling Township, however, in the last ten to fifteen years, people in Chicken Foot Village have abandoned subsistence farming. Many of the crops they produce are now sold on the market, and in most families, there is at least one person who has a paid job outside the village. In recent years, an increasing number of families have begun to rent out their land to poor Nuosu living across the valley. All in all, in the local context of a poor county in Southwest China, Chicken Foot Village has fared rather well economically. At the time of my fieldwork, there had been electricity for several years, and all the houses I visited had a television set. Judging by the ten families I interviewed in Chicken Foot Village, it seems clear that the general level of education was significantly higher than in Bustling Township. This is not so surprising in view of the fact that a junior middle school is just a fifteen-minutes walk from the village, and a "senior middle school" (*gaozhong*) and several technical secondary schools are located in the county capital, half an hour from the village by bus. In contrast to Bustling Township, the county-town, by virtue of its proximity, provides a job market, where acquired skills can be put to use, in this way greatly motivating young people to participate in the educational opportunities available.

As a result of broad participation in the Chinese educational system, Chinese language is understood and spoken by most people under the age of sixty in the village, although Premi is still the major language of communication within the village. Villagers also point to many other aspects of their lives as ethnic markers that distinguish them from surrounding ethnic groups such as the Han and the Nuosu. For example, on festive occasions, the women of Chicken Foot Village put on their traditional pleated skirts and arrange their hair in the typical Premi fashion, which involves braiding black woolen threads into it and winding it around the head. The Premi of Chicken Foot Village also have not adopted the custom of the surrounding Han of burying the dead, remaining loyal to the tradition of cremation and guiding the soul back to the ancestral lands. Furthermore, they honor their ancestors by offering some food to them before each meal on the iron tripod in the fireplace, and on the sacred offering stone next to it. Cremation ceremonies are now conducted exclusively by *yèma*, or Buddhist lay priests, without the traditional participation of a *hangui*. Unfortunately, the last practicing *hangui* of Chicken Foot Village had passed away only a short time before my first visit in 1998; as he had not had any students, the tradition died with him. Several young boys from the village had just entered the newly rebuilt Samye Gompa at Daxingzhen to become monks, and several people considered the defunct *hangui* tradition to be something rightly belonging to the past.

When discussing this tradition, the expression *mixin*, "superstition" or "confused beliefs," often popped up, reflecting familiarity with official Chinese discourse on nonmainstream religious practice. This did not mean that villagers interpreted official policy as condemning *hangui* ritual practice as superstition; although some villagers held such views themselves, many others were uncertain. As one sixty-three-year-old man exclaimed in exasperation: "What constitutes superstition and what constitutes religion is something we, common people, are not clear about!" (Shenme shi mixin, sheme shi zongjiao, women laobaixing bu qingchu!). But there are also other opinions on the *hangui* tradition of Chicken Foot Village and other Premi places in the area. A small number of elderly cadres from the county government, most of them originating from Chicken Foot Village, had become interested in many aspects of Premi culture. After they retired, this interest developed into a desire to "restore" what they saw as some of the most salient and important parts of this culture, the *hangui* tradition. One of them was Waija Dorje Tsering (Premi name), who had held a leading position in Ninglang's Chinese People's Political Consultative Conference. Another was Hu Jingming, also from the CPPCC and the son of Hu Wanqing, who was famed for informing Premier Zhou Enlai about the existence of the Premi in Yunnan and, as such, for being instrumental in bringing about official recognition of the Premi as a national minority.[11] On a subsequent visit in 2000, I found that these cadres had started a veritable *hangui* school in Chicken Foot Village and had contracted as the teacher an old friend of mine, Nima Anji from Walnut Grove. The *anji* tradition of Bustling Township had been "discovered" not only by a foreign anthropologist but also by urbanized Premi elites from the neighboring province.

The presentation of their restoration project in a modern PRC context is tellingly illustrated in a pamphlet issued in October 2000 to raise funds for the *hangui* school. It was distributed to those families in Chicken Foot Village whose members generated income by working outside the village:

Make your contribution to the continuation of the *hangui* religion!

From ancient times up to the present, [it has been the case that] a nationality that does not have religious beliefs is an ignorant nationality; the religious beliefs of the Pumi Nationality [Pumizu] is the "*hangui* religion." "*Hangui* religion" is the culture of the Pumi Nationality. The "*hangui*" is the person who takes care of the ceremonial customs among the social activities of the Pumi people. Whether in holding activities such as festival rites or marriage and funeral customs, gathering the people to discuss official business, going on military or punitive expeditions, and so on, all this was bound to be led by the "*hangui*" offering sacrifices. Over the long course of our history, he, with his religious rules, has provided ceremonial, ethical, and behavioral norms for conduct in human life; with his religious doctrines, he has nurtured the multiplying lives of our every generation, the traces of the civilized culture of our forefathers that have been kept until this day, making it hard for us to forget. At one time, it [*hangui* religion] constituted the spiritual pillar for the Pumi Nationality, for over the course of a people's long history, the old and rich ethnic traditional culture sometimes had its peculiarities. Nowadays, this can still be one of the important elements in constructing a "Socialist civilization with Chinese characteristics" [*Zhongguo tese de shehui zhuyi wenming*] and in establishing "a province with ethnic culture" [*minzu wenhua sheng*]. By taking advantage of the favorable situation to make use of the old and the contemporary, we can transform the old by getting rid of the rough while grasping the essence and by getting rid of the false while retaining the true. In order to serve the development of the economy and culture into the twenty-first century, it is also valuable to increase the popularity of one's own nationality.

As a result of several social factors, the continuation of the outstanding culture of the Pumi Nationality, the "*hangui* religion," has been broken—prayer halls, texts, and religious instruments have been completely destroyed—and this has resulted in the decline and confusion of the nationality, leading to ethnic self-confidence being strongly impaired. Although, ever since the Third Plenary Session of the Tenth Central Committee, our county has earnestly implemented the policies of "freedom of religious beliefs" and "respect for minority nationalities' customs," it has all along been unable to reverse the loss.

As former government and party cadres, the authors were clearly aware of how to frame their arguments within the limitations of prevailing official policies and discourses. Religious practice in China is strictly regulated, and in general, only practice defined as part of one of the five official religions is accepted. Folk religious practices such as ancestor cults have been officially frowned upon, but in the case of ethnic minorities, such practices can be defined as part of the ethnic minority's culture and therefore, in principle, are tolerated and protected by legislation such as the Autonomy Law for National Minorities (Shaoshu Minzu Zizhifa). The authors' statement that the "*hangui* religion" is the culture of the Pumi is therefore intended not so much to convince possible donors as to justify their project within the official framework. Furthermore, they firmly place the project within the modernization discourse of the post-Mao period by referring to the focus on nationalism (Chinese characteristics) and the provincial-level drive to commodify ethnic culture in order to attract tourists (establish a province with ethnic culture).[12] They express their strong conviction that the so-called *hangui* religion can be adapted to fit this framework.

The rest of the pamphlet is addressed to possible donors:

On the grounds of pressing demands and hopes of elderly fellow townspeople over the last many years, we have been looking everywhere for a teacher who is carrying on the "*hangui*" tradition. In the autumn of 1999, we engaged the famous teacher of religious scriptures [Nima Anji] from Muli County in Sichuan, and with the help of the cadres [names of three cadres], it was decided in consultation with the popular will to run a class to carry on the tradition of "*hangui* religion" in [Chicken Foot Village]. The time limit will be three years, and a monthly salary of ¥600 amounts to a total of ¥21,600 for the three years. When we have come to the end of the teaching period, comrade [name of cadre] also promised to give the teacher ¥2,000 and a big riding mule as a farewell present for his return home.

The teaching of carrying on the tradition of the "*hangui* religion" starts at this year's "Grave Sweeping" festival. Currently there are five apprentices, and starting in the spring of next year there will be seven; altogether, there will be two classes with more than ten apprentices. We plan to construct a scripture hall and purchase scriptures and religious instruments. When this cost is added to the remuneration for the scripture teacher, expenses will be pretty high. At the moment, our home village has barely attained the level of having adequate warm clothing and enough to eat; it still has not escaped from poverty. If we are only able to rely on the income of the peasants, we will not be able to achieve major undertakings; instead, we must rely on the assistance of our fellow villagers who work outside the village.

The Pumi Nationality, standing on its own in the forest of nationalities in the world, must continuously seek its own road to subsistence and development, knowing the main principles and looking after the interests of the nation, knowing its past, recognizing its present, and looking into the future. At present, it is the springtime season for greatly developing nationality culture; we must not let the opportunity slip. We hope that all those working outside the township—the Party and government cadres, workers and staff members, enterprise managers, merchants with breadth of vision, and intellectuals—will follow with interest the development of our hometown and the progress of our nationality. As to giving a fitting amount of support, give what you can afford: [if you have] a lot, [you can give] a couple of thousand; [if you have] a little, [you can give] a few hundred. But for the continuation of the "*hangui* religion" of our fellow townsmen and our nationality, please make some contribution!

Fellow townsmen, in order to rescue the culture of the *"hangui* religion" of the Pumi Nationality, we hope that in your different job positions you will carry on our concerted effort, strive for solidarity, have the courage to assume your social duties, and [carry on] our nationality's traditional spirit of almsgiving. Our fellow townsmen look forward to your close and long friendship.

Responsibility for management of the funds will be borne by the retired county-town cadre [name of cadre]. Please, fellow townsmen, hand your contribution over to him before New Year's Day.

Expecting to see you at Spring Festival in our hometown,

I hereby wish you a successful project!

Village committee of [Chicken Foot Village]

5 October 2000

The campaign had brought in ¥10,000 by the end of 2001. Somebody donated as much as ¥3,500, but most people gave ¥100–300. The first class, which started in the spring of 2000, was held in the existing school buildings of Chicken Foot Village, after normal classes were finished. Later, the local people refurbished a few unused buildings at the school to provide living quarters for Nima Anji and a room for teaching, practicing rituals, and keeping religious implements. The first five apprentices were all young men in their early twenties from Chicken Foot Village. Three had finished junior middle school, and one had even studied one year at senior middle school. Nima Anji was a demanding teacher, knowing that he had only three years to bring his students to a level that they would be able to conduct most rituals by themselves. In addition to learning to read and recite Tibetan texts, *hangui*-to-be were required to memorize countless rituals as well as all the intricacies of Premi cosmology as it had been transmitted in Walnut Grove. Most of this knowledge was entirely new to the apprentices, except for one student who had studied for four months in 1999 with an *anji* colleague of Nima Anji's in Walnut Grove. Not all apprentices were equal to the task, and during the first year, two of the five apprentices were kicked out. Given the yearly tuition fee of ¥650, regular fees for copies of ritual texts, and the prospect of having to invest in a full *"hangui* suit," the apprentices admitted that motivation had to be strong. This did not deter other hopefuls, and in the following years, the number of new apprentices increased steadily. In 2004, there were eight students in the two advanced classes and twelve in the beginners' class. Many of these students were around fifteen years old, or even younger, and came from Premi villages all over Ninglang County. Since many of these places were as far as several days' journey from Chicken Foot Village, these students boarded at the school. Two classes had finished the whole three-year course, and most of these first new *hangui* had returned to their villages to start their practice, while a few had stayed on to help teach the new classes.

The spiraling expansion of *hangui* teaching is certainly an expression of a larger interest in the *hangui* tradition among Premi in Ninglang. Although a select elite initiated the project, the response it provoked could indicate a more general concern with what Premi perceive to be important elements of their culture. In a modernizing society, such elements play a central role in the construction of ethnic identity. The *hangui* school is just one of several such activities taking place in Ninglang, not a few of which involve Nima Anji and the retired cadres. During my earlier visit, an altar to offer sacrifices to heaven was being constructed on a hilltop near Chicken Foot Village, and in the village itself, several families had received advice on how to turn one of the rooms in their houses into a *hlidzè^n*, or prayer hall. On my visit in 2004, I learned that Nima Anji, while still teaching in Chicken Foot Village, had moved into the house of one of the CPPCC cadres in Daxingzhen. They were collecting rituals—both the written Tibetan texts as well as the orally transmitted Premi "texts"—and planned to translate and publish them. Of the twelve kinds of ritual texts, they had found versions of ten, consisting of more than nine hundred parts. They still had not located any versions of rituals related to Premi medicine or those used for making people ill. As mentioned earlier, it was especially the latter category of Tibetan-language texts that had been destroyed during the Cultural Revolution. A publishing house had already agreed on a contract for a book, and out of philological considerations, the book would contain both the original "text" in the international phonetic alphabet and the translation in Chinese. In order to preserve the iconographic tradition, Nima Anji was also going to provide paintings used in the different rituals. Another retired cadre was working on a dictionary project and was on his way to Kunming to conclude a contract with a publishing house. Not all of the initiatives were as successful: an attempt to establish the Pumi Research Centre in Hongqiao on the road between Ninglang and the tourist spot of Lugu Lake collapsed due to lack of funds.[13]

It is probably too early to determine whether this interest in *hangui* tradition in Ninglang can be termed a genuine revival. Additional fieldwork is needed to find out whether newly educated *hangui* will come to play a role comparable to that of *anji* in Bustling Township. It is obvious that in spite of their different histories and different official ethnic classification, the Premi in Muli and Ninglang are culturally closely related. This is borne out by the fact that the most important *anji* from Bustling Township in Sichuan, Nima Anji, is at the center of the *hangui* resurrection project in Yunnan. At this level, the Ninglang elites who initiated this project do not care that Nima Anji is classified as a Tibetan. The Chinese state has recognized their separate ethnic identity of Premi as Pumizu, and Nima Anji is a crucial means of infusing this identity with meaningful cultural content. Their project is therefore entirely in line with the official discourses on religion and ethnic identity. As things stand at the start of the new millennium, none of the Tibetan elites in Muli would include Nima Anji in any project to revitalize religious practice in their county. For that, his ritual expertise is not only entirely redundant but, to some extent, presents a threat to the officially sanctioned version of Muli as a culturally Tibetan territory.

CONCLUSION

The Tibetan borderland communities examined in this study have revitalized traditional religious practice in a context of recent changes in the political, economic, and social reality. The specific shape of this process of revitalization can be understood only in a local cultural context and by clearly distinguishing between the different social actors involved. The particular form of social organization of Premi communities, the political and religious history of Muli, and modern discourses on religion and ethnic identity were all instrumental in molding the different expressions of this revival. But form can belie content and meaning. Ritual practice in the villages did not diverge fundamentally *in form* from the practices of Buddhist monks or the practices taught in the *hangui* school in Chicken Foot Village. In several aspects, village rituals, such as the reciting of Buddhist texts, had been directly taken from Buddhist practice, and the teachings at the *hangui* school were based on village ritual practice. Basic differences became apparent when examining the way ritual practice was understood and conceptualized by different categories of people in Premi society. To the educated elites, ritual and religion were key factors in constructing a modern ethnic identity within the context of the Chinese state and its official discourses. To the villagers, ritual practice was inextricably bound up in their religious beliefs and cosmological understanding, and as such, it was a more tightly integrated component of the cultural fabric of their community.

Although Bustling Township's position in the mountains of the Southwest is rather extreme in terms of geographical isolation, its present-day experiences of economic and social remarginalization are nevertheless shared by many communities in the poor rural areas of China. After the failure of the extremist policies of the Mao period, with their radical collectivization and intense ideological indoctrination, Deng Xiaoping gradually changed direction after he came to power at the end of the 1970s. For ethnic minorities, this meant that they could practice their religion openly again and that more space became available in which to express cultural divergence from mainstream Han society. The modernization process Deng initiated was focused not on political liberalization but on economic reform.

After more than two decades of increasing economic liberalization, living standards have risen all over China. At the same time, the modernization process has made people in many of the more remote rural areas aware of the unequal pace of economic development. Through increased mobility and the spread of media, people have learned about the growing differences in living standards between East and West China, between countryside and urban areas, and between ethnic minorities and the Han majority. The partial deregulation of agricultural prices in recent years has resulted in a drop in rural incomes in several areas and accentuated this divide. Few communities in rural China manage to obtain a satisfying living from farming alone, and many families count on members who work in urban areas to supplement their incomes. Members of ethnic minorities, who in general have a low level of formal education, often are not very proficient in speaking Chinese, and have poorly developed networks in the urban areas, are at a clear disadvantage when competing for jobs with their Han neighbors.

In this context, the central government's 1999 decision to ban logging in the natural forests of the Southwest represented a major economic setback for the poor Premi and Na villagers of Bustling Township. Almost overnight, the sole source of jobs outside the village was effectively eliminated. This development took place at a time when the social safety net of the Communist state had been going through a prolonged period of disintegration. The villagers saw that the state was shedding its responsibility to safeguard people's subsistence while simultaneously denying these people the means to better their living conditions by themselves. Having already squandered its ideological hegemony through the excesses of the Cultural Revolution, the state and the Party were no longer able to fulfill their role as protectors of the people's livelihood. In Bustling Township, as elsewhere in rural China, the combination of increasing economic uncertainty and more liberal policies on religion and other cultural practices stimulated a revival of religious practice.

Yet this study goes beyond demonstrating what other researchers have already shown, namely, that traditional ritual practices are in the process of being restored. It also looks beyond the socioeconomic context of this restoration and instead aims to understand the particular shape the revival has taken and why this has been different for different social actors. Conceptualizing religion is a challenging task, even in the relatively delimited context of the practices and cosmological beliefs of a numerically small ethnic group in Southwest China, and rather than enter into a broad epistemological debate on what constitutes religion or belief, this volume approaches local practices and cosmology through an empirically based analysis of two existing local concepts. One is the concept of *anji* or *hangui*, a term used by Premi villagers to designate a set of rituals practiced within the village as well as the ritual experts themselves. The other concept is associated specifically with the practices and beliefs found in the Tibetan Buddhist monastery. Throughout the research, it became apparent that the two concepts were often difficult to distinguish or separate and, moreover, that the entire assumption of the duality of religion among the Premi—and conceivably for several other ethnic groups in this area of Southwest China—needed to be modified. Although the starting point of a bipolar relationship between Buddhism and *anji* practice proved to be in agreement with official state discourse as reflected in the views of local elites and Buddhist monks, it was inadequate for understanding religious practice and belief within the context of the Bustling Township villages. Nevertheless, precisely because it exposed the discrepancy in conceptualizations of religion between these different social groups, this starting point, however fallacious, was an important methodological device.

For the local elites, the drive to revitalize religion was less a direct reaction to changing socioeconomic realities than a wish to establish a communal identity within the larger modernizing Chinese society. This project was framed within the official discourse on *minzu* and religion. In Muli, the Premi government cadres and teachers identified Tibetan Gelug Buddhism as a cornerstone of their *minzu* identity. In this way, they subscribed fully to the official line that viewed the former political role of Buddhism in Muli as an expression of the Tibetan ethnicity of its inhabitants. The project initiated by local elites among the Premi of neighboring Yunnan, to revive *hangui/anji* practices in the rural villages, could be related to their official *minzu* status. Because the Yunnan Premi were classified not as Tibetans but as a separate *minzu*, the Premi elite denied the role of Tibetan Buddhism in Premi society and viewed the *anji* practices of Bustling Township as one of the few surviving examples of true Premi culture.

In contrast, the official discourse on ethnic identity and religion was much less pervasive among the villagers of Bustling Township. This was due to several factors, such as limited participation in state education, the scarcity of people working outside the village, and the geographical isolation of Bustling Township. Villagers did not conceive of Buddhism as standing in opposition to practices mediated by the village ritualists, the *anji*. The teachings and practices of the Buddhist monks, when at all distinguished from *anji* practices, were characterized as *ch'wi-p'ö*, or "doing good things." Practicing *ch'wi-p'ö* was viewed as detached from the everyday concerns of the villagers. It was reserved for special categories of people, such as those who wanted to devote their lives to doing good (i.e., monks) or who had a semidivine quality (i.e., living deities). Those practicing *ch'wi-p'ö* were nevertheless viewed as competent in addressing the ritual needs of the villagers.

In the villages of Bustling Township, ritual practices were first of all the manifestation of a shared cosmological understanding. While the recent revival of these teachings and practices must be understood in the context of changes in the socioeconomic reality of modern China, religious practices and beliefs in Bustling Township cannot be reduced to the mechanical strategy of compensating for a drop in income or the collapse of the social security system. Religious practices and beliefs among the Premi in the villages of Bustling Township are also an organic part of an entire symbolic universe of meaning that has been reproduced over generations, what Catherine Bell terms the "enduring cultural structures" (1997). They make sense in the total context of social organization and are therefore, for example, closely linked to $dzè^n$, or houses. Even the disruptive events of the Cultural Revolution could not fundamentally change local cosmological understanding. Religious practices disappeared from the surface for some time, and people had no choice but to put their trust in Mao to protect them from evil spirits and provide abundant harvests. When farmers could no longer hold the annual ceremony asking the water deities for rain, rituals dedicated to the cult of Mao appeared. Yet there is little evidence that Maoism ever replaced people's fundamental conceptualization of the natural world, and when the Communist state ceased to fulfill its task of taking care of the people's livelihood and withdrew on the ideological level at the end of the 1970s, *anji* practice resurfaced. Traditional ritual activity slowly took off again with the help of the few surviving ritual experts and some old monks who had left the monastery and were living in the villages. Rituals were pieced together again through bits and pieces of texts that had been hidden, through the memories of the villagers and ritual experts, and especially through the remarkable zeal and creativity of one *anji* ritualist, Nima Anji of Walnut Grove. Families who had enjoyed a short reprieve from their terrible fate of being possessed by *brö* demons were thrown back into social isolation, and the deities punished one family with insanity for having defied and insulted them.

Ritual practice and social organization are interrelated in the villages of Bustling Township, with religion and ritual centered on a belief in the *me-drö*, or ancestral souls, and a plethora of deities, both categories of beings that interfere directly in people's daily lives. The hearth and the iron tripod in every house constitute the core place for worshipping. Here the inhabitants of the house make offerings and pray every day to the ancestors who lived and died in the house. This aspect of the house as a place of worship, and of its inhabitants as a ritual unit, shows that village religious beliefs and practices are strongly connected to social organization and, more particularly, to the system of constructing and maintaining relatedness. Although patrilineal clans are a very prominent feature of Premi society in Bustling Township, customs such as fraternal polyandry and sororal polygyny, as well as the existence of named houses, point to a system of social organization reminiscent of what Claude Lévi-Strauss has called *sociétés à maison*. The house as a built construction serves as a temple where its inhabitants maintain relationships with their ancestors' souls and solidify affinal relationships between those born in there and those who enter through marriage by the performance of common rituals. In addition, the house is a place thick with symbolic meaning. The *gujhi-jhata^n*, or central pillar, to which the platform with the hearth is attached, connects the *dzè^n* with heaven and earth, while the objects placed in the hollow of the offering stone, symbolize the house's potential to provide its inhabitants with prosperous lives, an important asset in increasingly uncertain times. As it is for the Tibetans of Gyelthang, a house in Bustling Township is "a cosmologically meaningful structure designed to maintain an efficient relationship with the powers of the outside world" (Corlin 1980: 91).

From the villagers' perspective, both official Chinese discourses on superstition, religion, and ethnic identity and the views of the monks from the monastery on the orthodoxy of Gelugpa beliefs and practices are, for all practical purposes, irrelevant. This is not to say that these larger contexts are not important in shaping local religious practice. For centuries, *anji* ritualists have integrated elements from Tibetan Buddhism and, to some extent, Bön into their practices. It is precisely because of the flexibility and inventiveness of *anji* ritualists that a ritual system has survived in the shadow of large, well-organized, and rationalized ideological systems such as Gelugpa Buddhism (or, for that matter, Maoism). But the practice of reciting the texts of these traditions, or importing some names and concepts of Tibetan deities, has not been matched by fundamental changes in the more basic aspects of religious practice or belief. Premi souls still travel to ancestral lands and are not reincarnated, and deities and evil spirits are still propitiated with blood offerings.

In his critique of a functionalist theory of religion, Clifford Geertz held that sociological and cultural processes had to be treated on equal terms. Ritual constitutes both a pattern of meaning (culture) and a form of social interaction (Geertz 1973: 142). *Anji* practice in Bustling Township is not only the expression of a shared symbolic universe, including a shared cosmological understanding, but also a means of establishing and maintaining community. Émile Durkheim held that "religious representations are collective representations that express collective realities; rites are ways of acting that are born only in the midst of assembled groups and whose purpose it is to evoke, maintain, or recreate certain mental states of those groups" (Durkheim and Fields 1995: 9). Participation in common rituals creates a sense of belonging during times when there are few options for establishing alternative forms of communal identity for poor subsistence farmers in the mountains of the Southwest. First, at the level of the $dzè^n$, rituals express, strengthen, and establish community. At the extended level of the village, common residence in clearly bounded villages and the sharing of cosmological beliefs establish "community" as a naturally given thing. This is nevertheless a truth with modifications as shown by the families in Walnut Grove who were viewed as possessed with brö demons and consequently were excluded from communal rituals. Living in the village is a condition but not a guarantee for belonging to the local community. Membership in the community cannot be chosen, and it can be rejected only by physically leaving the village.

People who have actually done so, or those who live in less bounded villages that are more closely integrated into the larger, individualized Chinese society, must construct a sense of belonging to a community. Individuals have to make an active choice among categories of available identities. These choices are nevertheless more limited in China than in societies with more democratic political systems. In post-Mao China, the state continues to be successful in convincing educated elites to construct their identities in line with its official discourse. Being aware of its potential as a marker of ethnic identity, members of the Premi elites have focused their projects on religion. In Muli, educated Premi accept their state classification as Tibetans, which is based on the integration of the pre-Communist elite into the Tibetan Buddhist Gelugpas. They take pride in being included in a community that is viewed within official Chinese discourse on ethnic minorities as one with an advanced culture, with its own script and famous icons such as the Potala Palace in Lhasa. Supported by the official ethnic classification of all Muli Premi as Tibetans, Muli elites do not have to worry about the obvious discrepancies between their views and Premi culture as it is expressed and lived in mountain villages such as Bustling Township.

The community construction project initiated by the group of enthusiastic Premi cadres and intellectuals in Yunnan is more demanding. Being members of the official Pumi *minzu*, they have identified the *hangui* religion as their central ethnic marker. It is up to them to convince the rest of the Premi in Yunnan to take up again a belief and a practice that had all but disappeared from the province. To them, to use Bauman's words, "'community' stands for the kind of world which is not, regrettably, available to us—but which we would dearly wish to inhabit and which we hope to repossess" (2001: 3).

EPILOGUE

In the autumn of 2006, I passed through Ninglang and Yongning on my way to visit Khe'ong Monastery (Kangwu) in eastern Muli. I used the opportunity to pay a visit to the *hangui* school in Chicken Foot Village and look up Hu Jingming and the other retired Premi cadres in Ninglang. I learned that Nima Anji was on his way from Walnut Grove to Ninglang and was distressed that my schedule would make it impossible to await his arrival. Remembering my missed opportunity with one of Yunnan's last *hangui* almost twenty years earlier, and my frustration when I arrived just a couple of days too late to participate in the funeral of the oldest *anji* of Bustling Township, I concluded that either fate or the water deities relished sabotaging my encounters with *hangui* or *anji*. Great was my joy, then, when, having arrived in Yongning, I almost literally bumped into Nima Anji on the one and only street. Both he and I were in town for only one night, headed in opposite directions, so I was lucky indeed!

Not only in Chicken Foot Village, but also in Walnut Grove, small and larger changes had taken place during the last two years. At the *hangui* school, the second of two four-year classes was approaching graduation. Soon, eight more *hangui* would return to their villages and start practicing. Since their teacher, Nima Anji, was often absent, the second class received most of its instruction from a graduate from the first class.

Chicken Foot Village itself counted seven practicing *hangui*. The activities of the retired cadres were not limited to organizing *hangui* teaching. They not only organized three large ceremonies every year in Chicken Foot Village but in 2006, with ¥100,000 in funding from the local government, made Ninglang the host town of the "official" Premi New Year celebration. This event attracted more than five hundred guests from all over the region. Hu informed me that they also had plans to start a museum of Premi culture in the tourist spot of Lugu Lake, near Yongning. They would need an investment of US$150,000 and were confident that they would quickly earn the money back by attracting three hundred paying visitors per day. According to Hu, this goal was realistic, considering that the Dongba Museum in Lijiang, dedicated to the traditional culture of the Naxi people, received two thousand visitors per day. Lugu Lake was famous for its Mosuo or Na people, with their matrilineal culture, but, Hu explained, the Mosuo did not have much to show in terms of cultural artifacts, and a museum of Premi culture would fill the gap perfectly.

Nima Anji had not been sitting idle either since I had last met with him in 2004. The work of collecting and translating written and oral tradition continued. Nima Anji had also taken the *hangui/anji* tradition beyond China's borders through his participation in two international conferences on Asian minorities in Thailand and Vietnam. In Walnut Grove, the people's living standard had improved somewhat owing to the government campaign of planting trees on sloping land. For a period of five to eight years, depending on the kind of tree, they were paid ¥200 annually for each *mu* they planted. Nima Anji himself had planted three *mu* with walnut trees. The money the villagers received for this work was pooled by two or three families who then bought small power stations and television sets. Even the ostracized families, those considered to be possessed with *brö* demons, now had access to TV. According to Nima Anji, one of the consequences was an improvement in Chinese-language skills, which might come in handy when young farmers leave Walnut Grove in search of jobs after the tree-planting campaign ends and the price of walnuts does not allow families to maintain a decent standard of living.

GLOSSARY

ABBREVIATIONS

C Chinese
T Tibetan
P Premi
AC autonomous county (*zizhixian*)
AP autonomous prefecture (*zizhizhou*)

a (P) I, me
agu (P) mother's brother
ama (P) mother
ane (P) father's sister
anfushi (C) 安抚使 pacification commissioner
anji (P) Premi ritual expert
apo^n (P) father, father's brother, father's sister's husband, mother's sister's husband, wife's father

arè (P) we
arje (P) home-distilled spirits

Ba'er (C) 巴耳 or 八尔 name of the ruling clan of Muli
baise (T) 'bad-sras (?) local administrator under the Muli *tusi* or head lama
baixing (C) 百姓 the common

people (lit., "the hundred family names")

Bajia (C) 八家 name of a village in Labai Township, Ninglang Yi AC

Banawa (C) 巴纳瓦 name of a village in Labai Township, Ninglang Yi AC

baoban maimai hunyin (C) 包办买卖婚姻 arranged mercenary marriage

bap'u (P) ancestors

Bari (T) 'ba 'ri name of the Premi ruling clan in Muli, Tibetan form of "Bar"

barzung rabyampa (T) 'bar-bzung rab-'byams-pa local administrator under the Muli *tusi* or head lama

Batang (C) 巴塘 name of town and county in Kham/Sichuan

bazong (C) 把总 hereditary rank held by administrators of border regions under the Muli *tusi*

bekha (T) bas-kha central pillar of a house in Gyelthang

bianzhi (C) 编制 authorized personnel, the establishment of posts

Biqi (C) 比奇 name of a village in Yongning Township, Ninglang Yi AC

bo^n (P) dpon-po head lama (in Muli)

Bön (T) bon Tibetan religion

Bönpo (T) bon-po adherent of Bön

brö demon (P) type of disease-causing demon

bu-dzu (P) place for cremation of a corpse

ch'ako^n (P) room, in a house, reserved for monks and for reading scriptures; also called *hlije^n*

ch'am (T) 'cham Tibetan Buddhist festival

Chamdo (T) chab-mdo town in Kham, Tibet Autonomous Region

chantsö (T) phyag-mdzod manager (administrator under the Muli *tusi* or head lama)

che (P) food

che-drö (P) offerings of food or wine (lit., "food for the souls")

Chen Xialing (C) 陈遐龄 name of a frontier commissioner/warlord

chö (T) chos dharma; Buddhism

cho^n (P) north

chongcao (C) 虫草 caterpillar fungus (*cordyceps sinensis*), a medicinal fungus; short for *dong-chong xia-cao*

Ch'ruame (P) local self-appellation for Premi-speaking populations in some areas of Muli; also called Chra-me (Rock) (official *minzu* name: Zangzu)

ch'ü (P) wind direction

chuzhong (C) 初中 junior middle school

ch'wi-p'ö (P) doing good things; monastic Buddhism

Cuiyu (C) 翠玉 name of a township in Ninglang Yi AC

cunmin xiaozu (C) 村民小组 villagers' small group, corresponding to "natural village" in Muli

cunminzu (C) 村民组 village group

cunweihui (C) 村委会 administrative village

cunxiao (C) 村校 village school

cunzhang (C) 村长 village leader

Dajianlu (C) 打箭炉 Chinese rendering of "Dartsendo," name of a town in Kham/Sichuan

Daocheng (C) 稻城 name of a town and county in Kham/Sichuan

dap'u (P) master, leader

Dartsendo (T) dar-rtze-mdo name of a town in Kham/Sichuan; called Kangding in Chinese

Daxingzhen (C) 大兴镇 name of the capital of Ninglang Yi AC

dazeze (P) of the same descent

dazhongyi (C) 大仲译 Tibetan-language secretary (in the administration of the Muli *tusi*)

dedrwè-p'ö (P) doing bad/evil things

depa (T) sde-pa local hereditary ruler (in pre-PRC Tibet)

desi (T) sde-srid regent (in pre-PRC Tibet)

dianban (C) 佃班 administrative post under the *tusi* or head lama in Muli

dianke (C) 佃客 administrative post under the *tusi* or head lama in Muli

Diantou (C) 甸头 village in Ludian Township, Yulong Naxi AC

difangzhi (C) 地方志 local gazetteer, local history

dizhu (C) 地主 landlord (PRC social-class designation)

dongba (C) 东巴 Naxi ritualist; Chinese transliteration of *dtô-mbà* or *dobbaq*

dong-chong xia-cao (C) 东虫夏草 winter insect, summer plant (see *chongcao*)

Dongfeng (C) 东风 name of a village in Ninglang Yi AC

drè^n (P) platform (in the main room of a Premi house); bed (in North Village)

Drenpa Namkha (T) dran-pa nam-mkha name of a sage in Bön religion

Drepung (T) 'bras-spungs name of a famous monastery outside Lhasa

drwama (P) offering stone (in a Premi house)

dzasa (T) dza-sag highest-level

administrator under the *tusi* or head lama in Muli; called *mengong* in Chinese

dzè-k'o (P) state, country; called *guojia* in Chinese

dzè^n (P) house (in North Village)

dzè^n-hsi (P) new house

dzè^n-mè (P) house name

dzè^n-p'o (P) "splitting the house," when a son moves out to establish his own neolocal residence

Eya (C) 俄亚 name of a township in Muli Tibetan AC

fangzhi (C) 方志 gazetteer

fengjian da lama (C) 封建大喇嘛 feudal high monk (PRC social-class designation)

fengsu xiguan (C) 风俗习惯 customs and habits

Fojiao Xiehui (C) 佛教协会 Buddhist Association

fu (C) 府 prefecture (during the Qing)

fu (P) north

funong (C) 富农 rich peasant (PRC social-class designation)

fupin (C) 扶贫 poverty alleviation

ga (P) household group (in Uphill and Downhill)

Gaige Kaifang (C) 改革开放 Reform and Opening Up policies

gaitu guiliu (C) 改土归流 replacement of native chieftains with Chinese administrators

Gala (C) 嘎拉 name of a village in Yongning Township, Ninglang Yi AC

Gami (P/C) 呷迷 local name for Kham Tibetans in Muli (official *minzu* name: Zangzu)

ganbu (C) 干部 cadre

Ganden Ngamcho (T) dga'-ldan nga-mchod Tibetan Buddhist festival

Ganden Shedrub Namgyel Ling (T) dga'-ldan bshad-grub rnam-rgyal gling full name of Muli Monastery

Ga^n-nyè (P) name for the Nuosu people

gaozhong (C) 高中 senior middle school

Ge Zu Ge Jie Renmin Daibiao Huiyi (C) 各族各界人民代表会议 Conference of Representatives of People of All Ethnic and Other Groups (CRPEOG)

Gelugpa (T) dge-lugs-pa name of a school of Tibetan Buddhism

geming zuzhe (C) 革命组织 revolutionary organization

geshe (T) dge-bshes the highest Buddhist scholarly degree

gompa (T) dgon-pa monastery
Gongaling (C) 贡嘎岭 name of a mountain in Kham/Sichuan
Guabie (C) 瓜别 name of a village in Yanyuan County, Sichuan
guan shijia (C) 官世家 aristocratic family of officials (Chinese title)
guca (C) 故擦 attendant (administrative post under the *tusi* or head lama of Muli); called *kuchar* in Tibetan
gujhi-jhataⁿ (P) central pillar (in a Premi house)
Guludian (C) 古鲁甸 name of a village in Labai Township, Ninglang Yi AC
guojia (C) 国家 country, nation, state
Guojia Minwei Minzu Wenti Wu Zhong Congshu (C) 国家民委民族问题五种丛书 National Committee of Nationalities' Five Series on (Minority) Nationality Questions
Guojia Zongjiao Shiwuju (C) 国家宗教事务局 State Administration of Religious Affairs
guoying linchang (C) 国营林场 state-run logging company
guoying muchang (C) 国营牧场 state-run livestock farm
guzyo (P) honored one (honorific designating incarnate lama); called *tulku* in Tibetan
gwèⁿ-gwèⁿ (P) cousins and siblings older than ego

gyelpo (T) rgyal-po king
Gyelthang (T) rgyal-thang name of a county in Yunnan; called Zhongdian or Xianggelila in Chinese

haijiao (C) 海椒 chili pepper
Han (C) 汉 name for the "default" ethnic majority in China; called Hsyè in Premi
Han Jiayang (C) 韩甲央 name of the gatekeeper, or *dzasa*, for the seventeenth and eighteenth head lamas (1888–1960)
hangui (P) 汗归 Premi ritual specialist
Hanzu (C) 汉族 the Han *minzu* (see also Han)
haozhi (C) 号纸 official charter (certificate of native ruler)
He Guoguang (C) 贺国光 name of a Nationalist general, governor of Xikang (1885–1969)
He'erdian (C) 合尔甸 name of a village in Labai Township, Ninglang Yi AC
hla (P) deity; also used to designate living persons considered to be deities, called "living deities" in this book
hli-dzèⁿ (P) prayer hall
Hongqiao (C) 红桥 name of a township in Ninglang Yi AC
hongzhao (C) 红照 red permit (certificate of concession for

land use rights in pre-PRC Muli)
hsin-drwè (P) iron tripod (in the fireplace, used for cooking)
Hsyè (P) name for the Han
hu (C) 户 household
Hu Ruoyu (C) 胡若愚 name of a commander in Long Yun's army
Hu Zongnan (C) 胡宗南 name of a deputy commander in the Nationalist Southwest military and administrative headquarters
hualip'e (P) fireplace (in a Premi house)
huofo (C) 活佛 an incarnate lama (lit., "living Buddha"); called *tulku* in Tibetan
huofo zhengshu (C) 活佛证书 "living Buddha" certificate

jabyè (P) designation for a monk who has returned from the monastery to live in the village and who keeps his vows; possibly from the Tibetan term *trapa*
Jamyang Sangpo (T) 'jam-dbyangs bzang-po name of the first head lama and second *tulku* of Muli (b. 1585, r. 1648–56)
jhü (P) clan
jhü-me (P) clan name
Jianchang Wei (C) 建昌卫 Ming period name for present-day Xichang, Sichuan
Jiang Jieshi (C) 蒋介石 Chiang Kai-shek (1887–1975)
Jianli lüse jingji qiang sheng, minzu wenhua sheng (C) 建立绿色经济强省, 民族文化省 "Establish a strong province with a green economy and a province with ethnic culture"
jiating lianchan chengbao zerenzhi (C) 家庭联产承包责任制 household contract responsibility system
Jiayang Zhigu (C) 甲央旨古 name of the ninth *tulku* of Muli (1905–1973)
jima (P) main room (in a Premi house)
Jinmian (C) 金棉 name of a township in Ninglang Yi AC
jiu (P) village
Jiuhe (C) 九河 name of a township in Ninglang Yi AC
Jiulong (C) 九龙 name of a county in Sichuan
Jueluo (C) 觉洛 name of a village in Yanyuan County, Sichuan

k'a (P) household group (in Walnut Grove)
kadra[n] (P) iron trident on top of a Premi house
k'ame (P) house name
Kangwu (C) 康坞 name of a township in Muli Tibetan AC

Kangxi (C) 康熙 Qing reign period, 1662–1723

Karma Kagyupa (T) kar-ma bka'-brgyud-pa name of a school of Tibetan Buddhism

kempo (T) mkhan-po abbot

Kham (T) khams name for the region of eastern Tibet, now mainly in western Sichuan

Khamba (T) khams-pa person from Kham

kuchar (T) sku-bcar attendant (administrative post under the *tusi* or head lama of Muli)

Kulu Gompa (T) khe'ong dgon-pa name of a monastery in Muli

kwasèⁿ (P) name of a tree that grows at high altitude

la (T) bla soul; life; spiritual essence

Labai (C) 拉佰 name of a township in Ninglang Yi AC

labrang (T) bla-brang monastic household; residence of high monks in a monastery

Lakua (C) 拉垮 name of a village in Labai Township, Ninglang Yi AC

lama (T) bla-ma spiritual teacher; a respectful term for a monk

Lamuzi (C) 拉木兹 local name for the Namuyi

Lhakhangteng Ganden Dargye Ling (T) lha-khang-steng dga'-ldan dar-rgyas-gling name of a monastery in Muli

Liangshan Yizu Zizhizhou (C) 凉山彝族自治州 Liangshan Yi AP

Liewa (C) 列瓦 name of a township in Muli Tibetan AC

Lihèⁿ (P) Premi name for the Na in the Yongning area

Lijiang (C) 丽江 name of a municipality in Yunnan

Lin Jiayong (C) 林甲镛 name of a lord of Bar (1914–1960)

lingdao ganbu (C) 领导干部 leading cadres

Liⁿwu (P) Yongning (lit., "the place of the Lihèⁿ")

Liru (C) 里汝 name of an ethnic group in Sichuan; also called Niru (official *minzu* name: Zangzu)

Litang (C) 理塘 name of a town and county in Kham/Sichuan

Liu Wenhui (C) 刘文辉 name of a western Sichuan warlord (1895–1976)

Lobsang Gedün (T) blob-bzang dge-'dun name of the translator of *The History of the Dharma in Muli* (Muli chöchung)

Lobsang Thutob (T) blo-bzang mthu-stobs name of the sixth head lama of Muli (r. 1726–59)

Long Yun (C) 龙云 name of a Yunnan warlord, governor (1928–45)

Ludian (C) 鲁甸 name of a township in Yulong Naxi AC
lunhuan (C) 轮换 rotate (between posts within the government or the Party)
Luobo (C) 倮波 name of a township in Muli Tibetan AC
Luoshui (C) 落水 name of a village in Yongning Township, Ninglang Yi AC
lwéjabu (P) water deities

maise (C) 麦色 administrative post under the *tusi* or head lama in Muli
mao (C) 毛 currency, equal to ¥0.1
me (P) person
me-drö (P) a person's soul, which is believed to continue its existence after the person's death
Meng Kun (C) 孟坤 name of a vice-commander in Long Yun's army
Mengguzu (C) 蒙古族 the Mongol *minzu*
mengong (C) 门公 gatekeeper (the highest post under the *tusi* or head lama in Muli)
miè (P) what? which?
Miji Si (C) 米吉寺 name of a monastery
minban (C) 民办 operated or paid for by the local people
Ming (C) 明 Chinese imperial dynasty, 1368–1644
mingong (C) 民工 a usually temporary laborer working on public project
Mingyin (C) 鸣音 name of a township in Yulong Naxi AC
Minzhu Gaige (C) 民主改革 Democratic Reforms
minzu (C) 民族 ethnic group or "nationality"; minority ethnic group (short for *shaoshu minzu*)
Minzhu Guanli Weiyuanhui (C) 民主管理委员会 Democratic Management Committee
minzu xiang (C) 民族乡 minority *minzu* township
minzu zizhixian (C) 民族自治县 minority *minzu* autonomous county
minzu zizhizhou (C) 民族自治州 minority *minzu* autonomous prefecture
mixin (C) 迷信 superstition
modyè (P) butter tea
Mosuo (C) 摩梭 Han name for the Na; Han name, in pre-PRC writings, for the Naxi and the Na
Moxie (C) 摩些 Han name, in pre-PRC writings, for the Naxi and the Na
mu (C) 亩 unit of measure comprising .0667 hectare or about one-sixth of an acre
mu (P) name for a kind of wild fowl
Mu Ding (C) 木定 thirteenth generation of the Mu kings of Lijiang (1477–1526)

Mu Qin (C) 木嵚 twelfth generation of the Mu kings of Lijiang (1429–1485)
Mu shi huan pu (C) 木氏宦谱 *Official Chronicles of the Mu Clan*
Mu Tian Wang (C) 木天王 Heavenly Mu King
Mu Wenfu (C) 穆文富 name of a Tibetan Communist cadre
Mu Zeng (C) 木增 nineteenth generation of the Mu kings of Lijiang (1587–1646)
muchang (C) 牧场 state-run livestock farm (short for *guoying muchang*)
Mudiqing (C) 木底箐 name of a township in Ninglang Yi AC
Muge Samten (T) dmu-dge-bsam-gtan name of a famous Tibetan scholar
mugong (C) 木工 carpentry; woodworker
muguan (C) 木官 administrative post under the *tusi* or head lama in Muli
Muli (C) 木里 name of an autonomous county in Sichuan
Muli chöchung (T) mu-li chos-'byung *The History* [or, *The*] *Emergence of the Dharma in Muli* (compiled by Ngawang Khenrab in 1735)
Muli Zangzu zizhixian (C) 木里藏族自治县 Muli Tibetan AC
Muli Zangzu Zizhixian Weisheng Xuexiao (C) 木里藏族自治县卫生学校 School of Hygiene of Muli Tibetan AC
Muli Zangzu Zizhixian Zongjiao Shiwuju Zhuren (C) 木里藏族自治县宗教事务局主人 Director of the Religious Affairs Bureau of Muli Tibetan AC
Muli Zangyi Yuan (C) 木里藏医院 Muli Hospital for Tibetan Medicine
muxi shehui de canyu (C) 母系社会的残余 remnants of matrilineal society

na (P) substance of the female line (lit., "flesh")
Na self-appellation of ethnic group concentrated in the area around Yongning and Lugu Lake in Ninglang County, Yunnan, and in adjacent areas in Sichuan (Muli and Zuosuo Counties); also called Hli-khin (Rock), Mosuo, Naze, Nyè-me (in Premi) (official *minzu* names: Naxizu [in Yunnan] and Mengguzu [in Sichuan])
nadzawè^{n}wu (P) caterpillar fungus (*cordyceps sinensis*), a medicinal fungus, parasitic on the ghost moth caterpillar; called *yartsa gunbu* in Tibetan

and *dong-chong xia-cao* or *chongcao* in Chinese

Nahiⁿ local self-appellation for Naxi living in Bustling Township and possibly other areas in Sichuan and Yunnan (official *minzu* name: Naxizu)

Namuyi (C) 纳木衣 self-appellation for ethnic group living in Liangshan Prefecture and Aba Prefecture (Jiulong County), Sichuan; also called Namuze (official *minzu* name: Zangzu)

Naxi name of ethnic group living mainly in northwestern Yunnan, with some small populations in Sichuan and the Tibetan Autonomous Region; also called Na-khi (Rock), Nyè-me in Premi (official *minzu* name: Naxizu)

Naxizu (C) 纳西族 the Naxi *minzu*

neri (T) gnas-ri Tibetan mountain cult (lit., "mountain abodes")

Neten Tsultrim Sangpo (T) gnas-brtan tshul-khrims bzang-po name of the Mongol who became *kempo* of Wachin Monastery in 1584 and later also of Kulu Monastery

Ngawang Khenrab (T) ngagdbang mkhyen-rab name of the compiler of *The History and Emergence of the Dharma in Muli* (Muli chöchung)

ngoⁿ (P) west

niè (P) you

Ninglang Yizu Zizhixian (C) 宁蒗彝族自治县 Ninglang Yi AC

Ningyuan fu (C) 宁远府 name of a Qing period prefecture

Nongye Xuexiao (C) 农业学校 Agricultural School

norbu rimpoche (T) nor-bu rin-po-che precious jewel, a motif from Tibetan Buddhist iconography

Nomihan (Manchu) Dharma King (official title); called nuomihan (诺米汗) in Chinese

nungk'e (P) thread cross, a ritual object

Nuosu self-appellation for ethnic group in Sichuan, mainly in Liangshan Prefecture, including Muli County and adjacent Ninglang and Lijiang Counties, Yunnan; also called Lolo, Gaⁿ-nyè in Premi (official *minzu* name: Yizu)

Nyè-me (P) Black People, name for the Na, the Naxi, and the Rek'ua

onmatsang (T) dbon-ma-tshang local hereditary title of Muli rulers during the Ming; called *guan shijia* in Chinese

peitong (C) 陪同 official assistant who accompanies a foreign researcher

Pema Rinchin (T) pad-ma rin-chen name of present *tulku* of Muli

pep'ei (P) term for cousins and siblings younger than ego

pönpo (T) dpon-po head lama or *tusi* (lit., "master," "lord")

Pöpa (T) bod-pa self-appellation for the Tibetan people

Premi (T) most common self-appellation for people speaking Premi language; also called Ch'ruame, Ba (Na and Naxi), P'rumi, Prmi, Xi-fan, Ozzu (Nuosu) (official *minzu* names: Pumizu [in Yunnan], Zangzu [in Sichuan])

Premi-hli (T) the Premi language

pri (T) barley beer

Pumizu (C) 普米族 the Pumi *minzu*

putonghua (C) 普通话 standard Chinese

putong xiang (C) 普通乡 "normal" (i.e., not a minority *minzu*) township

Qianlong (C) 乾隆 Qing reign period, 1736–96

Qing (C) 清 Chinese dynasty, 1644–1912

qu (C) 区 district; in some areas of China, the administrative level between county and township

raka (P) substance of the male line (lit., "bone")

rèdzeng rèda (P) mountain deities

Rek'ua self-appellation for a people living in Muli who are closely related culturally and linguistically to the Naxi and the Na; also called Rerkua, Zher-khin (Rock) (official *minzu* name: Naxizu)

Ren Da zhuxi (C) 人大主席 chairman of the National People's Conference (short for Renmin Dabiao Dahui zhuxi 人民代表大会主席)

Renmin Dabiao Dahui (C) 人民代表大会 National People's Conference

ro (P) rooster

rongban (C) 绒班 administrative post under the *tusi* or head lama in Muli; called *rongpo rabjampa* in Tibetan

rongpo rabjampa (T) rong-po rab-'byams-pa monk sent by a monastery to administer a village in pre-PRC Muli

Sakyapa (T) sa-skya-pa name of a school of Tibetan Buddhism

Samten Sangpo (T) bsam-gtan

bzang-po second head lama of Muli (r. 1656–79)

San Fan Zhi Luan (C) 三藩之乱 Rebellion of the Three Feudatories (1673–81)

san-shi-san zhong fudan (C) 三十三种负担 the thirty-three burdens

Sangye Gyatso (T) snags-rgyas rgya-mtsho name of the envoy sent to Muli by the third Dalai Lama in 1580

Sanjiacun (C) 三家村 name of a village in Mudiqing Township, Ninglang Yi AC

saⁿroa (P) local ritualist who has knowledge of Buddhism but does not keep Buddhist vows

sarra (P) small bench (part of the ritual setup for making offerings in a Premi house)

set'u (P) small table (part of the ritual setup for making offerings in a Premi house)

shang bao, xia bi (C) 上报, 下批 report to the higher authorities, grant permission to the lower authorities (short for "Wang shang baogao, wang xia pizhun" 往上报告, 往下批准)

shangceng (C) 上层 upper strata

shaoshu minzu (C) 少数民族 minority *minzu*

shaoshu minzu diqu (C) 少数民族地区 minority *minzu* area

shaoshu minzu zhongdianban (C) 少数民族重点班 special class reserved for members of minority *minzu*

she (P) substance of the female line (lit., "flesh")

shep'a (P) evil spirits

Sherab Nyipo (T) shes-rab snyings-po The Heart Sutra

shifan xuexiao (C) 师范学校 normal school (teacher training school)

shiye (C) 师爷 Chinese-language secretary (administrative post under the *tusi* or head lama in Muli)

Shu Yuanyuan (C) 舒源远 name of the last *bazong* of Baiwu (1916–1963)

Shuhiⁿ self-appellation for ethnic group of two thousand to three thousand people in Shuiluo Township in Muli County; also called Shimi, Shu-khin (Rock), Shumu, Xumi, Shiheng (official *minzu* name: Zangzu)

Shuiluo (C) 水洛 name of a township in Muli Tibetan AC

si fan (C) 四反 Four Antis (a political campaign)

si jiu (C) 四旧 Four Olds (from the Cultural Revolution slogan "Smash the Four Olds")

soma (P) spirit medium; called *sungma* in Tibetan

Sonam Gyatso (T) bsod-nams

rgya-mtsho name of the third Dalai Lama (1543–1588)
songrong (C) 松茸 pine mushroom
Songziyuan (C) 松子院 name of a village in Jiuhe Township, Yulong Naxi AC
sungdü (P/T) srung-mdud knotted thread worn around the neck or arm for protection
sungma (T) srung-ma spirit medium
syè (P) east

Taian (C) 太安 name of a township in Yulong Naxi AC
tamen shi yige danwei de (C) 他们是一个单位的 "they are all in the same work unit"
Tang Jiyao (C) 唐继尧 name of a Yunnan warlord (1881–1927)
Tashilhunpo (T) bkra-shis lhun-po name of a major Gelugpa monastery, situated in Shigatse and seat of the Panchen Lama
Tianbao (C) 天保 short for Tianranlin Baohu Gongcheng (Natural Forest Protection Program)
Tianranlin Baohu Gongcheng (C) 天然林保护工程 Natural Forest Protection Program
tirè (P) spring; place where water comes out
tönpa (T) ston-pa teacher

Tönpa Shenrab (T) ston-pa gshen-rab name of the founder of the Bön religion
Tonghailuo (C) 通海洛 name of a village in Jiuhe Township, Yulong Naxi AC
Tongzhi (C) 同治 Qing reign period, 1862–74
trapa (T) grwa-pa monk
trungyi (T) trung-yik Tibetan-language secretary (administrative post under the head lama or *tusi* in Muli)
Tsewang Rigzin (T) tshe-dbang rig-'dzin name of a Bön sage
tshokhang (T) tshogs-khang main assembly hall in a monastery
Tsongkhapa (T) tsong-kha-pa name of the founder of the Gelug school of Tibetan Buddhism (1357–1419)
Tubchen Chamling (T) thub-chen byams-gling name of a monastery in Lithang
tuguan (C) 土官 local official in pre-PRC Southwest China
Tuigeng Huanlin (C) 退耕还林 Return Farmland to Forest, official campaign and policy
tulku (T) sprul-sku incarnate lama
Tuokua (C) 拖垮 name of a village in Labai Township, Ninglang Yi AC
Tuoqi (C) 拖奇 name of a village

in Yongning Township, Ninglang Yi AC

tusi (C) 土司 hereditary native ruler in pre-PRC Southwest China

ulag (T) 'u-lag traditional form of corvée labor in pre-PRC Tibet

umdze (T) dbu-mdzad master of ritual, ceremony (one of the leading positions in a monastery)

Wachang (C) 瓦厂 name of a district in Muli Tibetan AC

Wachin Gompa (T) wa-cing dgon-pa name of a monastery in Muli

Wadu (C) 瓦都 name of a village in Yongning Township, Ninglang Yi AC

Wa'erzhai (C) 瓦尔寨 name of a village in Muli Tibetan AC

Wang Peichu Qudian (C) 王佩楚取典 name of a high official in Muli (1912–1951)

wei (C) 卫 military station (administrative division under the Ming)

Weixi (C) 维西 name of a county in Yunnan

Welchen Meri (T) dbal-chen me-ri name of a Bön deity

Women wei shenme zhu-zhang zongjiao ziyou? (C) 我们为什么主张宗教自由? "Why do we advocate religious freedom?"

Wu Sangui (C) 吴三桂 general who rebelled against the Qing (1612–1678)

Wu Shifan (C) 吴世璠 grandson of Wu Sangui

wu-hsi (P) Premi New Year purification ceremony

wuqu (C) 乌取 administrative post under the *tusi* or head lama in Muli

wushu (C) 巫术 witchcraft, sorcery

xiaceng (C) 下层 lower strata

xiang (C) 乡 township

Xiang Cicheng Zhaba (C) 项此称扎巴 name of the sixteenth head lama (r. 1924–34), also known as Miji Tulku

Xiang Longpu (C) 项隆普 name of the fifteenth head lama (r. 1902–24)

Xiang Niancha (C) 项拈查 name of the ninth head lama (r. 1781–1800)

Xiang Peichu Zhaba (C) 项陪初扎巴 name of the nineteenth head lama (r. 1950), Muli County leader

Xiang Songdian Chunpin (C) 项松典春品 name of the eighteenth head lama (r. 1944–49)

Xiang Songlang Zhashen (C) 项松郎扎什 name of the thirteenth head lama (r. 1868–90)

Xiang Zhaba Songdian (C) 项扎巴松典 name of the seventeenth head lama (r. 1935–44)

Xiang Zhashi (C) 项扎史 name of the twelfth head lama (r. 1849–67), also known as Palden Gyatso (*dpal-dan rgya-mtsho*)

Xiangcheng (C) 乡城 name of a county in Sichuan

Xianggelila (C) 香格里拉 name of a county in Yunnan

xiangzhang (C) 乡长 township leader

xiaomaibu (C) 小卖部 small shop

Xibu Da Kaifa (C) 西部大开发 Opening Up the Western Regions, official campaign and policy

Xichang (C) 西昌 name of the capital of Liangshan Yi AP

Xichang Minzu Ganbu Xuexiao (C) 西昌民族干部学校 Xichang Cadre School for Minority Nationalities

Xichuan (C) 西川 name of a township in Ninglang Yi AC

Xifan (C) 西番 Chinese name, used mainly before 1949, primarily for Premi but also for some smaller ethnic groups, such as Shimi, Liru, Ersu, and Namuyi, all living in the southeastern borderlands of ethnic Tibet (official *minzu* names: Pumizu [in Yunnan], Zangzu and Mengguzu [in Sichuan])

Xinan Zhangguan Gongshu (C) 西南长官公署 Southwest Military and Administrative Headquarters (Nationalist administration)

xingzheng jiguan (C) 行政机关 administrative organs (in the Party or government)

xingzhengcun (C) 行政村 administrative village (administrative level under township)

Xinyingpan (C) 新营盘 name of a township in Ninglang Yi AC

Xishuangbanna (C) 西双版纳 Sipsong Panna, name of a former independent kingdom in Yunnan, now a Dai autonomous prefecture

xuanweishi (C) 宣慰使 control commissioner (Qing title)

Xumi (C) 虚迷 name of an ethnic group

Yanyuan Xian (C) 盐源县 name of a county in Liangshan Yi AP, Sichuan

yartsa gunbu (T) dbyar-rtswa dgun-'bu caterpillar fungus (*see* nadzawèⁿwu)

yèma (P) Buddhist lay priest; Buddhist monk, from the Tibetan term *lama*

yinxin (C) 印信 official seal
Yiren (C) 夷人 former Chinese name for non-Han in Southwest China
yizèⁿgu (P) name of a Premi religious ceremony
Yizu (C) 彝族 the Yi *minzu*
Yongning (C) 永宁 name of a township in Ninglang Yi AC
Yongzheng (C) 雍正 Qing reign period, 1723–36
you luohou sixiang de (C) 有落后思想的 "those with backward thinking"
yuegu (C) 约古 name of an ethnic group
yüllha (T) yul-lha god of the locality
Yunnan fu (C) 云南府 historic place-name for Kunming
Yunnan Minzu Daxue (C) 云南民族大学 Yunnan Nationalities University
Yunnan Sheng (C) 云南省 Yunnan Province

Zangzu (C) 藏族 the Tibetan *minzu*
Zhao Erfeng (C) 赵尔丰 name of a Qing governor-general (1845–1911)
zheixie fengjian mixin huodong (C) 这些封建迷信活动 "these activities of feudal superstition"
zhengchang de zongjiao huodong (C) 正常的宗教活动 normal religious practice
Zhongdian (C) 中甸 name of a county in Yunnan, recently renamed Xianggelila
zhongdian fupin xian (C) 重点扶贫县 key poverty county
Zhongguo shaoshu minzu jianshi (C) 中国少数民族简史 *Short Histories of the Minority* Minzu *of China*
Zhongguo shaoshu minzu jianzhi congshu (C) 中国少数民族简志丛书 *Series of Short Surveys of the Minority* Minzu *of China*
Zhongguo shaoshu minzu shehui lishi diaocha (C) 中国少数民族社会历史调查 *Materials from the Investigation of the Society and History of China's Minority* Minzu
Zhongguo shaoshu minzu yuyan jianzhi (C) 中国少数民族语言简志 *Short Records of the Languages of the Minority* Minzu *of China*
Zhongguo shaoshu minzu zizhi difang gaikuang (C) 中国少数民族自治地方概况 *Surveys of Autonomous Areas of the Minority* Minzu *of China*

Zhongguo tese de shehui zhuyi wenming (C) 中国特色的社会主义文明 Socialist civilization with Chinese characteristics

Zhongguo Zangyuxi Gaoji Foxueyuan (C) 中国藏语系高级佛学院 Chinese Higher Institute of Tibetan Buddhism

Zhonghua minzu (C) 中华民族 the Chinese nation

Zhonglu (C) 仲路 name of a village in Mingyin Township, Yulong Naxi AC

Zhongluo (C) 中罗 name of a village in Mingyin Township, Yulong Naxi AC

zhongxin wanquan xiaoxue (C) 中心完全小学 (central) full primary school

zhongzhuan (C) 中专 technical secondary school

Zhou Kangding Shifan Xuexiao (C) 定师范学校 Prefectural Normal School in Kangding

ziran chongbai (C) 自然崇拜 worship of nature

zirancun (C) 自然村 natural village

zizhu hunyin (C) 自主婚姻 marriage in which partners choose each other by their own free will

Zongjiao Shiwuju (C) 宗教事物局 Religious Affairs Bureau

zuzhang (C) 组长 leader of an administrative village (level under the township)

zyè (P) wind demons

NOTES

INTRODUCTION

Chapter epigraph from the 1982 Communist Party Document 19, cited in MacInnis 1989, 25–26.

1   "Communist Party Document 19" is formally titled *Guanyu woguo shehuizhuyi shiqu zongjiao wenti de jiben guandian he jiben zhengce* (Basic viewpoints and policies toward the question of religion during the Socialist Period in our country) and contains important guidelines for Party members, including recommendations for facilitating the reconstruction of religious buildings and institutions and for educating clergy (see, e.g., Potter 2003, 319).

2   In this book, I will try to maintain the distinction between "religion" and "(religious) beliefs," with the former referring to social practices and institutions.

3   In some areas of Muli and Ninglang, the pronunciation was *nanjhi*. I will use *anji* to designate the religious experts operating in my field site in Muli and *hangui* to designate their colleagues in Ninglang. The latter form has found its way into the Chinese ethnography of the Premi.

4   "Bustling Township" and the other names on map 2 are fictitious names. I explain the use of fictitious names further on in the introduction.

5   The term "Bön" has different connotations. Besides being the designation of the pre-Buddhist religion of Tibet, it is also the name of a religion that

developed in Tibet in the tenth and eleventh centuries and has existed uninterruptedly until today alongside Buddhism with its own textual tradition and monastic system (see, e.g., Kværne 1996, 9–10; Samuel 1993, 10–12).

6   The Lòlop'o is one of several ethnic groups or linguistic communities that have been classified by the Chinese state as Yi; this category also includes the Nuosu, who are close neighbors of the Premi (for further discussion, see chapter 2).

7   This is of course not unique to China. See, for instance, Paul Dresch on the problems of conducting anthropological fieldwork in the Arab world. In many countries of the Middle East, the prying of the foreign anthropologist is associated with spying, the more so when he or she speaks Arabic well, yet if one does not speak Arabic well, one is not considered worthy of being told anything of any significance (Dresch 2000).

8   In 2004, I interviewed the *tulku*, or incarnate lama, of Muli, Guzyo Pema Rinchin, and lived with a family in Bustling Township's North Village; in 2006 and 2007, I twice visited Chicken Foot Village, met with central informants such as Nima Anji, interviewed monks at the monastery of Kulu in Muli, and made shorter trips to other Premi areas such as Jiulong County in Sichuan and Lanping Bai and Pumi Autonomous County in Yunnan.

9   Between 1987 and 1995, I visited Premi villages in what was then Lijiang County (now Lijiang City and Yulong County), Songziyuan in Taian Township, Zhongluo and Zhonglu in Mingyin Township, Tonghailuo in Jiuhe Township, and Diantou in Ludian Township. During the same time period, I also visited the following Premi villages in Yunnan, all in Ninglang County: in Yongning Township, Tuoqi, Biqi, Bajia, Wadu, Gala (all in the vicinity of Yongning Town), Mudiqing, and Luoshui, and in Labai Township, Guludian, Tuokua, Banawa, and He'erdian. In addition, I visited Zuosuo Township, in neighboring Sichuan.

10   Chinese government regulations require that foreign researchers be accompanied in the field by an assistant, usually a researcher or student from the Chinese institution responsible for the project. This assistant is often required to write a report on the activities of the foreign researcher.

11   Muge Samten, a famous Tibetan scholar, argued in an article published in 1981 and translated by Janet Upton, that it would be absurd to consider the Premi of Muli anything else but Tibetans. He does so using an argument that is apparently self-explanatory, that is, by not calling them Premi or Pumi but Bod-mi, which means "Tibetan people." Furthermore, there are even those "who are diligently planning to make Muli [County] a non-Tibetan [County]" (Upton 2000: 8).

1 ∞ MULI

1. The current official appellation "Muli" is probably an early Chinese rendering of "Mi-li," one of the appellations of the area used in Premi and many Tibetan sources (rMi-li) before the Communist takeover (Rock 1947: 356; Kessler 1982–: 13). Another Tibetan appellation—used, for example, in the autobiography of the fifth Dalai Lama of 1677—is "rMu-le" (Ahmad 1970: 60). Today the official Chinese name is Muli, and official publications in the Tibetan language have adopted the name Mu-li.

2. See especially Rock 1925 and Rock 1930. Besides Davies and Rock, only a few other Westerners had passed through Muli around the turn of the twentieth century: the Swedish missionary Edvard Amundsen passed through Muli in 1899 (Amundsen 1900), and the Austrian botanist Heinrich Handel-Mazetti—stuck in Southwest China during the First World War—made a short trip through Muli to collect plant samples (Handel-Mazzetti 1927).

3. Chinese maps depicted Muli as officially part of Yanyuan County until the early 1950s.

4. Muli was the first new territory added to the Chinese empire since the conquest of the Southwest by Kublai Khan in the thirteenth century, and in the Ming dynasty, it was under the nominal administration of the Jianchang "military station" (*wei*), with its center located at the present-day town of Xichang, capital of Liangshan Prefecture. Before the Mongol conquest, it was part of the territories of the Dali Kingdom, and before that, it was ruled by the Nanzhao Kingdom, which had taken over the area from the Tibetans (*Muli Zangzu zizhixian zhi* 1995: 113).

5. The *Official Chronicles of the Mu Clan* (Mu shi huan pu) states that the eleventh Mu king, Mu Qin, conquered several of the villages in the Shuiluo River valley in the western part of Muli in the second half of the fifteenth century. His grandson, Mu Ding, added a considerable number of villages, also in Shuiluo (Rock 1947: 110, 114).

6. The core of this area corresponds roughly to the present-day town of Lijiang and the counties of Yulong, Weixi, and Xianggelila (Shangri-la, called Zhongdian until 2001), all in northwestern Yunnan.

7. Although this Bönpo monastery is newly built, it is likely that a monastery existed on the site before, since it is inconceivable that the Bönpo would have been allowed to establish themselves in the Mu territory at that time. Today there are no Bönpo in Muli, but there is still a small monastery with a few monks near the town of Zuosuo in Yunnan one or two stages (one stage is

one day's travel by mule or walking) from Liewa, and one with ten monks in nearby Ga'er in Jiulong County.

8   It appears that the monastery already existed but had been a Bön center (*Ganze zhou zhi* 1997: 316).

9   In Tibetan, *bari* (*'ba' ri*) (*Muli chöchung* 1993: 18, line 11). Rock has *Bar-ri* (1947: 357).

10 Other sources on Muli argue that the *tusi* system started in 1648 with the rule of the first head lama (see, for example, *Muli Zangzu zizhixian zhi* 1995: 543). Nevertheless, *History of the Dharma* mentions that the father of the boy who would become the first head lama already held the golden seal of hereditary native chieftainship, a title locally called (*w*)*onmatsang*, translated in Chinese as *guan shijia*, "aristocratic family of officials" (*Muli chöchung* 1993: 4, line 17 [Chinese part]; 18, line 15 [Tibetan part]). The area controlled by the Bar clan at that time was situated around their manorial estate in the southeast of Muli and was considerably smaller (in that it did not, for example, include the Shuiluo River valley).

11 Although the Qing designated only men and their paternal line as *tusi*, during the Ming there were quite a number of women *tusi* among the Yi in the Southwest (Herman 1997: 51).

12 The presence of several Naxi villages in Muli today may be traced to this strategy, as could the ruins of watchtowers in the Shuiluo River valley and a few other places.

13 In paintings, Mu Zeng is depicted as a monk, suggesting he was at least initiated as a Buddhist monk (Rock 1947: 161). He is also credited with establishing or rebuilding several of the monasteries and temples around Lijiang (ibid.: 206, 210).

14 Although the Mu kings were strong supporters of the Karma Kagyu School from at least the end of the fifteenth century, the autobiography of the third Dalai Lama mentions that the king of Sa-tham (Lijiang) provided laborers and artisans for the construction of the Chokhorling monastery at Lithang and even invited the third Dalai Lama to come to Lijiang (Ahmad 1970: 59). At that time, large parts of Lithang were under the control of the Mu kings (Xu 1993: 265).

15 Referred to in Shakabpa's *Tibet*, which remarks that Tibetans at the Simla conference in 1913-14 used the records of this census to refute Chinese claims to these areas in eastern Kham (1967: 113).

16 Data on the administration of Muli before 1949 are drawn from the *History of the Dharma* (*Muli chöchung* 1993: e.g., 56, 57) and the *Annals of Muli Tibetan Autonomous County* (*Muli Zangzu zizhixian zhi* 1995: 544-48).

17　The Baiwu *bazong* was of Naxi origin, and his territory was situated in what is now Yanyuan County. See Harrell 2001: 134 and *Muli Zangzu zizhixian zhi* 1995: 948.

18　See chapter 3 for a discussion of whether the position of *baise* corresponds to that of *besé* in Walnut Grove.

19　The Wu Sangui Rebellion, also called the Rebellion of the Three Feudatories (San Fan Zhi Luan), took place from 1673 to 1681 in Southwest China. Wu Sangui, a Han general who had helped the Manchu defeat the Ming, rebelled in 1673 and joined forces with the remnants of the Ming in the south. The rebellion ended in 1681 with the fall of Yunnan Fu (Kunming) and the suicide of Wu Shifan, Wu Sangui's grandson (see, e.g., Wakeman 1985).

20　An extensive presentation of the available Tibetan and Chinese sources on communications between the fifth Dalai Lama and the Qing court regarding Wu Sangui is in Ahmad 1970: 205–29. These documents, including the Dalai Lama's autobiography and the dynastic history of the Qing, seem to leave little doubt about the Dalai Lama's hesitant attitude.

21　One of the consequences of this change of policy was the annexation of Dartsendo (today Kangding), to the northeast of Muli, after closer examination of the border region revealed that this area had been administered by the Ming (ibid.: 225–29).

22　Within the Qing military native chieftain system, *anfushi* is a mid-level rank, at 5b (in the eighteen-level system ranging from 1a to 9b) (Herman 1993: 26).

23　Rock mistakenly transcribes the character as Hang (see, e.g., 1947: 357). From this point onward, I refer to Muli rulers only by the Chinese name form, although it is clear from the sound of the characters Chinese sources give for the names of the head lamas that the part of the name following the family name Xiang is undoubtedly Tibetan, as, for example, Xiang Songlang Zhashen.

24　The *tusi* was required to send tribute to Beijing on regular occasions but was not required to participate personally in the mission.

25　This is how his name is cited in the *Annals of Yanyuan County* (Gu 1894: 13). The *Annals of Muli Tibetan Autonomous County* gives the name as Xiang Zhashen (*Muli Zangzu zizhixian zhi* 1995: 543).

26　In the Qing system of administrative grades, level 3a—the rank of *xuanweishi*—was the sixth-highest position out of a total of eighteen (Hucker 1985: 95; Herman 1993: 26).

27　The large monasteries of Bathang and Chatring were completely destroyed in 1905 and 1906, respectively, after they rose in rebellion, and all surviving monks were summarily executed (Teichman 1922: 21–22).

28 Local hereditary rulers in Kham were called either *depa* or *gyelpo*. *Depa*, or governors, were lay administrators and were often less independent from Lhasa than were *gyelpo*, or kings. The Qing had invested both *depa* and *gyelpo* with *tusi* titles (see, e.g., Coleman 2002: 33; Samuel 1993: 74–75).

29 Banditry was one of the major scourges of Western travelers to the region, and their travelogues abound with descriptions; see, for example, Bacot 1912: 148–49 and Rock 1931: 14. Spengen 2002 gives an informative overview of these descriptions.

30 At the end of the Qing, there were still 150 *tusi* in the whole of Sichuan, but according to Gong Yin, only 50 had any real authority, and those were mostly *tusi* of smaller areas (1992: 175).

31 Eric Teichman, who did not visit Muli, noted the area's special administrative status, but he mistakenly designated it as "a Tibetan native state under the suzerainty of the Yunnanese Government" (1922: 204). Although the Muli head lama did enter into an alliance with the Yunnan warlord Long Yun at one point, Muli was never officially administered by Yunnan.

32 At that time, Chen Xialing was stationed at Dartsendo as frontier commissioner, but since he acted rather independently to preserve his own power base (as did many of the other high-ranking Chinese officials in the region), the term "warlord" would be more appropriate. Chen was a longtime survivor of the theater of the Sino-Tibetan border region and had held various positions in the region since the days of Zhao Erfeng (see ibid.: 47, 50, 57).

33 The warlord of Yunnan, Tang Jiyao, was forced to relinquish power by his three commanders, Long Yun, Hu Kuyu, and Zhang Ruji, in 1930. Immediately afterward, the commanders turned against one another in the struggle for control of Yunnan. Long won out over Hu and chased him and the remnants of his troops in the direction of Muli (*Muli Zangzu zizhixian zhu* 1995: 78–79). This was the start of Long Yun's rule as warlord of Yunnan. He was an ethnic Yi and Liu Wenhui's enemy (Peng 2002: 65).

34 "Nomihan" or "Nominhan" is a Manchu title that means "Dharma King."

35 Although both Liu Wenhui and Jiang Jieshi were members of the Nationalist Party, Liu was part of its reformist wing, which hoped to oust Jiang from power (Peng 2002: 65). This explains why Xiang Cicheng Zhaba sought support directly from Nanjing.

36 Ethnic categories are explained more specifically in the glossary.

37 This traditional form of corvée existed all over Tibet and Kham and obligated local people to provide transportation services to those whom the local ruler designated as entitled to such services. In Muli, this meant one family must provide one mule or horse, or two persons, for covering a distance of half a stage (a half day of traveling, usually between ten and fifteen kilometers or six and nine miles). Providing food, water, and encampment or lodging was also part of corvée duties (Liu 1939: 67).

38 One social division in the highly stratified Nuosu society in Liangshan was between the aristocratic Black Nuosu and the majority White Nuosu, which was in itself stratified (see, e.g., Sichuan sheng Liangshan Yizu shehui diaocha ziliao xuanji 1987).

39 This was an initiative by Hu Zongnan, deputy commander of the Nationalist Southwest Military and Administrative Headquarters (Xinan Zhangguan Gongshu), and He Guoguang, the governor of the province of Xikang (*Muli Zangzu zizhixian zhi* 1995: 84).

40 This paragraph draws from the *Annals of Muli Tibetan Autonomous County*, an officially sanctioned version of Muli history and contemporary conditions. I have corroborated some of the facts through talks with government officials but have not been able to interview surviving witnesses of these events outside the Bustling Township area. When stripped of ritual remarks such as "the PLA troops received a warm welcome from all people of all ethnic and religious groups," the inner logic of the narrative of the Communist takeover of Muli is nevertheless consistent and corresponds to better-researched cases on the United Front policy (see, e.g., Goldstein 1998: 23).

41 In view of the fact that the label "Tibetan" is also used in Liangshan to designate other Tibeto-Burman speakers such as Premi or Namuyi, Mu's real ethnic affiliation is unclear. Mu later held several high-ranking positions within the Prefectural People's Congress of Liangshan and its Chinese People's Political Consultative Conference (CPPCC). He was still around for the fiftieth anniversary of the Liangshan CPPCC in Xichang in March 2006. http://zx.lsz.gov.cn/showdetailokok.aspx?infoid=26259 (accessed 14 May 2006).

42 In 1993, the provincial government of Sichuan posthumously recognized Wang Peichu Qudian as a revolutionary martyr (*Muli Zangzu zizhixian zhi* 1995: 940).

43 One *jin* equals five hundred grams or about one pound.

44 See, for example, the work by Lin Yaohua, one of the progenitors of ethnic classification work in China (1987) as well as the recent reappraisals of this

process of state-controlled labeling by Nicholas Tapp (2002) and the authors whose work is collected in a separate issue of *China Information*, edited by Thomas Mullaney (Gros 2004; Mackerras 2004; Mullaney 2004a, 2004b; Caffrey 2004).

45 One article on the Naxi of Eya in the southwestern corner of Muli, by the Naxi scholar Guo Dalie, was published in the volume on the Naxi (Guo 1986).

46 These are mainly Zhongguo Shehui Kexue Yuan Minzu Yanjiu suo and Guojia Minzu Shiwu Weiyuanhui Wenhua Xuanchuansi 1994: 813; Li 1986; and Sun 1983.

47 The *Annals of Muli Tibetan Autonomous County* acknowledges that the Tibetans of Muli call themselves by different names and lists the townships inhabited by these different categories of Tibetans (*Muli Zangzu zizhixian zhi* 1995: 833).

48 Altogether, the proportional figures exceed the total figure of 35,000 because some townships are inhabited by more than one group and, except for Shuiluo, the *Annals of Muli Tibetan Autonomous County* does not distinguish between these groups at the township level.

49 The text contains a strong defense of the concept of *Zhonghua minzu* (the Chinese nation), an attempt by some Chinese intellectuals in the 1990s to defend the indivisibility of the peoples living within the current political borders of China and Taiwan on the basis of "natural" or even racial grounds. In the text, Long also launches a vitriolic attack on Western writings on China.

50 For a discussion of the terms "elite" and "minority elite," see chapter 5.

51 Xiang Zhaba Songdian became a member of Sichuan's CPPCC in 1956, and Lin Jiayong participated in the 1957 National People's Congress in Beijing, where he had a personal meeting with Chairman Mao Zedong's secretary, who conveyed to him Mao's support of his progressive work in Muli. In that same year, Lin participated in an important meeting on ethnic minority work in Qingdao, where he would meet Zhou Enlai, Mao, and Ulanfu (*Muli Zangzu zizhixian zhi* 1995: 946–47).

52 1 *mu* equals 0.0667 hectare or one-sixth of an acre.

53 See, for example, Smith 1996: 399–412.

54 The last rebel surrendered in 1974 and was given amnesty (*Muli Zangzu zizhixian zhi* 1995: 94).

55 Xiang Zhaba Songdian financed the building of Muli's first hydropower station in 1957, among other things (ibid.: 951).

56 Xiang Zhaba Songdian died in 1964 and Xiang Songdian Chunpin in 1961. Lin Jiayong and former gatekeeper Han Jiayang had died the year before, in 1960. Former *bazong* Shu Yuanyuan, who played a central role in establishing the first two "state-run livestock farms" (*guoying muchang*) in Muli, died of cancer in 1963 at the young age of forty-seven (ibid.: 948).

57 The Four Olds (Si Jiu) are old thoughts, old culture, old customs, and old habits.

2 ∾ BUSTLING TOWNSHIP

1 In 1998, production was 3.3 tons per hectare, while the national average was 3.7 tons. For the national figure on wheat yield, see, for example, the Web site of the US Department of Agriculture, http://www.pecad.fas.usda.gov/highlights/2006/01/china_27jan2006/ChinaWheatArea.htm (accessed 20 March 2006). This was a year of exceptionally bad yields in China. The local government compiled but did not publish the township figures. For the entire county of Muli, only figures up to 1990 were available, and these showed a wheat yield that was markedly lower than the national average. This is probably because the northern townships are much higher above sea level and consequently have lower yields, reducing the total average yield for all of Muli.

2 In Shuiluo, a township in the west of Muli, the rate was between 0.7 and 1.1 *mu* per person in a family in 1982 (see Naef 1998: 56). This means that the quality of the land in Bustling Township was rather low, even by Muli standards.

3 Muli itself was classified as a "key poverty county" (*zhongdian fupin xian*) in Sichuan and received special allocations from the province (*Muli Zangzu zizhixian zhi* 1995: 928). These funds were distributed to families officially registered as poor and were earmarked for special purposes such as the purchase of seedlings or breeding of livestock and help with medical expenses. In 1998, 42 percent of the households in Bustling Township received such support; the allocations were discontinued in 1999 (interview with the Party secretary in Bustling Township).

4 Its Latin name is *cordyceps sinensis*. In Chinese, the fungus is called *chongcao*, a shortened form of the Chinese translation of the Tibetan name, *dong-chong-xia-cao* (winter insect, summer plant), which refers to the life cycle of the fungus: after living underground as host to the larva of a white ghost

moth, the fungus breaks through the head of the caterpillar and appears above ground to spread its spores. This shoot, still attached to the empty body of the caterpillar, is used as medicine.

5   In 2004, prices were considerably higher in the shops of the major tourist city of Lijiang: *chongcao* sold for ¥40–80 per gram, and a 250-gram package of *songrong* went for ¥120. Collection of medicinal plants has become an important source of income for the whole region of Southwest China, and in Muli, it has reached the limits of sustainability for several species, according to ethnobotanist Karoline Weckerle (pers. comm.).

6   China enacted this radical prohibition on logging in the natural forests of seventeen Chinese provinces in 1998, after the disastrous flooding of the Yangzi.

7   A large company in Yunnan organized this enterprise. Each tree could provide up to several kilos of resin, which the workers tap into plastic bags that are then emptied into large containers. These containers are picked up at regular intervals by trucks making the difficult journey to Bustling Township and, for that matter, to many other places in the pine-covered regions of Southwest China.

8   See also chapter 1 for a general discussion of ethnic classification in Muli and the glossary for the different ethnic categories used in this book.

9   An ethnic group in Sichuan became classified as Mongol (Mengguzu) even though it had no apparent cultural similarities with the people living on the grasslands of Inner Mongolia because the Na chieftains legitimated their rule by claiming descent from Mongol officers of Kublai Khan who were "left behind" to administer the area (McKhann 1998: 33; Harrell 2001: 218).

10   On the Na of Ninglang County in Yunnan, see chapter 5.

11   Joseph Rock has written an article on the Rek'ua and their ritual practice, calling them "Zher-khin" (1938). Rock calls the Na "Hli-khin"; the Shuhi[n] or Xumi from Shuiluo Township in Muli he calls "Shu-khin" and considers them to be a sub-branch of the "Zher-khin." Charles McKhann—who uses the spelling "Rerkua"—has classified the Rek'ua as a separate ethnic category but one that is closely related to the Naxi (1998).

12   The spelling *dtô-mbà* was introduced by Joseph Rock. This religious practice has also been rendered in Western literature as *dongba* (Chinese pinyin transcription) or *dobbaq* (using the so-called Naxi pinyin, a romanized spelling designed for use in literacy campaigns among the Naxi). It is also the name of the religious specialists at the center of this ritual practice. *Dtô-mbà* is the

indigenous religion of the Naxi people of the Lijiang and Zhongdian areas of northern Yunnan and the adjacent areas in Sichuan. A comprehensive corpus of ritual texts written in pictographs has brought the Naxi a certain fame in China and the West, to such a degree that it is now possible to talk about the field of Naxi Studies (Pan 1998; Jackson and Pan 1998; Mathieu 2003).

13 I am concerned here mainly with the immediate periphery around my area of research in the south of Muli. This includes, besides southern Muli, the northern half of Ninglang County in Yunnan and the adjacent areas of Yanyuan County in Sichuan. In the larger periphery of southwestern Sichuan and northwestern Yunnan, there are large areas where non-Han languages dominate in small market towns and administrative centers; these are mainly areas with a concentrated Nuosu (Yi) or Tibetan (Khampa) population.

14 Even in regions with a large non-Han majority, such as the Tibetan Autonomous Region, local people lose out at all levels of the job market to inmigrating Han who are better skilled (Benjor 2001: 181).

15 In Party or "government administrative organs" (*xingzheng jiguan*), the term *bianzhi* translated as "authorized personnel" or "the establishment of posts," refers to the number of personnel authorized by the higher authorities (see Brødsgaard 2002: 363–64).

16 It was only coincidence that the township head for Bustling Township was Premi. Since the majority of the population in Bustling Township were officially designated as Tibetan, they belonged to the same *minzu* for which the autonomous county had been created and were therefore only a "normal township" (*putong xiang*). In order to show official consideration for the special needs of other minority *minzu*, five so-called *minzu* townships (*minzu xiang*) had been established in Muli in areas where these other *minzu* made up a large proportion of the township population (although not necessarily the majority): two Na (Menggu), two Miao, and one Naxi. Except for receiving extra funding from the Commission of Ethnic Affairs of Liangshan Yi Autonomous Prefecture (Liangshan Yizu Zizhizhou Minzu Weiyuanhui) (in 1998, this amounted to ¥130,000, divided among the thirteen *minzu* townships of the whole prefecture), the only obvious difference between a "normal" township and a *minzu* township was that in the latter the township head had to be of the same *minzu* as the one for which the autonomous township had been created.

17 The campaign is also called Tuigeng Huanlin Huancao (Return Farmland

to Forest and Grass), and its major aim is to stop or reverse the deterioration of the natural environment and protect water resources (see, e.g., Ye, Chen, and Fan 2003). According to a Tibet Information Network Testimonies report of 17 August 2004, since 1999–2000, farmers all across the Tibetan Plateau have been urged and—according to some of the testimonies—sometimes forced by the government to plant trees and scrub on farmland. http://www.tew.org/development/tin.testimonies.08.17.04.html (accessed 20 March 2006).

18 The campaign was also launched in other places in Muli. According to the ethnobotanist Karoline Weckerle, people in the township of Shuiluo in the western part of Muli were also planting chestnut trees on their contracted lands (pers. comm.).

19 In a restricted publication on the work of the civil administration in Muli, propagation of Chinese marriage laws is put forward as an area in which a lot of work has been done but also one in which a lot remains to be done, promoting monogamy being one of the major tasks. According to this book, another challenge linked to the issue of polygamy is marriage registration (not registering a marriage is one way of keeping the state at bay): in a 1998 survey, of 9,626 marriages in Muli County, 34.5 percent were "not registered" (*wei dengji*), only 10 percent were "concluded with the mutual consent of both partners" (*zizhu hunyin*), and 2.22 percent were so-called "arranged mercenary marriages" (*baoban maimai hunyin*), in which the bride had been bought by the groom's family (see Muli Zangzu Zizhixian Minzhengju 1998: 111–13).

20 Unlike many other ethnic minority regions that had fully complied with national standards on organizing local elections (see, e.g., Benjor 2001: 88), Bustling Township had to wait until 2005 before residents could propose their own candidates.

21 This is not necessarily the standard situation. In a comparative study of ten villages dispersed throughout rural China, Stephan Feuchtwang points out that according to regulations in Yunnan, officials at the administrative village level should *not* originate from the village in which they are posted (1998). In the Tibetan Autonomous Region, in contrast, candidates for the village committees were proposed and chosen by the villagers, at least in some counties in the 1996–98 period (see Benjor 2001: 88).

22 National statistics showed that in 2002, 90 percent of Chinese had completed the nine years of compulsory education. Even leaving aside for a moment the thought that this figure is undoubtedly the result of overreporting, there are

still 450 counties in China that had not fully implemented the law of 1986 on compulsory education (see, e.g., *Renmin ribao*, 3 November 2003, 14 March 2003). Ethnic minority areas, which make up a large part of these areas, were given more time to reach the required level (see Hansen 1999: 22, describing the situation in Yunnan, where all minority areas were supposed to establish six years of compulsory education by the year 2000). In a speech at the Chinese Women's Ninth National Congress on 2 September 2003, Premier Wen Jiabao vowed to make nine years of compulsory education available to all children in China by 2008 (*Renmin ribao*, 3 September 2003).

23 According to Regulation 51 of the Autonomy Regulations adopted at the First Meeting of the Seventh Session of the National People's Congress of Muli County in 1990 (ratified by the National People's Congress of Sichuan in 1992), "Tibetan-language courses will be established, alongside the centralized curriculum, in secondary schools with a majority of Tibetan students, in minority classes [*shaoshu minzu zhongdianban*], and in primary schools in townships with a concentrated Tibetan population, aiming to enable the student to master both spoken and written Tibetan and Chinese" (Dai Zuomin 1992: 24). This regulation stipulates further that where other ethnic minorities constitute a majority, classes or courses in their spoken and written languages are to be started. This can apply only to the Nuosu/Yi in Muli, but I have no data on the existence of any formalized courses in their language. The six Nuosu (out of 201 pupils) at the district junior middle school of the district in which Bustling Township is situated had no other option than to participate in Tibetan classes.

24 This seems to be the case in other places in Muli as well and is apparently related to the fact that Premi is quite different from standard Tibetan. A comparative investigation reveals that among the ninety (Kham) Tibetan speakers of Xiangyang Village in Donglang Township, thirteen people could read Tibetan, while among two communities with a total of 176 Premi speakers in the townships of Kala and Taoba, only one person could be found who was able to read Tibetan (Zhongguo Shehui Kexue Yuan Minzu Yanjiu Suo 1994: 423).

25 Despite its name, this school was established to train teachers for the whole prefecture of Garze, not just Kangding County. Its full name is Prefectural Normal School at Kangding (Zhou Kangding Shifan Xuexiao). Although Muli County is not in Garze Prefecture, the school accepts students from Muli because there are no schools for educating Tibetan-language teachers in Liangshan Prefecture.

3 ❧ THE PREMI HOUSE

1. In order to distance themselves from traditional kinship theories, several anthropologists have argued for using the term "relatedness" (see, e.g., Bodenhorn 2000; Carsten 2000; Edwards and Strathern 2000; Hutchinson 2000). Carsten holds that the use of this new term signals openness to indigenous idioms, and it facilitates comparisons "without relying on an arbitrary distinction between biology and culture" (2000: 3).

2. The pronunciation of *dzè*ⁿ differed slightly throughout Bustling Township.

3. When discussing the organization of landownership in certain western Polynesian societies, Stevan Harrell defines "household" in the sense not of a co-resident group but of a group that "eats together," that is, the "processing group" (1997: 242).

4. Levine keeps to the concept of the corporate household in analyzing Nyinba society and positions herself against, among others, Carter (1984) when she holds that it is a mistake to interpret the fact that because common residence necessarily precedes the establishment of the domestic group, such co-residence is therefore generative of social relationships "where no such ties existed before" (1988: 128).

5. For Naxi kinship, see, for example, McKhann 1992; for the Na, see Wang and Zhan 1988, Zhou and Zhan 1988, Yan and Liu 1986, Yan 1986, and Yan and Song 1983.

6. In his examination of the *numaya* institution among the Kwakwaka'wakw (Kwakiutl) people in what is now British Columbia, Canada, Lévi-Strauss turned to history and found similarities with European noble houses of medieval times as well as other institutions like those in Japan in the Heian period (794–1192). He defined such a "house" as a *personne morale* or corporate body "holding an estate made up of both material and immaterial wealth, which perpetuates itself through the transmission of its name, its goods, and its titles down a real or imaginary line, considered legitimate as long as this continuity can express itself in the language of kinship or of affinity and, most often, of both" (1983: 17).

7. See, for example, Howell 1995: 151, 169; Carsten and Hugh-Jones 1995: 10; and Sparkes and Howell 2003.

8. This constitutes one of the four ideal types of terminologies distinguished by Lowie in the generation of ego's parents, that is, "bifurcate merging." The other three are "generational," "lineal," and "bifurcate collateral" (Lowie 1928, cited in Barnard 1996: 477).

9   Due to some initial confusion on my part regarding Premi relationship terminology, I cannot eliminate the possibility that there were a few more cases of cross- and parallel-cousin marriages among the forty-six registered marriages in Walnut Grove.
10 This study is cited in Ma 2001: 83.
11 In their separate studies of two neighboring villages in the west of Muli, Naef and Schiesser each mention a few cases of polygamy. In his house survey of the eighty-two marriages in a Menggu village, Naef registered four cases of sororal polygyny and only one case of fraternal polyandry (1998: 52–53). Schiesser registered a slightly higher occurrence among the seventy-six marriages in a Premi village: five polyandrous and four polygynous marriages (2000: 183). Liu Longchu found seven cases of polygyny among 130 Naxi households in Eya Township in Muli in 1982 (1986).
12 This does not differ from other regions in China. While regular rounds of complete land redistribution have become rare, minor rounds of readjustment do occur in many places in the countryside, usually every five years, for example, in relation to changes in family size. As in Bustling Township, major redistribution apparently did not take place in Benjor's field site, making land use rights more stable and predictable.
13 The ashes and bone remains of the deceased Ts'uop'i are placed on Shogu-na^{n}basa^n, a mountain on the border between Yunnan and Sichuan.
14 The symbolic association of the number seven with female and nine with male is widespread among Tibeto-Burmans. Populations as diverse as the Gurung in Nepal and the Lisu in northern Thailand, for example, hold the belief that women have seven souls and men nine (Macfarlane 1981: 56; Larsen 1984: 117). The Naxi funeral pyre for women traditionally has seven layers of logs, while there are nine for men (Shih 1998: 120). The same is true for the Na (Mathieu 1998: 220) and the Nuosu (Stevan Harrell, pers. comm.).
15 It is possible to identify the places mentioned in the beginning of the ritual, but as the recitation continues, the identification of these places with actual, present-day, place-names becomes more questionable. Educated Premi and Chinese historians and anthropologists have analyzed and compared many different so-called *kai lu* (opening of the road) ceremonies and proposed many different locations for the Premi's place of origin, several of which are situated in present-day Qinghai. There is supposed to be a place called Zhewo in Qinghai that is said to be identical to Jewopöjeda^n (Hu Jingming, pers. comm.).
16 The *nungk'e* is made with threads of different colors and is also known to other peoples in the region, such as the Naxi and the Tibetans. In Naxi,

it is *naká* (see Fang and He 1981: 346) or *Na-k'wai* (Rock 1952: 52), and in Tibetan it is *nam mkha* or *mdos* (see also Beer 1999: 322). It serves as a temporary dwelling for divinities during rituals, as, for example, in Naxi ritual, in which it symbolizes the hill Ts'a-nyî-gyû-k'ò mbù, the residence of the king of the demons of love suicide and suicide by hanging (see He and He 1998: 146). Moreover, through the symbolism of the ensnaring net, the *nam mkha* are also often used to keep evil spirits away. After some time, the *nam mkha* are often burned, thereby destroying the trapped evil spirits (Nebesky-Wojkowitz 1993: 369–97).

17 According to the African Nyakusa, the spirits of the dead survive underground in the place of the shades (*ubusyuka*), whence they emerge to visit surviving relatives in their dreams and affect their lives (Wilson 1957: 17).

18 See Aziz 1978: 51–57 as well as Levine 1988: 41–45 for the Tibetan Nyinba in Nepal.

19 This is one of the arguments that led Shih to believe that the *tusi* family of Yongning was originally of Premi origin, a plausible explanation for the special status of the Premi in his territory (2001: 394–95).

20 Several sources (Yan 1993: 38; Shih 2001: 390) mention that the Premi practice the patronymic linkage system common among Tibeto-Burmans. Under this system, the last one or two syllables of the father's name are the first one or two syllables of the son's name (Lo 1945). This system was not in use in Bustling Township, perhaps because of the prevalence of Tibetan names.

21 House names become an integral part of personal names, so this practice might be the reason some ethnographers have mistakenly concluded that the Premi use the patronymic linkage system (see preceding note). On the one hand, if the son in a house that carries the name of his father uses this name as the first part of the name of his neolocal residence, this would make it seem as if he were following the patronymic linkage system. On the other hand, the possibility cannot be excluded that the custom of inserting the name of one's native house into the name of one's own house is a vestige of a once prevalent patronymic linkage system.

22 *Drwè* is the word for the three stones on which the cooking pot was placed in former days, before the use of iron (*hsin*).

23 I am grateful to Toni Huber for pointing this out to me.

24 Such symbolism is known from other societies that rely heavily on little-worked timber for house building. In Southeast Asia, the life-giving symbolism of posts that follow the direction of the growing tree is supported by the opposite phenomenon of inverting the posts in constructions related, for example, to funerals (Domenig 2003).

4 ~ PREMI COSMOLOGY

1 Samten Karmay, personal communication, 17 June 2002.
2 See Zhongguo Ge Minzu Zongjiao yu Shenhua Da Cidian Bianshen Weiyuanhui 1990: 495. According to Rock, the name of the mythical founder of the Naxi *dtô-mbà* religion, Dtô-mbà Shilo, is derived from Tibetan. *Dtô-mbà* is equivalent to *tönpa*, "teacher," and Dtô-mbà Shi-lo would refer to the founder of Bön religion, Tönpa Shenrab (1937: 7–8). The Premi pronunciation of *shenro* lends support to the argument that the religious traditions of the peoples of the southeastern periphery of historic Tibet have been influenced by Bön practices and beliefs.
3 In Walnut Grove today, a very smart girl may be called a *zènbuma*, in reference to the disguised *shep'a* king who managed to trick Dingba Shenro into marrying him.
4 Although other ethnic groups in the region also told versions of this story, to my knowledge their stories do not end with the wild chicken putting the lofty Dingba Shenro in his place.
5 *Brö* demons are supposed to have originated among the Na. In the area of Wenquan, to the north of Yongning, where the first infected bride came from, the local Premi children wear small bags with medicinal herbs around their necks to protect them from *brö* demons carried by their Na classmates.
6 This is why some of the more educated Premi identify *brö* demons with *gu*, or poison spirits, traditionally associated with the Miao people (see Diamond 1988).
7 The phenomenon of demons entering a household with a new bride is also known among Mongolian nomads, where it is explicitly related to such uncertainties (Maria Tatár, pers. comm., April 2004).
8 For the sake of clarity, I use the term *yèma* only to refer to the Buddhist lay priest residing in the village, and the term *anji* only to designate the non-Buddhist ritual specialist.
9 The ritual use of the text translated by Lopez is prescribed as "a cure for a wide range of calamities, misfortunes, dangers, and afflictions, including epidemic, possession by demons, sick livestock, loss of wealth and property, dying under a bad star, false accusations, and bad dreams" (Lopez 1997: 511).
10 While Muli Gompa demands that all monks reside at the monastery, the monks of the subordinate monastery of Zhamei in Yongning all live at home and go to a monastery only on certain ritual occasions (see chapter 5).

11   Harrell notes that the Na and Premi in Yanyuan County to the south of Muli use the term *djaba* (2001: 199).

12   Although Bön distinguishes between deities and famous teachers who have obtained divine status (Kværne 1996: 116, 119–20), such distinctions are not made by *anji*, who consider all of them to be powerful deities that can be invoked.

13   This exposé on ritualists and mediums among Naxi, Na, Tibetans, and other ethnic groups of the region includes a graphic description of a séance carried out by a famous Tibetan *sungma* in Yongning, organized for the purpose of casting a spell on an invading rebel army.

14   The available figures on the number of resident monks at Muli Gompa for the period 1930–50 are not consistent. According to the *Annals of Muli Tibetan Autonomous County* (*Muli Zangzu zizhixian zhi* 1995), after 1919 the number never again reached 300; in contrast, Liu Lirong, who stayed one month in Muli in 1938, put the figure at approximately 1,500 at that time (1939); Joseph Rock mentions 700 monks during his visit in 1924 (1925). This last estimate is close to the quota of 770, or one-tenth the number of monks in Drepung. Several of the surviving monks or Buddhist lay priests who were in Muli Gompa at the time it was shut down in 1959 put the number of resident monks at 600–700. On the total monk population of Muli in various periods, see chapter 3. It should also be kept in mind that few statistics differentiate between fully ordained monks and novices.

15   On a short revisit in 2004, I was told by some of the monks that the number of monks had risen to around seventy, but I was unable to obtain the precise number of monks officially registered and the quota of monks allowed. Such a rise would be significant for the overall development of monasticism in Muli, but the number of monks from Bustling Township, as far as I could verify, was the same as in 1999.

16   Wang Yangzhong, Director of the Religious Affairs Bureau of Muli Tibetan Autonomous County (Muli Zangzu Zizhixian Zongjiao Shiwuju Zhuren), pers. comm. All these monasteries belong to the Gelug sect, except for one in the north of Muli, which belongs to the Sakya sect.

17   On two official delegation visits to China in 2002 and 2004, within the framework of a human rights dialogue between Norway and China, the State Administration of Religious Affairs acknowledged the general policy of not allowing organized religious education of children. This is, arguably, in violation of the United Nations Convention on the Rights of the Child, ratified by China, since such a policy may be viewed as limiting children's right to practice religion (Lothe, Arnesen, and Wellens 2002). At the

same time, actual implementation of this policy was not rigid. In response to a question on several child-monks we had seen in Tibetan monasteries, Thubten, director of the State Administration of Religious Affairs for the Tibetan Autonomous Region, answered: "When I visit a monastery and see a child-monk, I close my eyes."

18 The others are Islam, Protestantism, Catholicism, and Daoism.
19 In particular, Documents 6, 144, and 145 specify how religious practice must be administered and controlled by the government and the Party in order to promote stability. Furthermore, they state that foreign intervention in religious practice in China, even from Taiwan, must be curbed (Potter 2003: 319–21).
20 See, for example, the article by Ye Xiaowen, the longtime leader of the State Administration of Religious Affairs, "Why We Advocate Religious Freedom" (Women wei shenme zhuzhang zongjiao xinyang ziyou) (Ye Xiaowen 1999).
21 Interestingly, there is no mention of China having only five religions.
22 See Goldstein 1998: 159; and Wei Jing 1989: 61.
23 See note 15.
24 State Council General Office Document 39 of 1991 contains "Circular on the Relevant Items Concerning the Reincarnation of Living Buddhas in Tibetan Buddhism" (referred to in *Muli Zangzu zizhixian zhi* 1995: 906).
25 Between 1987 and 2004, the institute educated more than four hundred *tulku*, and the staff grew to thirty-eight. But ambitions are even higher. According to Vice Director Li, the institute plans to augment its teaching capacity so that it will be able to offer a standardized *geshe* degree (the highest level of education in Buddhist studies within the Gelug School) for monks from all Tibetan and Mongol areas of China. One underlying motivation is to counter the trend of monks from Tibet traveling to India to study for this degree because they believe the level of *geshe* studies is not sufficiently high in Tibet. Such a move was not uncontroversial, and the institute dispatched a delegation of two *tulku* to monasteries in Tibet in an attempt to convince local clergy to support these plans (Li Guoqing, pers. comm., June 2004).
26 Although the Gelugpa monastic tradition accepts the establishment of monasteries for Buddhist nuns, there are none in Muli, and there were no plans to establish any at the time of my most recent visit in 2004.
27 In an article on hail protection ceremonies, Anne C. Klein and Khetsun Sangpo discuss the view that such ceremonies are dirty business because they involve the harming of malevolent spirits, a violation of the Mahayana spirit (1997: 539).

28 For a study on the concept of syncretism, see the essays and the introduction in Stewart and Shaw 1994. An interesting alternative approach to coexisting religious traditions has been explored in another volume that focuses on Shinto and Buddhism in Japan (Teeuwen and Rambelli 2003).

29 A comparable Tibetan version tells of the contest between Buddhist Milarepa and Naro Bonchung, a Bönpo, or adherent of the Bön religion (Dás 1881).

30 Such stories are also told among the Na. Like the Premi, they participate in Tibetan Buddhism but also call on the services of non-Buddhist ritualists, the *ddaba* or *Nda-pa* (see also chapter 5). Unlike the *anji*, these religious experts use only orally transmitted "texts." According to Na legends, the *ddaba* did have texts written on ox hide, but once, when they had no food, they were forced to eat their texts. As a result, all of their knowledge is in their stomachs (see, e.g., Rock 1938: 174; or Mathieu 1998: 210–11).

31 See Samuel 1993. Per Kværne distinguishes three significations for the use of Bön in Western scholarship: (1) the pre-Buddhist religion of Tibet; (2) the religion that appeared in Tibet in the tenth and eleventh centuries, is still prevalent in some parts of Tibet, and has many points of similarity with Buddhism; and (3) a designation for popular beliefs in Tibet, including divination and the worship of local deities (1996: 9–22).

32 It is interesting to note that, in accordance with the policy practiced during the time of the "Lama Kingdom," leading monks limit the universalist claims of Tibetan Buddhism to the assertion that Buddhism should be the religion of the Tibetans, and possibly the Naxi and the Menggu, but not the Yi or the Han. As explained in chapter 1, since the Yi/Nuosu and Han populations in Muli were counted as commoners, they were not forced to send their third sons to the monasteries.

5 ∾ MODERNITY IN YUNNAN

1 These two figures are based on Public Security data from Yunnan for the year 2000 as found in "Report on an Investigation into the Socioeconomic Development of the Pumi in Yunnan" (Yunnan Sheng Minzu Shiwu Weiyuanhui Pumi Jingji he Shehui Fazhan Wenti Diaoyanzu 2002: 178). They tally with the results of the PRC's fifth population census of the same year.

2 This case is a thorn in the eye for Chinese evolutionist theory, because it clearly undermines the deterministic argument that human society passes

through fixed stages of development, whereby a matrilineally organized society always precedes a patrilineal one.

3   Wang and Yan trace this change to the year 1863, when the *tusi*, prompted by a particular case, ruled that the Premi practice of killing babies born out of wedlock was henceforth forbidden. Even if a woman refused to marry, the resulting child could not be killed (1990: 194).

4   In Na and Premi, the monastery is called "Jamige." Its full Tibetan name is Thar-lam dgan-ldan Thub-stan bde-bskyid gling (see also Rock 1959: 807).

5   In 2006, there were around twenty monks and novices living at the monastery. As mentioned earlier, many informants did not differentiate between novices and fully ordained monks, a difference that easily involves up to seven or eight years of study. My use of the term "monk" as a translation of the word *yèma* covers both categories as well.

6   According to the abbot, the local people made available seven *mu* of land and also supplied the manpower for the construction of the monastery. The county government provided ¥20,000, the Provincial Committee on Ethnic Affairs (Sheng Minzu Weiyuanhui) ¥20,000, the Provincial Religious Affairs Bureau (Sheng Zongjiao Shiwuju) ¥30,000, and the town government ¥16,000.

7   One of the standard Chinese ethnographies of the Na, the 450-page-long *The Matrilineal System of the Yongning Naxi* (Yongning Naxizu de muxizhi) (Yan and Song 1983) includes only thirteen pages on Na religious practices. Two chapters by Shih and Mathieu in *Naxi and Moso Ethnography* (Oppitz and Hsu 1998) on the Na and the Naxi are based on more recent ethnography and are concerned with religion among the Na. *Mosuo Daba Culture* (Mosuo daba wenhua), a volume with Chinese translations of *ddaba* ritual "texts," was published in 1999 (Lamu Gatusa 1999).

8   This was part of a larger survey on Premi religious practice involving villages in the two counties of Lijiang and Ninglang. Villages surveyed in Ninglang include the following: in Labai Township, Guludian, Tuokua, Banawa, and He'erdian; in Yongning, Gala, Luoshui (Lugu), Tuoqi, Biqi, Bajia, and Wadu; in Mudiqing, Sanjiacun, Xiaocun, Zhongcun, Dacun, and Sanwangcun; and in Hongqiao, Lakua.

9   In the Premi areas of Lijiang County, the survey found that people in many Premi villages called on the services of a Naxi *dtô-mbà* ritualist (Wellens 1998).

10 Mentuhui (The Society of Disciples) is a Christian-inspired millenarian sect especially prevalent in poor rural areas. In Southwest China, it was wide-

spread in certain minority areas—especially among the Nuosu (Yi) (see Luobu 1998)—until the government conducted a series of crackdowns in the wake of the anti-Falungong campaigns in 1999 and the early 2000s. In Ninglang, it was mainly prevalent among the Nuosu; in Tuoqi near Yongning, three Nuosu committed suicide after a campaign in 2003. One of my monk informants in Tuoqi claimed that Premi and Na were not susceptible to such cults because of their adherence to Buddhism. Nevertheless, I collected several tales of Na and Premi who suffered because of their involvement with Mentuhui. Believing that the end is near, people slaughter all their domestic animals for food, stop working their land, and burn material goods. This makes post-crackdown readjustment very hard and places a terrible strain on the extended family, which is forced to pool resources in order to repair the financial situation of affected households.

11 Hu Jingming, pers. comm. Story also referred to in Harrell 2001: 211.
12 This is part of a slogan used in official campaigns or speeches in Yunnan to promote development: "Establish a strong province with a green economy and establish a province with ethnic culture" (Jianli lüse jingji qiang sheng minzu wenhua sheng).
13 Hu had previously told Stevan Harrell that they were planning to finance this project with iron-ore and timber revenues from Muli (2001: 213). The 1999 ban on logging deprived these cadres of an important source of funding.

BIBLIOGRAPHY

Ahmad, Zahiruddin. 1970. *Sino-Tibetan Relations in the Seventeenth Century.* Rome: Istituto italiano per il Medio ed Estremo Oriente.

Amundsen, Edward. 1900. "A Journey through South-West Sechuan." *Geographical Journal* (June and November): 620–25, 531–37.

Anagnost, Ann S. 1994. "The Politics of Ritual Displacement." In *Asian Visions of Authority: Religion and the Modern States of East and Southeast Asia*, edited by Charles F. Keyes, Laurel Kendall, and Helen Hardacre. Honolulu: University of Hawai'i Press.

Aris, Michael. 1992. *Lamas, Princes, and Brigands: Joseph Rock's Photographs of the Tibetan Borderlands of China.* New York: China Institute in America.

Asad, Talal, ed. 1973. *Anthropology and the Colonial Encounter.* London: Ithaca Press.

Aziz, Barbara Nimri. 1978. *Tibetan Frontier Families: Reflections of Three Generations from D'ing-ri.* New Delhi: Vikas.

Bacot, Jacques. 1912. *Le Tibet révolté: Vers Népémakö, la terre promise des tibétains* (Tibet in revolt: Toward Népémakö, the Tibetans' promised land). Paris: Librairie Hachette.

Barnard, Alan. 1996. "Relationship Terminology." In *Encyclopedia of Social and Cultural Anthropology*, edited by A. Barnard and J. Spencer. London: Routledge.

Bauman, Zygmunt. 2001. *Community: Seeking Safety in an Insecure World, Themes for the 21st Century.* Cambridge: Polity.

Beer, Robert. 1999. *The Encyclopedia of Tibetan Symbols and Motifs.* Boston: Shambhala.

Bell, Catherine. 1997. *Ritual: Perspectives and Dimensions.* New York: Oxford University Press.

Benjor (aka Ben Jiao). 2001. "Socio-economic and Cultural Factors Underlying the Contemporary Revival of Fraternal Polyandry in Tibet." PhD diss., Case Western Reserve University, Cleveland.

Blondeau, Anne-Marie. 1997. "Que notre enfant revienne! Un rituel méconnu pour les enfants morts en bas-âge" (Let our child return! A little-known ritual for children dying at a very young age). In *Les habitants du Toit du Monde: Hommage à Alexander W. Macdonnald,* edited by S. Karmay and P. Sagant. Nanterre, France: Société d'Ethnologie.

Bodenhorn, Barbara. 2000. "'He Used to Be My Relative': Exploring the Bases of Relatedness among Iñupiat of Northern Alaska." In *Cultures of Relatedness: New Approaches to the Study of Kinship,* edited by J. Carsten. Cambridge: Cambridge University Press.

Bourdieu, Pierre. 1977. *Outline of a Theory of Practice.* Cambridge: Cambridge University Press. Originally published as *Esquisse d'une théorie de la pratique, précédé de trois études d'ethnologie kabyle* in 1972.

Brødsgaard, Kjeld Erik. 2002. "Institutional Reform and the Bianzhi System in China." *China Quarterly* 170: 362–86.

Caffrey, Kevin. 2004. "Who 'Who' Is, and Other Local Poetics of National Policy." *China Information* 18 (2): 243–74.

Carsten, Janet. 2000. "Introduction: Cultures of Relatedness." In *Cultures of Relatedness: New Approaches to the Study of Klinship,* edited by J. Carsten. Cambridge: Cambridge University Press.

Carsten, Janet, and Stephen Hugh-Jones. 1995. Introduction. In *About the House: Lévi-Strauss and Beyond,* edited by J. Carsten and S. Hugh-Jones. Cambridge: Cambridge University Press.

Carter, Anthony. 1984. "Household Histories." In *Households: Comparative and Historical Studies of the Domestic Group,* edited by E. J. Arnould, R. R. Wilk, and R. M. Netting. Berkeley: University of California Press.

Certeau, Michel de. 1984. *The Practice of Everyday Life.* Translated by S. Rendall. Berkeley: University of California Press.

Chau, Adam Yuet. 2005. "The Politics of Legitimation and the Revival of Popular Religion in Shaanbei, North-Central China." *Modern China* 31 (2): 236–79.

Coleman, William M., IV. 2002. "The Uprising at Batang: Khams and Its Significance in Chinese and Tibetan History." In *Khams pa Histories: Visions of People, Place and Authority—PIATS 2000: Tibetan Studies: Proceedings of the Ninth Seminar of the International Association for Tibetan Studies, Leiden 2000*, edited by L. Epstein. Leiden: Brill.

Corlin, Claes. 1980. "The Symbolism of the House in rGyal-thang." In *Tibetan Studies in Honour of Hugh Richardson: Proceedings of the International Seminar on Tibetan Studies in Oxford, 1979*, edited by M. Brauen and P. Kværne. Warminster, UK: Aris & Phillips.

Dai, Yingcong. 1996. "The Rise of the Southwestern Frontier under the Qing, 1640–1800." PhD diss., University of Washington, Seattle.

Dai Zuomin, ed. 1992. *Muli Zangzu zizhixian zizhi tiaoli* (Autonomous regulations of Muli Tibetan Autonomous County). Chengdu: Sichuan Sheng Minzu Chubanshe.

Dargay, Eva K. 1988. "Buddhism in Adaptation: Ancestor Gods and Their Tantric Counterparts in the Religious Life of Zanskar." *History of Religions* 28 (2): 123–34.

Dás, Sarat Chandra. 1881. "Dispute between a Buddhist and a Bonpo Priest for Possession of Mount Kaila'sa and Lake Ma'nasa." *Journal of the Asiatic Society of Bengal* 50: 206–11.

Davies, Henry Rodolph. 1909. *Yün-Nan, the Link between India and the Yangtze*. Cambridge: Cambridge University Press.

Dean, Kenneth. 2003. "Local Communal Religion in Contemporary South-east China." *China Quarterly* 174: 338–59.

Diamond, Norma. 1988. "The Miao and Poison: Interactions on China's Southwest Frontier." *Ethnology* 27 (1): 1–25.

Domenig, Gaudenz. 2003. "Inverted Posts for the Granary: Opposition and Reversal in Toba Batak Architecture." In *The House in Southeast Asia: A Changing Social, Economic and Political Domain*, edited by S. Sparkes and S. Howell. London: RoutledgeCurzon.

Dorfman, Diane. 1996. "The Spirits of Reform: The Power of Belief in Northern China." *Positions: East Asia Cultures Critique* 4 (2): 253–89.

Dresch, Paul. 2000. "Wilderness of Mirrors: Truth and Vulnerability in Middle Eastern Fieldwork." In *Anthropologists in a Wider World: Essays on Field Research*, edited by P. Dresch, W. James, and D. Parkin. New York: Berghahn Books.

Durkheim, Émile, and Karen E. Fields. 1995. *The Elementary Forms of Religious Life*. New York: Free Press.

Edin, Maria. 2003. "State Capacity and Local Agent Control in China: CCP Cadre Management from a Township Perspective." *China Quarterly* 173: 35–52.

Edwards, Jeanette, and Marilyn Strathern. 2000. "Including Our Own." In *Cultures of Relatedness: New Approaches to the Study of Kinship*, edited by J. Carsten. Cambridge: Cambridge University Press.

Fang Guoyu and He Zhiwu. 1981. *Naxi xiangxing wenzi pu* (Glossary of Naxi pictographs). Kunming: Yunnan Renmin Chubanshe.

Faure, David. 2007. *Emperor and Ancestor: State and Lineage in South China*. Stanford, Calif.: Stanford University Press.

Feuchtwang, Stephan. 1998. "What Is a Village?" In *Cooperative and Collective in China's Rural Development: Between State and Private Interest*, edited by E. B. Vermeer, F. N. Pieke, and Woei Lien Chong. Armonk, N.Y.: M. E. Sharpe.

———. 2000. "Religion as Resistance." In *Chinese Society: Change, Conflict and Resistance*, edited by E. J. Perry and M. Selden. London: Routledge.

———. 2001. *Popular Religion in China: The Imperial Metaphor*. Richmond, Va.: Curzon.

Fjeld, Heidi. 2007. "The Rise of the Polyandrous House: Marriage, Kinship and Social Mobility in Rural Tsang, Tibet." PhD diss., University of Oslo.

Ganze zhou zhi (Annals of Garze Prefecture). 1997. Chengdu: Sichuan Renmin Chubanshe.

Geertz, Clifford. 1973. *The Interpretation of Cultures: Selected Essays*. New York: Basic Books.

Gellner, David N. 1997. "For Syncretism: The Position of Buddhism in Nepal and Japan Compared." *Social Anthropology* 5 (3): 277–91.

Germano, David. 1998. "Re-membering the Dismembered Body of Tibet: Contemporary Tibetan Visionary Movements in the People's Republic of China." In *Buddhism in Contemporary Tibet: Religious Revival and Cultural Identity*, edited by M. C. Goldstein and M. Kapstein. Berkeley: University of California Press.

Goldstein, Melvyn C. 1971. "Stratification, Polyandry, and Family Structure in Central Tibet." *Southwestern Journal of Anthropology* 27 (1): 64–74.

———. 1976. "Fraternal Polyandry and Fertility in a High Himalayan Valley in Northwest Nepal." *Human Ecology* 4 (3): 223–33.

———. 1978. "Adjudication and Partition in the Tibetan Stam Family." In *Chinese Family Law and Social Change in Historical and Comparative Perspective*. Seattle: University of Washington Press.

———. 1998. "The Revival of Monastic Life in Drepung Monastery." In *Buddhism in Contemporary Tibet: Religious Revival and Cultural Identity*, edited by M. C. Goldstein and M. Kapstein. Berkeley: University of California Press.

Gong Yin. 1992. *Zhongguo tusi zhidu* (The Chinese *tusi* system). Kunming: Yunnan Minzu Chubanshe.

Gros, Stéphane. 2004. "The Politics of Names: The Identification of the Dulong (Drung) of Northwest Yunnan." *China Information* 18 (2): 275–302.

Gu Peiyuan. 1894. *Yanyuan xian zhi juan jiu: Wubei zhi: Tusi* (Annals of Yanyuan County, chapter 9: Condition of the armed forces: *Tusi*).

Guo Dalie. 1986. "Muli Eya Naxizu gaikuang" (Survey on the Naxi in Eya in Muli). In *Naxizu shehui lishi diaocha* (Investigation into the society and history of the Naxi). Kunming: Yunnan Minzu Chubanshe.

Handel-Mazzetti, Heinrich. 1927. *Naturbilder aus Südwest-China: Erlebnisse und Eindrücke eines österreichischen Forschers während des Weltkrieges* (Pictures of nature in Southwest China: Adventures and impressions from an Austrian researcher during the world war). Vienna: Österreichischer Bundesverlag für Unterricht, Wissenschaft und Kunst.

Hansen, Mette Halskov. 1999. *Lessons in Being Chinese: Minority Education and Ethnic Identity in Southwest China*. Seattle: University of Washington Press.

Harrell, Stevan. 1997. *Human Families, Social Change in Global Perspective*. Boulder, Colo.: Westview Press.

———. 2001. *Ways of Being Ethnic in Southwest China*. Seattle: University of Washington Press.

He, Limin, and Shicheng He. 1998. "The *Dtô-mbà* Ceremony to Propitiate the Demons of Suicide." In *Naxi and Moso Ethnography: Kin, Rites, Pictographs*, edited by M. Oppitz and E. Hsu. Zurich: Völkerkundemuseum Zürich.

Herman, John E. 1993. "National Integration and Regional Hegemony: The Political and Cultural Dynamics of Qing State Expansion, 1650–1750." PhD diss., University of Washington, Seattle.

———. 1997. "Empire in the Southwest: Early Qing Reforms to the Native Chieftain System." *Journal of Asian Studies* 56 (1): 47–74.

Hillman, Ben. 2004. "The Rise of the Community in Rural China: Village Politics, Cultural Identity and Religious Revival in a Hui Hamlet." *China Journal* (51): 53–73.

Holmberg, David H. 1989. *Order in Paradox: Myth, Ritual, and Exchange among Nepal's Tamang*. Ithaca, N.Y.: Cornell University Press.

Holy, Ladislav. 1996. *Anthropological Perspectives on Kinship*. London: Pluto Press.

Howell, Signe. 1995. "The Lio House: Building, Category, Idea, Value." In *About the House: Lévi-Strauss and Beyond*, edited by J. Carsten and S. Hugh-Jones. Cambridge: Cambridge University Press.

Hsu, Elisabeth. 1998. "Moso and Naxi: The House." In *Naxi and Moso Ethnography: Kin, Rites, Pictographs*, edited by M. Oppitz and E. Hsu. Zurich: Völkerkundemuseum Zürich.

Huber, Toni. 1998. *The Cult of Pure Crystal Mountain: Popular Pilgrimage and Visionary Landscape in Southeast Tibet.* New York: Oxford University Press.

Hucker, Charles O. 1985. *A Dictionary of Official Titles in Imperial China.* Stanford, Calif.: Stanford University Press.

Hutchingon, Sharon Elaine. 2000. "Identity and Substance: The Broadening Bases of Relatedness among the Nuer of Southern Sudan." In *Cultures of Relatedness: New Approaches to the Study of Kinship*, edited by J. Carsten. Cambridge: Cambridge University Press.

Jackson, Anthony, and Anshi Pan. 1998. "The Authors of Naxi Ritual Books, Index Books and Divination." In *Naxi and Moso Ethnography: Kin, Rites, Pictographs*, edited by M. Oppitz and E. Hsu. Zurich: Völkerkundemuseum Zürich.

Jäschke, H. A. 1998 (1881). *A Tibetan-English Dictionary.* Reprint. Richmond, Va.: Curzon Press.

Jing, Jun. 1996. *The Temple of Memories: History, Power, and Morality in a Chinese Village.* Stanford, Calif.: Stanford University Press.

Jing, Wei, ed. 1989. *100 Questions about Tibet.* Beijing: Beijing Review Press.

Kapstein, Matthew T. 2000. *The Tibetan Assimilation of Buddhism: Conversion, Contestation, and Memory.* Oxford: Oxford University Press.

Kessler, Peter. 1982-. *Laufende Arbeiten zu einem ethnohistorischen Atlas Tibets (EAT)* (Work in progress on an ethnohistorical atlas of Tibet [EAT]). Rikon: Tibet-Institut.

Klein, Anne C., and Khetsun Sangpo. 1997. "Hail Protection." In *Religions of Tibet in Practice*, edited by D. S. Lopez. Princeton, N.J.: Princeton University Press.

Kværne, Per. 1996. *The Bon Religion of Tibet: The Iconography of a Living Tradition.* Boston: Shambhala.

Lamu Gatusa, ed. 1999. *Mosuo daba wenhua* (Mosuo *daba* culture). Kunming: Yunnan Minzu Chubanshe.

Larsen, Hans Peter. 1984. "The Music of the Lisu of Northern Thailand." *Asian Folklore Studies* 43: 41–62.

Leach, Edmund. 1970. *Political Systems of Highland Burma: A Study of Kachin Social Structure.* London: Athlone Press.

Lévi-Strauss, Claude. 1982. *The Way of the Masks.* Translated by S. Modelski. London and Seattle: Jonathan Cape and University of Washington Press.

Levine, Nancy E. 1988. *The Dynamics of Polyandry: Kinship, Domesticity, and Population on the Tibetan Border.* Chicago: University of Chicago Press.

Lewis, I. M. 1996. *Religion in Context: Cults and Charisma.* Cambridge: Cambridge University Press.

Li Shaoming. 1986. "Liu jiang liuyu de minzu kaocha shuping" (Review of the investigation into the ethnic groups in the valleys of the Six Rivers). *Xinan minzu xueyuan xuebao* (Journal of Southwest Nationalities Institute) 1: 38–43.

Lin Yaohua. 1987. "Zhongguo Xinan diqu de minzu shibie" (Ethnic classification in Southwest China). In *Yunnan shaoshu minzu shehui lishi diaocha ziliao huibian* (Collection of materials on the investigation into the society and history of the minority nationalities of Yunnan). Kunming: Yunnan Renmin Chubanshe.

Litzinger, Ralph A. 2000. *Other Chinas: The Yao and the Politics of National Belonging.* Durham, N.C.: Duke University Press.

Liu Lirong. 1939. "Xikang Muli xuanweisi zheng-jiao gaikuang" (Situation of politics and religion in Muli Pacification District in Xikang). *Xinan bianjiang* (The southwestern border regions) 8: 64–70.

Liu Longchu. 1986. "Sichuan sheng Muli xian Eya Naxizu yiqiduofuzhi hunyin jiating shi xi" (Preliminary analysis of the polyandrous household of the Naxi in Eya in Sichuan's Muli County). *Minzu yanjiu* (Ethnic studies) 4: 25–32.

Lo, Ch'ang-p'ei. 1945. "The Genealogical Patronymic Linkage System of the Tibeto-Burman Speaking Tribes." *Harvard Journal of Asiatic Studies* 8 (3/4): 349–63.

Long Xijiang. 1991. "Liangshan Zhou jingnei de 'Xifan' ji yuanyuan tantao" (Inquiry into the "Xifan" of Liangshan Prefecture and their origin). *Xizang yanjiu* (Tibetan studies) 1: 26–36 (vol. 1); 3: 56–65 (vol. 2).

———. 1997. "Lun Zhongguo tese de minzu lilun" (Discussing the Chinese characteristics of ethnic theory). www.unirule.org.cn/Academia/neibu99-12-long.htm.

Lopez, Donald S. 1997. "Exorcising Demons with a Buddhist Sutra." In *Religions of Tibet in Practice*, edited by D. S. Lopez. Princeton, N.J.: Princeton University Press.

Lothe, Egil, Knut Espen Arnesen, and Koen Wellens. 2002. "Report from a Visit to China by a Delegation from the Olso Coalition." Oslo: The Oslo Coalition on Freedom of Religion or Belief.

Lowie, R. H. 1928. "A Note on Relationship Terminologies." *American Anthropologist* 30: 263–68.

Luobu Heji. 1998. "Bixu jinzhi xiejiao zuzhi 'Mentuhui' zai Liangshan de fanlan" (The unchecked spread in Liangshan of the evil cult of "Mentuhui" must be stopped). *Liangshan yixue* (Liangshan Yi studies) 6: 21–22.

Ma Rong. 2001. "Marriages and Spouse Selection in Tibet." *Development and Society* 30 (1): 79–117.

Macfarlane, Alan. 1981. "Death, Disease and Curing in a Himalayan Village." In *Asian Highland Societies in Anthropological Perspective*, edited by C. von Fürer-Haimendorf. New Delhi: Sterling.

MacInnis, Donald E. 1989. *Religion in China Today: Policy and Practice*. Maryknoll, N.Y.: Orbis Books.

Mackerras, Colin. 2004. "Conclusion: Some Major Issues in Ethnic Classification." *China Information* 18 (2): 303-13.

Mathieu, Christine. 1998. "The Moso *ddaba* Religious Specialists." In *Naxi and Moso Ethnography: Kin, Rites, Pictographs*, edited by M. Oppitz and E. Hsu. Zurich: Völkerkundemuseum Zürich.

———. 2003. *A History and Anthropological Study of the Ancient Kingdoms of the Sino-Tibetan Borderland—Naxi and Mosuo*. Lewiston, N.Y.: Edwin Mellen Press.

McKhann, Charles F. 1992. "Fleshing Out the Bones: Kinship and Cosmology in Naxi Religion." PhD diss., University of Chicago.

———. 1998. "Naxi, Rerkua, Moso, Meng: Kinship, Politics and Ritual on the Yunnan-Sichuan Frontier." In *Naxi and Moso Ethnography: Kin, Rites, Pictographs*, edited by M. Oppitz and E. Hsu. Zurich: Völkerkundemuseum Zürich.

Metcalf, Peter. 2002. *They Lie, We Lie: Getting On with Anthropology*. London: Routledge.

Mueggler, Erik. 2001. *The Age of Wild Ghosts: Memory, Violence, and Place in Southwest China*. Berkeley: University of California Press.

Muli chöchung (mu-li chos-'byung) (The history [or, the emergence] of the dharma in Muli). 1993. *Muli zheng-jiao shi, 1580-1735* (The history of the politics and religion of Muli, 1580-1735). Translated by Lobsang Gedün, compiled by Ngawang Khenrab. Chengdu: Sichuan Minzu Chubanshe.

Muli Zangzu zizhixian gaikuang (Survey of Muli Tibetan Autonomous County). 1985. Chengdu: Sichuan Renmin Chubanshe.

Muli Zangzu Zizhixian Minzhengju, ed. 1998. *Muli Zangzu zizhixian minzheng zhi: 1953-1995* (Annals of the civil administration of Muli Tibetan Autonomous County: 1953-1995). Xichang (printed).

Muli Zangzu zizhixian zhi (Annals of Muli Tibetan Autonomous County). 1995. Chengdu: Sichuan Renmin Chubanshe.

Mullaney, Thomas S. 2004a. "Ethnic Classification Writ Large: The 1954 Yunnan Province Ethnic Classification Project and Its Foundations in Republican-era Taxonomic Thought." *China Information* 18 (2): 207-41.

———. 2004b. Introduction: "55 + 1 = 1 or the Strange Calculus of Chinese Nationhood." *China Information* 18 (2): 197-205.

Mumford, Stan Royal. 1989. *Himalayan Dialogue: Tibetan Lamas and Gurung Shamans in Nepal*. Madison: University of Wisconsin Press.

Naef, Roland. 1998. *Das Haus bei den Lianmu-Menggu (Südwest-China): Zugänge zu einer Ethnologie des Hauses*. Lizentiatsarbeit, Ethnologisches Seminar, Universität Zürich, Zurich.

Nebesky-Wojkowitz, Réne de. 1993. *Oracles and Demons of Tibet: The Cult and Iconography of the Tibetan Protective Deities*. Kathmandu: Tiwari's Pilgrims Book House.

Netting, Robert McC., Richard R. Wilk, and Eric J. Arnould. 1984. Introduction. In *Households: Comparative and Historical Studies of the Domestic Group*. Berkeley: University of California Press.

Ninglang Yizu zizhixian zhi (Annals of Ninglang Yi Autonomous County). 1993. Kunming: Yunnan Minzu Chubanshe.

Oppitz, Michael, and Elisabeth Hsu, eds. 1998. *Naxi and Moso Ethnography: Kin, Rites, Pictographs*. Zurich: Völkerkundemuseum Zürich.

Pan, Anshi. 1998. "The Translation of Naxi Religious Texts." In *Naxi and Moso Ethnography: Kin, Rites, Pictographs*, edited by M. Oppitz and E. Hsu. Zurich: Völkerkundemuseum Zürich.

Paper, Jordan. 1994. "Religion." In *Handbook of Chinese Popular Culture*. Wesport, Conn.: Greenwood Press.

Peng Wenbin. 2002. "Frontier Process, Provincial Politics and Movements for Khampa Autonomy during the Republican Period." In *Khams pa Histories: Visions of People, Place and Authority—PIATS 2000: Tibetan Studies: Proceedings of the Ninth Seminar of the International Asociation for Tibetan Studies, Leiden, 2000*, edited by L. Epstein. Leiden: Brill.

Penny, Benjamin. 2005. "The Falun Gong, Buddhism and 'Buddhist Qigong.'" *Asian Studies Review* 29 (1): 35–46.

Peter, Prince of Greece and Denmark. 1963. *A Study of Polyandry*. The Hague: Mouton.

Pieke, Frank N. 2004. "Contours of an Anthropology of the Chinese State: Political Structure, Agency and Economic Development in Rural China." *Journal of the Royal Anthropological Institute* 10: 517–38.

Potter, Pitman B. 2003. "Belief in Control: Regulation of Religion in China." *China Quarterly* 174: 317–38.

Ramble, Charles. 1990. "How Buddhist Are Buddhist Communities? The Construction of Tradition in Two Lamaist Villages." *Journal of the Anthropological Society of Oxford* 21 (2): 185–97.

Rock, Joseph Francis. 1925. "The Land of the Yellow Lama: National Geographic

Society Explorer Visits the Strange Kingdom of Muli, beyond the Likiang Snow Range of Yünnan Province, China." *The National Geographic Magazine* 47: 447–91.

———. 1930. "The Glories of the Minya Konka: Magnificent Snow Peaks of the China-Tibetan Border Are Photographed at Close Range by a National Geographic Society Expedition." *The National Geographic Magazine* 58 (4): 385–437.

———. 1931. "Konka Risumgongba, Holy Mountain of the Outlaws." *The National Geographic Magazine* 60 (1).

———. 1937. "The Birth and Origin of Dto-mba Shi-lo, the Founder of Mo-so Shamanism, According to Mo-so Manuscripts." *Artibus Asiae* 7: 5–52.

———. 1938. "The Zher-khin Tribe and Their Religious Literature." *Monumenta Serica* 3: 171–90.

———. 1947. *The Ancient Na-khi Kingdom of Southwest China.* Cambridge, Mass.: Harvard University Press.

———. 1952. *The Na-khi Naga Cult and Related Ceremonies.* Vol. 4, Serie Orientale Roma. Rome.

———. 1959. "Contributions to the Shamanism of the Tibetan-Chinese Borderland." *Anthropos* 54: 796–818.

Samuel, Geoffrey. 1993. *Civilized Shamans: Buddhism in Tibetan Societies.* Washington, D.C.: Smithsonian Institution Press.

Schiesser, Markus. 2000. "Haus und Raum bei den Siweng-Pumi in Südwest-China" (House and space among the Siweng-Pumi in Southwest China). Lizentiatarbeit, Ethnologisches Seminar, Universität Zürich, Zurich.

Scott, James C. 1986. "Everyday Forms of Peasant Resistance." In *Everyday Forms of Peasant Resistance in Southeast Asia*, edited by J. C. Scott and B. J. T. Kerkvliet. London: Cass.

Shakabpa, W. D. 1967. *Tibet: A Political History.* New Haven: Yale University Press.

Sheils, Dean. 1975. "Toward a Unified Theory of Ancestor Worship: A Cross-Cultural Study." *Social Forces* 54 (2): 427–40.

Shih, Chuan-kang. 1993. "The Moso: Sexual Union, Household Organization, Ethnicity and Gender in a Matrilineal Duolocal Society in Southwest China." PhD diss., Stanford University.

———. 1998. "Mortuary Rituals and Symbols among the Moso." In *Naxi and Moso Ethnography: Kin, Rites, Pictographs*, edited by M. Oppitz and E. Hsu. Zurich: Völkerkundemuseum Zürich.

———. 2001. "Genesis of Marriage among the Moso and Empire-building in Late Imperial China." *Journal of Asian Studies* 60 (2): 381–412.

Sichuan sheng Liangshan Yizu shehui diaocha ziliao xuanji (Selections from the investigation into the society of the Yi of Liangshan in Sichuan). 1987. Chengdu: Sichuan Sheng Shehui Kexue Yuan Chubanshe.

Smith, Warren W. 1996. *Tibetan Nation: A History of Tibetan Nationalism and Sino-Tibetan Relations.* Boulder, Colo.: Westview Press.

Sparkes, Stephen, and Signe Howell, eds. 2003. *The House in Southeast Asia: A Changing Social, Economic and Political Domain.* London: RoutledgeCurzon.

Spengen, Wim van. 2002. "Frontier History of Southern Kham: Banditry and War in the Multi-ethnic Fringe Lands of Chatring, Mili, and Gyethang, 1890–1940." In *Khams pa Histories: Visions of People, Place and Authority—PIATS 2000: Tibetan Studies: Proceedings of the Ninth Seminar of the International Association for Tibetan Studies, Leiden 2000,* edited by L. Epstein. Leiden: Brill.

Sperling, Elliot. 1976. "The Chinese Venture in K'am, 1904–1911, and the Role of Chao Erh-feng." *The Tibet Journal* 1 (2): 10–36.

Spiro, Melford E. 1967. *Burmese Supernaturalism: A Study in the Explanation and Reduction of Suffering.* Englewood Cliffs, N.J.: Prentice-Hall.

Stewart, Charles, and Rosalind Shaw. 1994. *Syncretism/Anti-Syncretism: The Politics of Religious Synthesis.* London: Routledge.

Sun Hongkai. 1983. "Liu jiang liuyu de minzu yuyan ji qi xi shu fenlei: Jian shu Jialing Jiang shangyou, Yalu Zangbu Jiang liuyu de minzu yuyan" (The languages of the [minority] *minzu* of the valleys of the Six Rivers and their classification: Discussing the languages of the [minority] *minzu* living in the valley of the upper reaches of the Jialing River and in the valley of the Yarlung Zangbo River). *Minzu xuebao* (*Minzu* journal) 3: 99–273.

Tapp, Nicholas. 2002. "In Defence of the Archaic: A Reconsideration of the 1950s Ethnic Classification Project in China." *Asian Ethnicity* 3 (1): 63–84.

Teeuwen, Mark, and Fabio Rambelli, eds. 2003. *Buddhas and Kami in Japan: Honji Suijaku as a Combinatory Paradigm.* London: RoutledgeCurzon.

Teichman, Eric. 1922. *Travels of a Consular Officer in Eastern Tibet: Together with a History of the Relations between China, Tibet and India.* Cambridge, U. K.: A University Press Publication.

Thomas, Philip. 1996. "House." In *Encyclopedia of Social and Cultural Anthropology,* edited by A. Barnard and J. Spencer. London: Routledge.

Turner, Victor. 1967. *The Forest of Symbols: Aspects of Ndembu Ritual.* Ithaca, N.Y.: Cornell University Press.

———. 1977. *The Ritual Process: Structure and Anti-Structure: The Lewis Henry Morgan Lectures, 1966, Presented at the University of Rochester, Rochester, New York.* Ithaca, N.Y.: Cornell University Press.

Upton, Janet L. 2000. "Notes towards a Native Tibetan Ethnology: An Introduction to and Annotated Translation of dMu dge bSam gtan's Essays on Dwags po (Baima Zangzu)." *Tibet Journal* 15 (1): 3–26.

Vinding, Michael. 1998. *The Thakali: A Himalayan Ethnography.* London: Serindia Publications.

Wakeman, Frederic E. 1985. *The Great Enterprise: The Manchu Reconstruction of Imperial Order in Seventeenth-Century China.* Berkeley: University of California Press.

Wang Chengquan and Zhan Chengxu. 1988. "Ninglang xian Yongning qu Zhongshi xiang Naxizu fengjian lingzhuzhi, azhu hunyin he muxi jiating diaocha" (Investigation into the feudal lord system, the *azhu* marriage and matrilineal household of the Naxi of Zhongshi Township of Yongning District in Ninglang County). In *Ninglang Yizu zizhixian Yongning Naxizu shehui ji qi muxizhi diaocha* (Investigation into the society and the matrilineal system of the Naxi of Yongning in Ninglang Yi Autonomous County). Kunming: Yunnan Renmin Chubanshe.

Wang Shuwu and Yan Ruxian. 1990. "Yongning Wenquan xiang Pumizu hun sang xisu diaocha" (Investigation into the marital and funerary customs of the Pumi of Wenquan Township in Yongning). In *Jinuozu Pumizu shehui lishe zonghe diaocha* (Comprehensive investigation into the social history of the Jinuo and Pumi Nationalities). Beijing: Minzu Chubanshe.

Webb, Jen, Tony Schirato, and Geoff Danaher. 2002. *Understanding Bourdieu.* London: Sabe.

Weber, Max. 1964. *The Sociology of Religion.* Boston: Beacon Press.

Weckerle, Caroline. 1997. *Der Gebrauch von Planzen im Alltag der Nanman-Shimi.* Master's thesis, Diplomarbeit in Ethnobotanik, Institut für systematische Botanik, Universität Zürich, Zurich.

Wellens, Koen. 1998. "What's in a Name? The Premi in Southwest China and the Consequences of Defining Ethnic Identity." *Nations and Nationalism* 4 (1): 17–34.

Wilson, Monica. 1957. *Rituals of Kinship among the Nyakusa.* London: Oxford University Press.

Wylie, Turrel V. 1959. "A Standard System of Tibetan Transcription." *Harvard Journal of Asiatic Studies* 22: 261–67.

Xu Maoci. 1993. "Kangqu tusi zhidu de youlai he fazhan" (Origin and development of the *tusi* system in the Kham area). In *Sichuan zangxue yanjiu* (Sichuan Tibetology), edited by Yangling Duoji and He Shengming. Chengdu: Zhongguo Zangxue Chubanshe.

Yan Ruxian. 1986. "Qianyan" (Preface). In *Yongning Naxizu shehui ji muxizhi diaocha* (Investigation into the society and the matrilineal system of the Yongning Naxi), edited by Yunnan Sheng Bianjibu. Kunming: Yunnan Renmin Chubanshe.

———. 1993. "Pumizu de xingming jiegou ji qi laiyuan tantao" (Inquiry into the construction and origin of Pumi family names). *Minzu yuyan* (Languages of the [minority] *minzu*) 1: 37–41.

Yan Ruxian and Chen Jiujin. 1986. *Pumizu* (The Pumi). Beijing: Minzu Chubanshe.

Yan Ruxian and Liu Yaohan. 1986. "Yongning Wenquan xiang Naxizu muxizhi ji lingzhu jingji diaocha" (Investigation into the matrilineal system and feudal lord economy of the Naxi of Wenquan Township in Yongning). In *Yongning Naxizu shehui ji muxizhi diaocha* (Investigation into the society and the matrilineal system of the Yongning Naxi), edited by Yunnan Sheng Bianjibu. Kunming: Yunnan Renmin Chubanshe.

Yan Ruxian and Song Zhaolin. 1983. *Yongning Naxizu de muxizhi* (The matrilineal system of the Yongning Naxi). Kunming: Yunnan Renmin Chubanshe.

Yan Ruxian and Wang Shuwu. 1988. *Pumizu jian shi* (A short history of the Pumi). Kunming: Yunnan Renmin Chubanshe.

Yang Xuezheng. 1991. "Ninglang xian Pumizu zongjiao diaocha" (Investigation into the religion of the Pumi in Ninglang County). In *Yunnan shaoshu minzu shehui lishi diaocha ziliao huibian* (Collection of materials on the investigation into the society and history of the minority *minzu* of Yunnan). Kunming: Yunnan Renmin Chubanshe.

Ye Xiaowen. 1999. "Women wei shenme zhuzhang zongjiao xinyang ziyou" (Why we advocate freedom of religion). *Zhongguo zongjiao* (China religion) 1.

Ye Yanqiong, Chen Guojie, and Fan Hong. 2003. "Impacts of the 'Grain for Green' Project on Rural Communities in the Upper Min River Basin, Sichuan, China." *Mountain Research and Development* 23 (4): 345–52.

Yin Haitao. 1989. *Pumizu yanyu* (Sayings of the Pumi). Beijing: Zhongguo Minjian Wenyi Chubanshe.

Yunnan Sheng Minzu Shiwu Weiyuanhui Pumi Jingji he Shehui Fazhan Wenti Diaoyanzu, ed. 2002. "Yunnan Pumi jingji he shehui fazhan diaocha baogao" (Report on an investigation into the socioeconomic development of the Pumi in Yunnan). In *Pumi yanjiu wenji* (Collected works on the Pumi), edited by Hu Wenming. Kunming: Yunnan Minzu Chubanshe.

Zhongguo Ge Minzu Zongjiao yu Shenhua Da Cidian Bianshen Weiyuanhui. 1990. *Zhongguo ge minzu zongjiao yu shenhua da cidian* (Dictionary of the religion and mythology of every ethnic group in China). Beijing: Beijing Xueyuan Chubanshe.

Zhongguo Shehui Kexue Yuan Minzu Yanjiu Suo and Guojia Minzu Shiwu Weiyuanhui Wenhua Xuanchuansi, eds. 1994. *Zhongguo shaoshu minzu yuyan shiyong qingkuang* (The situation of language use among China's ethnic minorities). Beijing: Zhongguo Zangxue Chubanshe.

Zhou Yudong and Zhan Chengxu. 1988. "Ninglang xian Yongning qu Kaiping xiang Naxizu fengjian lingzhuzhi, azhu hunyin he muxi jiating diaocha" (Investigation into the feudal lord system, the *azhu* marriage and matrilineal household of the Naxi of Kaiping Township of Yongning District in Ninglang County). In *Ninglang Yizu zizhixian Yongning Naxizu shehui ji qi muxizhi diaocha* (Investigation into the society and the matrilineal system of the Naxi of Yongning in Ninglang Yi Autonomous County). Kunming: Yunnan Renmin Chubanshe.

INDEX

Amundsen, Edvard, 239n2
ancestor worship, 120–22, 126, 185
anji: and Buddhism, 7, 173–76, 179–87, 209, 214; difference with *yèma*, 149–51; during Cultural Revolution, 61, 159–62; lineage protector deity, 142; revival after Mao, 162; and rituals for exorcising evil spirits, 143, 147; and rituals for house construction, 122–23; and rituals for mountain deities, 141; and rituals for water deities, 139–40, 147; transmission of lineage, 153; use of texts in ritual, 151
Anti-Right Deviation campaign, 59–60
Aziz, Barbara, 96, 101, 116

Ba'er. *See* Bar clan
baise, 34–35
banditry/ bandits, 40, 43, 47, 55, 242n29

Bar clan, 27, 29–33, 38, 57, 111, 116, 154, 240n10
Bathang, 39
Bauman, Zygmunt, 216
bazong, 33–34, 52
Bell, Catherine, 119, 134, 213
Benjor, 103, 251n12
birth control, in Bustling Township, 86
Blondeau, Anne-Marie, 120
Bön(po), 28, 33, 151, 198, 239n7, 253n2, 256n31
Bourdieu, Pierre, 112, 186
brö demons, 145–46, 253nn5,6
Buddhism, 6, 7, 27, 28, 158; in Bustling Township, 172–73; coexistence with *anji* practices, 173–76, 179–87; coexistence with other religions, 176–77, 184, 192–93; influence on Premi cosmology, 122, 125, 135, 142; in Ninglang (Yunnan), 190–92; relationship

Buddhism (cont.) with Party-state, 167–71, 178; role as seen by Muli elites, 179; use of texts in ritual, 150, 152. *See also* Gelug(pa); Karma Kagyu(pa); Sakya; Theravada

Buddhist Association, 168, 169

Bustling Township: agricultural production in, 64–66; government administration of, 79–87; geography of, 64; ethnic groups in, 73–74; income generation in, 66–73; poverty alleviation in, 245n3

caterpillar fungus, 66, 245nn4,5

Certeau, Michel de, 186

Chau, Adam Yuet, 9, 163

Chen Xialing 42, 242n32

Chiang Kai-shek, 43

Chinese Communist Party, 3, 49, 167, 169, 171; in Bustling Township, 82–83

Chinese People's Political Consultative Conference, 52, 55, 169, 203

Christianity, 195

clan, 94, 98, 102; affiliation in Bustling Township, 105; exogamy, 102, 104, 106–7; origins in Bustling Township, 105–7; as ritual unit, 108, 109; segmentation, 107

community, 215–16

Confucius, 10

control commissioner, 38, 41

Corlin, Claes, 124

corvée, 46, 52, 115, 243n37

CPPCC. *See* Chinese People's Political Consultative Conference

cremation ceremony, 108–9, 141–42

crime: in Bustling Township, 83; in Muli during Republic, 46

Cultural Revolution, 60–62, 123, 146, 153, 165, 195, 213

Dalai Lama: 3rd, 28–29, 240n14; 5th, 26, 31, 32, 33, 35, 36, 37, 241n20; 13th, 42; 14th, 44

Dali Kingdom, 189, 239n4

Dargay, Eva, 121, 181

Davies, Major H. R., 25–26

ddaba (Na ritualist), 192–93, 194, 195, 256n30

Dean, Kenneth, 4

deities, 134–42; living, 156–58, 171, 183

Democratic Management Committee, 168, 170

Democratic Reforms campaign, 56–57, 116, 123, 165

Dingba Shenro, 143–44, 253nn3,4

disease: curing of, 139, 153–54, 162, 198; as drain on family economy, 67

Dresch, Paul, 238n7

dtô-mbà, 75–76, 106, 246n12, 253n2, 257n9

Durkheim, Émile, 215

dze^n, 94–95, 126, 141, 182, 185, 213. *See also* house

dze^n-me, 113–16

education (official): in Bustling Township, 87, 92–93; participation in, 87–89, 91, 202

elections, 248n20

elites, 52, 53, 55–57, 177–79, 215

ethics in research, 21–23

ethnic conflict, in Bustling Township, 78

ethnic identity, in Bustling Township, 75
evil spirits. See *shep'a*
exogamy, clan, 102, 104, 106–7
Eya, 35, 36, 251n11

Falungong, 4, 171, 258n10
family planning. See birth control
Feuchtwang, Stephan, 8, 248n21
fieldwork, as a research methodology, 12–13, 17–20
Fjeld, Heidi, 103
forests: management in Bustling Township, 84–85; and mountain deities, 141
Four-Antis movement, 58, 59, 165

gaitu guiliu, 36, 53
Gami, 54, 57, 58, 106
Geertz, Clifford, 176–77, 214
Gellner, David, 184
gender roles, 119, 158
genealogies, 105, 106, 112
Gelug(pa): conflict with Bön, 33; conflict with Karma Kagyu(pa), 29, 31, 33; establishment in Muli, 6, 24–25, 27, 29, 33; relationship with Muli elites, 54–55, 212
gold mining, 43
Goldstein, Melvyn, 49–50, 100–101
Great Leap Forward, 10, 59
Gushri Khan, 32, 35
Gyelthang, 25, 35, 36, 124, 214

habitus, 186
Han, in Bustling Township, 76–78
Handel-Mazetti, Heinrich, 239n2
hangui, 193–208. See also *anji*
hangui school, 5, 203–7, 217–18

Harrell, Stevan, 250n3, 254n11, 258n13
Heart Sutra, 150
Hillman, Ben, 9
The History of the Dharma in Muli (Ngawang Khenrab, comp.), 26–28
house (as unit of social organization), 96–97, 113, 116, 250n6; as corporate unit, 118–19; and ritual activity, 119–20, 122–31, 213; splitting of, 114, 117–18. See also *dze^n*
household responsibility system, 65–55
Hsu, Elisabeth, 96, 118
Hu Jingming, 51, 203, 217–18, 258n13
Hui, 9

inheritance, 114
interview, as a research methodology, 13–14
Islam, 9

Jamyang Sangpo, 30, 31, 32, 33
jhü. See clan
Jiang Jieshi. See Chiang Kai-shek
Jiayang Chunpin, 58, 59
Jiayang Zhigu, 49, 52
Jing Jun, 9
job-rotation system, 80–81

Kachin, 96, 116, 126
Kapstein, Matthew, 120
karma, 180, 185
Karma Kagyu(pa), 28, 31
Kham, 36, 37, 39–41
Khetsun Sangpo, 255n27
kinship, 94; terminology, 98–99, 116. See also relatedness
Klein, Anne C., 255n27

Kublai Khan, 189, 239n4, 246n9
Kulu Gompa, 29, 57
Kværne, Per, 256n31
Kwakwaka'wakw, 250n6

lama, 148
land: dividing of, 117–18, 251n12; -use policy, 84, 104
language use, in education, 77, 87, 89–92, 249n23
Levine, Nancy, 101, 250n4
Lévi-Strauss, Claude, 97, 98, 116, 214, 250n6
Lijiang, 26, 28, 32, 36, 240nn13,14, 257n9
Lin Jiayong, 51, 56, 244n51, 245n56
Litzinger, Ralph, 177, 178
Liu Lirong, 46, 254n14
Liu Longchu, 100, 251n11
Liu Wenhui, 43, 44, 242n35
Lobsang Thutob, 37
logging, 69
Lòlop'o, 10, 238n6
Long Xijiang, 54–55, 244n49
Long Yun, 43, 44, 242n31
Lopes, Donald S., 150
Lowie, R. H., 250n8
lunhuan. See job-rotation system

Manchu, 32
Maoism, 10, 11, 161, 213
marriage: age for, 97; ceremony, 98; cross-cousin, 98, 99; finding partner for, 102, 145–46; laws and registration of, 248n19; types of, 98. *See also* polyandry; polygyny
Mathieu, Christine, 192–93, 257n7
matrilineal society, 190, 257

McKhann, Charles, 96, 246n11
me-drö, 108–10, 126, 141, 213
Mentuhui, 195, 257n10
Metcalf, Peter, 19
Miao, 35, 253n6
modernity, 4
Mongols, 29, 35, 189, 246n9
Mu (ruling Naxi clan), 28, 31, 111
Mu Ding, 239n5
Mu Qin, 239n5
Mu Wenfu, 49, 50, 51, 243n41
Mu Zeng, 31, 32, 240n13
Mueggler, Eric, 10
Muge Samten, 238n11
Muli, 7, 25, 41, 46; ethnic make-up, 53–54; history before 1580, 28; relationship with Lhasa, 26, 32, 35, 38; relationship with Qing, 26, 35; religion in history of, 27
Muli chöchung. See *The History of the Dharma in Muli*
Muli Gompa, 55, 164–68, 170–73, 175; establishment of, 33, 164; number of monks at, 164–65, 254nn14,15
Muli Tibetan Automous County, establishment of, 50–52

Na, 73, 189–91, 253n5, 256n30, 257n7; kinship and descent, 96, 111–12
Naef, Roland, 81, 251n11
naming (of newborn children), 183
Nanzhou Kingdom, 239n4
nat cult, 184
National People's Congress, in Bustling Township, 83
Natural Forest Protection Program, 69, 84, 104, 246n6
Naxi, 28, 35, 73, 74, 75, 106, 240n12, 244n45; kinship system of, 96;

polyandry among, 100; polygyny among, 251n11; religious beliefs and ritual practice, 146n12, 252n16
Ndembu, 109–10
Neten Tsultrim Sangpo, 29, 30
Nima Anji, 15, 155, 157, 159, 163, 206, 208, 217–18
Nomihan, 43, 242n34
Nuosu, 21–22, 25, 34, 47, 57, 108, 189, 238n6, 243n38, 258n10; armed conflict with, 37, 47–48
Nyinba, 101, 250n4

offering stone, 126, 127
Opening Up the Western Regions (government policy), 63
orthodoxy, 7

pacification commissioner, 37
Panchen Lama, 42
People's Communes, 59
People's Liberation Army, 48–49, 58
PLA. See People's Liberation Army
political power, 82
polyandry, 85, 99–104, 118, 251n11
polygyny, 85, 99, 103, 251n11
praying, 126–27, 186; for male offspring, 138–39
Premi, appellation and distribution: in Bustling Township, 74–75; in Muli, 54; in Ninglang, 188–89
Premi language, xix, 14, 75, 189, 202
pseudonyms, use of, 20
Pumi(zu) (official *minzu* label of Premi in Yunnan), 54, 188. *See also* Premi, appellation and distribution

Qing, 32, 35, 38; control over Tibet, 37, 39

Red Guards, 60–61, 159, 160
reincarnation, 185, 199
relatedness, 94, 96, 250n1
religion, as social practice, 184; CCP view on, 3; regulation by the Party-state, 167–71, 237n1, 255n19
Religious Affairs Bureau, 168, 169, 170
Rek'ua, 73, 74, 75, 246n11
Rock, Joseph F., 26, 41, 154, 193, 194, 239n2, 246nn11,12, 253n2, 254n14

Sakya, 28, 191, 254n16
Samuel, Geoffrey, 24, 134, 184–85
Sangye Gyatso, 29, 30
Schiesser, Markus, 251n11
Scott, James, 19
sexual relations, 97, 101, 102, 104, 145
Sheils, Dean, 120–21
shep'a, 142–45
Shih Chuan-kang, 96, 112, 192, 252n19, 257n7
Shu Yuanyuan, 58, 59, 245n56
Shuhi[n], 54, 121
Shuiluo, 54, 106, 121, 245n2, 248n18
slaves, taking of, 47
social stratification, 111, 116
soma, 154–56
Sonam Gyatso. *See* Dalai Lama: 3rd
soul. *See me-drö*
Spiro, Melford, 184
State Administration of Religious Affairs, 167, 171, 254n17
superstition, concept of, 202

Teichman, Eric, 242n31
Theravada, 184
Tianbao. *See* Natural Forest Protection Program
Tibet: relation with Qing, 35, 36, 37, 38, 39; relation with Republic of China, 40; social transformation in, 103
Tibetan language, 249n24. *See also* language use, in education
"Tibetanization," 24
Tsongkhapa, 30, 31, 55, 191
Tuigeng Huanlin campaign, 84, 247n17
tulku, 148, 156, 255n25; official recognition by Party-state, 169–70; position of, in Muli, 27, 29, 30, 32, 33, 156
Turner, Victor, 109–10
tusi: defined, 30; number in Sichuan, 242n30; position in Muli, 30, 35, 42, 240n10; replacement by Qing administrators, 36; women holding position of, 240n11; in Yongning, 111, 252n19

ulag. *See* corvée
United Front policy, 49
uprising, in Kham (1956-59), 57–59

village committees, 86
villagers, small groups of, 86–87

Wachin Gompa, 29, 32
Waija Dorje Tsering, 203
Wang Chengquan, 193, 194
Wang Peichu Qudian, 48, 49, 50, 51, 54, 243n42
Wang Shuwu, 190, 257n3
Weber, Max, 176–77
Weckerle, Caroline, 121, 248n18
Wu Sangui Rebellion, 35–36, 241n19

Xiang Cicheng Zhaba, 41–44
Xiang Niancha, 37–38
Xiang Peichu Zhaba, 48, 50, 51, 52, 58
Xiang Songdian Chunpin, 48, 52, 245n56
Xiang Songlang Zhashen, 39
Xiang Zhaba Songdian, 42, 48, 58, 244n51, 245n56
Xiang Zhashi, 38–39
Xifan, 25, 46

yak breeding station, 65
Yan Ruxian, 111, 190, 257n3
Yang Xuezheng, 193, 196–200
Yanyuan, 41, 42, 44, 48, 50, 51, 241n17, 254n11
Yao, 177
yèma, 143, 147–52, 175–76, 182, 191
Yongning, 66, 102, 111, 171, 189, 190

za^{n}bala, 61, 122, 127–29, 161
Zangzu, official *minzu* label, 53–56, 73
Zhao Erfeng, 39–41
Zhamei Gompa, 190, 192, 193, 253n10, 257n4
Zhan Chengxu, 193, 194
Zhou Enlai, 203
Zuosuo, 44–45, 200, 239n7